Professional and Practice-based Learning

Volume 5

For further volumes:
http://www.springer.com/series/8383

Series Editors:

Stephen Billett, Griffith University, Australia
Christian Harteis, Paderborn University, Germany
Hans Gruber, University of Regensburg, Germany

Professional and practice-based learning brings together international research on the individual development of professionals and the organisation of professional life and educational experiences. It complements the Springer journal *Vocations and Learning: Studies in vocational and professional education.*

Professional learning, and the practice-based processes that often support it, are the subject of increased interest and attention in the fields of educational, psychological, sociological, and business management research, and also by governments, employer organisations and unions. This professional learning goes beyond, what is often termed professional education, as it includes learning processes and experiences outside of educational institutions in both the initial and ongoing learning for the professional practice. Changes in these workplaces requirements usually manifest themselves in the everyday work tasks, professional development provisions in educational institution decrease in their salience, and learning and development during professional activities increase in their salience.

There are a range of scientific challenges and important focuses within the field of professional learning. These include:

- understanding and making explicit the complex and massive knowledge that is required for professional practice and identifying ways in which this knowledge can best be initially learnt and developed further throughout professional life.
- analytical explications of those processes that support learning at an individual and an organisational level.
- understanding how learning experiences and educational processes might best be aligned or integrated to support professional learning.

The series integrates research from different disciplines: education, sociology, psychology, amongst others. The series is comprehensive in scope as it not only focusses on professional learning of teachers and those in schools, colleges and universities, but all professional development within organisations.

Rob F. Poell · Marianne van Woerkom
Editors

Supporting Workplace Learning

Towards Evidence-based Practice

 Springer

Editors
Prof. Rob F. Poell
Department of Human Resource Studies
Tilburg University
PO Box 90153
5000 LE Tilburg
Netherlands
r.poell@uvt.nl

Dr. Marianne van Woerkom
Department of Human Resource Studies
Tilburg University
PO Box 90153
5000 LE Tilburg
Netherlands
m.vanwoerkom@uvt.nl

ISSN 2210-5549
ISBN 978-90-481-9108-6
DOI 10.1007/978-90-481-9109-3
Springer Dordrecht Heidelberg London New York

e-ISSN 2210-5557
e-ISBN 978-90-481-9109-3

Printed on acid-free paper

Springer is part of Springer Science+Business Media (www.springer.com)

Series Editors' Foreword

This volume provides perspectives drawn largely from the field of human resource development that together discuss what constitutes support for assisting learning and learners in workplace settings. Learning through and for work has long been the concern of this discipline, and before it became of interest in many of the disciplines who now focus on workplaces as sites for learning. The volume adds a range of conceptions and perspectives from this field and does much to provide fresh and helpful insights about learning through and for work and, as such it contributes directly to the purpose of this book series. It also goes some way to rebut criticisms of this field.

Indeed, rightly or wrongly, fairly or unfairly, many researchers from the broad field of education are wary, if not quickly dismissive of the field of inquiry referred to as 'human resource development'. Concerns about development of human resources being for the purposes of others (e.g., capital, employers, business), an emphasis on quantitative inquiry that focuses on measurement of performance, and the often claimed lack of critical perspective has led to this field being seen by some as being reductive, narrow, and antithetical to the kinds of human interests that are central to much of social science. Yet, similar concerns have been and sometime are still expressed about workplace learning (i.e., that it is narrowly focused and economically driven etc., etc.,). So, a volume that offers human resource development accounts of workplace learning has some significant challenges in either fulfilling the expectations of critics or offering contributions that challenge easy criticisms of both the human resource and workplace learning field.

Although not explicitly setting out to achieve this goal, this edited volume goes some way to addressing the second of these challenges: confronting easy criticisms about being narrow, reductive and focused on the interests of others, not learners. Indeed, quite specifically, in the introductory section, the editors point to the problematic nature of both the human resource development perspective and workplaces as environments in which learning and development occur. Here, they rehearse early the dangers in simplistic views about the generation of knowledge for others' benefit and that learning environments per se will always have strengths and limitations in their contributions to individuals' development, and workplaces as sites of human development are no exception. These themes are taken up by the contributors.

Indeed, a theme that evolves through the collection of chapters is that rather than being set, predictable and pre-determined, that a range of personal and situational factors do much to mediate the learning that arises in workplaces and through efforts to promote and direct that learning. In short, this learning may or may not be what was intended by others. These sentiments are rehearsed convincingly across the first two sections and from contributions that have quite diverse focuses and content. An almost consistent set of findings evolve across these contributions about the indeterminacy of settings to be able to press for, secure, or translate their suggestions into change in humans. Instead, they emphasize the person-dependent ways in which development arises in spite of as well as through these experiences in workplace settings. Variously, these sections report that regardless of whether the workplace affords access to knowledge through working with others, learning technologies, team coaching, mentoring, or supervisory support that there can be no guarantee that what is afforded, projected, or suggested to learners is what they will learn. Instead, there was much that was person-dependent in both the process and outcomes of that learning. The explanation of that person-dependence is also consistently developed across the sections in that human attributes such as intentionality, interest, active participation, existing ways of knowing and knowledge are too central to processes of human development to simply be seen as an obstacle to realizing pre-specific outcomes or what others want to be learnt, or an inconvenience to the systematic and uniform development of knowledge. Instead, they are absolutely central to the process of human development regardless of the intentions of others, technology, and ordered experiences. Moreover, these contributions do more than suggest that what arises is a needing to account for personal and social factors. Even when learning is promoted through group processes, technology, expert coaching that the interdependency of both sets of factors comes to the fore, as do relations between them. Indeed, across the three sections the contributions suggest, and some quite explicitly so, that there is a need to consider the relational nature of what is suggested by social forms, partners, and artifacts and the ways these are engaged in quite individualist ways. Yet, could it be ever different than this. The wonder of humans and human development, and perhaps what makes us a distinct species, is our capacity for reflecting on what we do and being reflexive about it. Such qualities are hardly going to be held hostage by attempts to secure uniform and intended outcomes through instructional and pedagogic means.

So, through its diverse contributions, this volume demonstrates that the human resource development field is not pre-occupied with reproduction of the kinds of learning that others want. Perhaps they leave this for schooling. Instead, nuanced and complex accounts of human development are advanced and in ways that provide helpful critiques and advance understanding learning through and for work practice in open and critical ways.

Stephen Billett
Hans Gruber
Christian Harteis

May 2010

Contents

1 Introduction: Supporting Workplace Learning 1
Rob F. Poell and Marianne van Woerkom

Part I   Workplace Learning Interventions

2 Strategies of HRD Practitioners in Different Types of
Organization: A Qualitative Study Among 18 South
Australian HRD Practitioners 11
Karen Oostvogel, Marieke Koornneef, and Rob F. Poell

3 Conceptualising Participation in Formal Training and
Development Activities: A Planned Behaviour Approach 27
Ronan Carbery and Thomas N. Garavan

4 Experiences of E-Learning and Its Delivery Among
Learners Who Work: A Systematic Review 47
Christopher Carroll, Andrew Booth, Diana Papaioannou,
and Anthea Sutton

Part II   The Role of Social Support

5 Managerial Coaching as a Workplace Learning Strategy 71
Andrea D. Ellinger, Robert G. Hamlin, Rona S. Beattie,
Yu-Lin Wang, and Orla McVicar

6 Direct and Indirect Effects of Supervisor Support on
Transfer of Training 89
Derk-Jan Nijman and John Gelissen

7 Understanding the Relational Characteristics of Effective
Mentoring and Developmental Relationships at Work 107
Andrew D. Rock and Thomas N. Garavan

8 Learning How Things Work Here: The Socialization
of Newcomers in Organizations 129
Russell Korte

9   **Learning Vocational Practice in Relative Social Isolation:
    The Epistemological and Pedagogic Practices of
    Small-Business Operators**   147
    Stephen Billett

Part III Encouraging Collective Learning

10 **Team Coaching in Teacher Teams**   165
    Marianne van Woerkom

11 **Learning with the Intention of Innovating: Eleven Design
    Principles for Knowledge Productivity**   183
    Suzanne Verdonschot and Paul Keursten

12 **From Function-Based Development Practices
    to Collaborative Capability Building: An Intervention
    to Extend Practitioners' Ideas**   205
    Marika Schaupp

13 **Implications for Research and Practice**   225
    Rob F. Poell and Marianne van Woerkom

Index   231

Contributors

Rona S. Beattie Glasgow Caledonian University, UK, r.beattie2@gcal.ac.uk

Stephen Billett Faculty of Education, Griffith University, Australia, s.billett@griffith.edu.au

Andrew Booth University of Sheffield, School of Health and Related Research (ScHARR), Sheffield, S1 4DA, UK, a.booth@shef.ac.uk

Ronan Carbery Department of Personnel & Employment Relations, Kemmy Business School, University of Limerick, Ireland, Ronan.Carbery@ul.ie

Christopher Carroll University of Sheffield, School of Health and Related Research (ScHARR), Sheffield, S1 4DA, UK, c.carroll@shef.ac.uk

Andrea D. Ellinger University of Texas at Tyler, USA, aellinger@uttyler.edu

Thomas N. Garavan Department of Personnel & Employment Relations, Kemmy Business School, University of Limerick, Ireland, Thomas.Garavan@ul.ie

John Gelissen Department of Methodology & Statistics, Tilburg University, P.O. Box 90153 5000 LE Tilburg, The Netherlands, j.p.t.m.gelissen@uvt.nl

Robert G. Hamlin University of Wolverhampton, UK, r.g.hamlin@wlv.ac.uk

Paul Keursten Kessels & Smit, The Learning Company, Johannesburg, South Africa, keursten@kessels-smit.com

Marieke Koornneef Rijkswaterstaat, The Netherlands, Marieke.Koornneef@Rws.Nl

Russell Korte Assistant Professor, Human Resource Development, Fellow, Illinois Foundry for Innovation in Engineering, Education, University of Illinois at Urbana-Champaign, 1310 South 6th Street, Champaign, IL 61820, 217-333-0807, korte@illinois.edu

Orla McVicar Glasgow Caledonian University, UK, Orla.McVicar@gcal.ac.uk

Derk-Jan Nijman Department of Education, Working and Learning, IVA policy research and advice, Tilburg University, Warandelaan 2 PO Box 90153 5000 LE Tilburg, The Netherlands, djjmnijman@uvt.nl

Karen Oostvogel Voortgezet onderwijs raad, The Netherlands, Karenoostvogel@vo-raad.nl

Diana Papaioannou University of Sheffield, School of Health and Related Research (ScHARR), Sheffield, S1 4DA, UK, d.papaioannou@shef.ac.uk

Rob F. Poell Department of Human Resource Studies, Tilburg University, Tilburg, The Netherlands, r.poell@uvt.nl

Andrew D. Rock Department of Personnel & Employment Relations, Kemmy Business School, University of Limerick, Limerick, Ireland, andrew.rock@ul.ie

Marika Schaupp Finnish Institute of Occupational Health, Helsinki, Finland, marika.schaupp@ttl.fi

Anthea Sutton University of Sheffield, School of Health and Related Research (ScHARR), Sheffield, S1 4DA, UK, a.sutton@shef.ac.uk

Marianne van Woerkom Department of Human Resource Studies, Tilburg University, Tilburg, The Netherlands, m.vanwoerkom@uvt.nl

Suzanne Verdonschot Kessels & Smit, The Learning Company, Utrecht, The Netherlands, sverdonschot@kessels-smit.com

Yu-Lin Wang National Cheng Kung University, Taiwan, ywang@mail.ncku.edu.tw

Chapter 1
Introduction: Supporting Workplace Learning

Rob F. Poell and Marianne van Woerkom

The issue of workplace learning has received increasing attention from academics and practitioners alike since the 1990s. A body of knowledge is starting to accumulate about the question of how learning in the workplace might be encouraged. This book brings together a range of state-of-the-art research papers all addressing interventions to support learning in the workplace. The authors are experienced researchers in the field of HRD and workplace learning, who have an interest in making HRD and workplace learning practices more evidence based, through practically relevant research. Most chapters present new empirical research in an area that has gained much attention from HRD practitioners over the last decade but is relatively under-researched empirically.

During the 1990s, the workplace was rediscovered as a rich source of learning. Although people have always learned in the workplace, for most of the 20th century attention was focussed on formal schooling and off-the-job training. In the 1980s and 1990s, the limitations of these approaches to corporate education became apparent. The transfer of learning gained during formal courses to the workplace was generally found to be low, limiting the effectiveness of these relatively expensive training efforts. Both in organisational and vocational education contexts, closer links between learning and work were increasingly sought. Organisations in the 21st century need to take into account the emergence of the knowledge economy and further globalisation, an ageing workforce, fast technological developments and new forms of production and organisation of work. Vocational education is looking at offering more combined programmes of school and work to provide a better match with the labour market. All these developments contribute to the relevance of learning in the workplace, as many authors have indicated (Billett, 1994, 2001; Engeström, 2001; Eraut, Alderton, Cole, & Senker, 1998; Marsick & Volpe, 1999).

In essence, learning in the workplace is a natural and largely autonomous process derived from the characteristics of the work process and its inherent social

R.F. Poell (✉)
Department of Human Resource Studies, Tilburg University, Tilburg, The Netherlands
e-mail: r.poell@uvt.nl

R.F. Poell, M. van Woerkom (eds.), *Supporting Workplace Learning*, Professional and Practice-based Learning 5, DOI 10.1007/978-90-481-9109-3_1,
© Springer Science+Business Media B.V. 2011

interactions. Learning in the workplace is often implicit and sometimes even hard to differentiate from doing the daily work. This is its strength as much as it is a weakness. Transfer problems are far less likely to occur; fewer investments are needed for training materials and training personnel; and employees spend less time being unproductive. Besides these advantages, there are a number of potential disadvantages to workplace learning. Some workplaces are badly equipped for learning, both materially (time, space) and socially (coaching, support); creativity and innovation are not necessarily encouraged by forging close links between work and learning; employees may learn the 'wrong' things if there is no careful analysis, delivery and evaluation.

Despite the strengths of workplace learning as a mainly autonomous process, its potential disadvantages lead organisations to wanting to manage it as part of their broader HRD strategy. This can result, for instance, in new partnerships between HRD professionals, managers and employees; in structured on-the-job training programmes; and in Intranet-based performance support systems. There are limits, however, to the extent to which the complex dynamics of learning in the workplace can be guided in pre-determined desirable directions. HRD professionals have only limited possibilities to make workplaces better equipped for learning. In some organisations, especially small- and medium-sized enterprises, managers and employees have no support from dedicated HRD practitioners whatsoever. SMEs may nevertheless have the kind of flourishing workplace learning culture that some multinationals can only aspire to. Large organisations, then again, usually do a better job of providing their employees with career development opportunities, through more or less formalised coaching and mentoring schemes designed to encourage learning in the workplace.

It is this very tension between the need to encourage learning in the workplace and the desire to manage its complex dynamics that the book will address, as it investigates the following related questions based on conceptual and empirical research conducted by the authors:

- Which interventions can organisations make to encourage workplace learning?
- How can social support contribute to workplace learning?
- What measures can be taken to stimulate collective learning in the workplace?

Very few books in the field of HRD to date are grounded in evidence-based research. Most HRD books are essentially text books and not researchbased (though sometimes they are informed by research). HRD as an emerging field has a relatively theoretical knowledge base, which is reflected in the nature of its handbooks (Stewart & McGoldrick, 1996; Hargreaves & Jarvis, 1998; Wilson, 2005; Walton, 1999; Yorks, 2005; Sadler-Smith, 2006). The few research-driven books on HRD have been on very specific topics, for instance, HRD in the post-command economies of East and Central Europe after the fall of communism (Lee, Letiche, Crawshaw, & Thomas, 1996) or HRD in the health and social care sector (Sambrook & Stewart, 2007). Stewart, McGoldrick, and Watson (2001) focused on the research process and research design in HRD rather than on research findings, as did Swanson and Holton (1997). In general, therefore, the HRD literature lacks a strong empirical evidence base.

Much the same can be concluded about the topic of workplace learning. Although books in this area have been published as early as 1991 (Watkins) and even 1987 (Marsick), they predominantly focus on theory, how-to-do types of knowledge and sometimes mere advocacy (Rothwell, Sanders, & Soper, 1999; Stern & Sommerlad, 1999; Ashton & Sung, 2002). One good exception was Billett (2001), which was based on a series of empirical studies across a range of industries. Another exception was Marsick and Watkins (1990), which contained a number of single case studies on what they termed informal and incidental learning at the time. The empirical evidence base of the workplace learning literature, therefore, is rather limited as well.

Structure and Contents of the Book

All chapters in this volume are state-of-the-art research papers, authored by an international spread of leading scholars in the field. Taken in part from the Workplace Learning stream of the 2006 International Conference on HRD Research and Practice across Europe (held in Tilburg), which was coordinated by the editors, all contributions are highly selected.

The book is broken into three parts, preceded by one introductory overview chapter and concluded by one final implications chapter. Part I deals with Workplace Learning Interventions (three chapters), including HRD practitioners' strategies, training and development activities, and e-learning programmes. Part II comprises five chapters about the Role of Social Support in workplace learning, such as mentoring, coaching and socialisation practices, as well as the impact of (a lack of) social support. Part III addresses Collective Learning in the Workplace (three chapters), looking at teams, knowledge productivity and collaborative capability building. A summary of each chapter is provided below.

The *first part* of the book (Workplace Learning Interventions) kicks off with Chapter 2 written by Karen Oostvogel, Marieke Koornneef and Rob Poell. They present a qualitative study among 18 South Australian HRD practitioners working in different organisational types, aimed at investigating the actual strategies they employ in shaping their roles. Based on semi-structured interviews and using the Learning-Network Theory (Van der Krogt, 1998) as an interpretive framework, the results are presented against the backdrop of two similar studies conducted earlier in the United Kingdom and the Netherlands. Four different areas (referred to as action domains) emerged on which the South Australian HRD practitioners focused their strategies: 'participants', 'materials', 'informal style' and 'learning culture'. Most respondents focused their strategies mainly on organising learning activities for employees ('participants' and 'materials'). Few differences across types of organisation were found.

Ronan Carbery and Thomas Garavan are the authors of Chapter 3 , which deals with participation in formal training and development activities. Based on the theory of planned behaviour (Ajzen, 1991), an extension of the theory of reasoned action (Ajzen & Fishbein, 1970), the authors construct a model to explain training participation behaviour. They show how the latter is influenced by employees' intentions to participate, which in turn are influenced by three key aspects. The first key aspect is individuals' attitudes towards training and development (Participation Attitudes, e.g. achievement expectancies); the second is perceived social pressures to participate in training and development (Subjective Norms, e.g. perceptions of the transfer environment); and the third is how individuals deal with situations where they have certain intentions but cannot act upon those due to resource or other limitations (Perceived Behavioural Control, e.g. self-efficacy beliefs). These three aspects are shown to be predicted by general-person characteristics, for example, educational achievements and past career experiences.

The final chapter in the first part looks at employees' experiences of e-learning programmes and is authored by Christopher Carroll, Andrew Booth, Diana Papaioannou, Anthea Sutton and Ruth Wong. The aim of their systematic literature review was to evaluate the views and attitudes of work-based students towards the delivery of e-learning (both technologies and pedagogic approaches) so as to identify those techniques that most enhance the learning experience. Analysis of 41 key studies on the topic revealed that a number of factors that appeared to moderate the relationship between e-learning courses and learners' reported experiences thereof. The usability, applicability and attractiveness of the course and its materials all influence positively or negatively the learners' experiences, besides issues related to access, motivation, confidence with information technology, time pressures, flexibility and student isolation. Communication between students was most frequently reported; discussion forums and related media, such as group-working and prior socialisation through induction programmes, were the techniques most prominent across studies. The findings strongly support the social nature of learning.

The *second part* in this volume is concerned with the Role of Social Support and is headlined by a chapter on managerial coaching as an informal workplace learning strategy. The authors are five scholars from three continents: Andrea Ellinger, Bob Hamlin, Rona Beattie, Yu-Lin Wang and Orla McVicar. They contend that both coaching and mentoring can often be used to facilitate employee learning in the workplace and that managers are increasingly being encouraged to serve as coaches for their employees. The chapter integrates conceptual and empirical research on managerial coaching to develop a more comprehensive understanding of how managers as coaches can engage with their employees and facilitate their learning. Personal as well as contextual aspects can support the adoption of the coaching role or hinder or prevent managers serving in these developmental capacities, which then can ultimately hinder or prevent learning from occurring.

Chapter 6, authored by Derk-Jan Nijman and John Gelissen, deals with the direct and indirect effects of supervisory support on transfer of training. They present a multi-dimensional construct of supervisory support and thus relate various types of support (instrumental, informational, appraisal-related and emotional) to transfer motivation of trainees, the transfer climate and transfer outcomes. Based on empirical results, the authors conclude that the multi-dimensional conceptualisation of supervisor support is construct valid and useful in future research. Supervisor support turns out to have a small direct effect on transfer outcomes. It also contributes indirectly to transfer of training through the transfer climate and (indirectly) through trainees' motivation to transfer. The authors recommend that supervisors take better into account trainee's motivation and needs, especially as the levels of supervisory support were generally perceived as low.

Andrew Rock and Tom Garavan look at the relational characteristics of effective mentoring and developmental relationships at work in Chapter 7. They aim to incorporate various relational theories into a relational perspective on mentoring and other developmental relationships at work. They draw on a number of relational theories to understand the characteristics that make mentoring and other developmental relationships function effectively. Intense and meaningful developmental relationships at work are potentially invaluable for personal development and career success. The authors discuss seven theories that illuminate how developmental relationships function and highlight a number of characteristic qualities of highly effective relationships: trust; compatibility of relationship members; authenticity; dialogue, reflection and feedback; and relationship proximity. This perspective helps explain how supportive relationships can flourish and contribute to the enhancement of individual and relational career capital.

Chapter 8 by Russell Korte presents a qualitative study of the socialisation of newcomers in organisations. He claims that current scholarship views organisational socialisation as a learning process that is primarily the responsibility of the newcomer; however, recent learning research recognises the importance of the social interactions in the learning process. The study investigated how newly hired engineers at a large manufacturing company learned job-related tasks and the social norms of the organisation. From the perspective of social exchange theory, two major findings emerged from the data that indicated (a) relationship building was a primary driver of socialisation and (b) the work group was the primary context for socialisation. These findings challenge the current views of organisational socialisation by accentuating the relational processes at the local level that mediate learning during socialisation.

In the final chapter of the second part, Stephen Billett investigates the epistemological and pedagogic practices of small business operators, who often work and learn in relative social isolation. Although much is already understood about how learning progresses in situations that provide rich sources of direct social guidance (i.e. schools, colleges, workplaces), this is not the case for many people learning in 'poorer' contexts (e.g. shift workers, home workers, workers who are the sole experts in their workplace). Localised support and the agentic actions of these workers were, in this study, found to be central to learning in such circumstances. Suggestions are made in the chapter about the means by which other kinds of socially isolated workers might come to know and learn through their working life.

The *third part* of the book is about Encouraging Collective Learning and its first chapter, written by Marianne van Woerkom, looks at the effects of coaching leadership in teacher teams in the context of higher education, with team cohesion as a mediating variable. She reasons that a team leader acting as a coach can produce stronger attraction among team members, which in turn may lead to a greater willingness to share and discuss information and thereby to team learning. The study shows that team coaching does not lead directly to team learning but it can create conditions for team learning by helping the team members to build a collective commitment and to improve their interpersonal relationships. Also teams with clear boundaries and high interdependency among members experience more team learning than other teams. Team cohesion proves to be higher in teams with a high interdependency and clear boundaries. Therefore another way to stimulate team cohesion (and team learning) is creating a team structure in which team members really need to communicate and coordinate among each other to get the work done, and to be very clear about the team identity.

Chapter 11 sees Suzanne Verdonschot and Paul Keursten develop a set of 11 design principles for knowledge productivity. The latter concept refers to the processes through which new knowledge is developed, contributing to the gradual improvements and radical innovations of products, services and operating procedures. The aim of their study was to better understand the learning processes undertaken by employees with a view to realising knowledge productivity. The authors conducted a parallel study of ten cases in which various stakeholders aimed to find innovative solutions for intricate questions. The analysis yielded 11 characteristics of work environments that support learning with the intention of innovating, which are presented as 11 design principles: formulate an urgent and intriguing question, create a new approach, work from individual motivation, make unusual combinations, work from mutual attractiveness, build on strengths, create something together, give new meaning to signals, connect inside and outside worlds, mind communication, support competence development.

Part III closes with Chapter 12 by Marika Schaupp, who reports on an intervention study in which a Finnish road-building company goes from function-based development practices to collaborative capability building. She contends that distinctive and difficult-to-imitate capabilities have generally been recognised as the key source of competitive advantage of firms; however, theories of organisational learning have traditionally concentrated on the learning processes without an interest in the object and specific content of learning. The concept of capability turns the attention from individuals' skills and the process of learning to the collective mastery of a particular action. Studies on organisational capabilities, however, tend to ignore the practitioners' active contribution in capabilitybuilding and overlook the question of how capabilities could be developed intentionally and systematically. The chapter described an intervention to create a new understanding of the nature of capabilities and new collaborative capability-building practices between functional specialists, such as HRD practitioners and systems developers.

In the concluding chapter of the book, Rob Poell and Marianne van Woerkom reflect on the implications for research and practice of all the chapters that make up the volume.

References

Ajzen, I. (1991). The theory of planned behaviour. *Organizational Behaviour and Human Decision Processes, 50*, 179–211.
Ajzen, I., & Fishbein, M. (1970). The prediction of behavioural intentions in a choice situation. *Journal of Experimental Social Psychology, 5*, 400–416.

Ashton, D. N., & Sung, J. (2002). *Supporting workplace learning for high performance working.* Geneva, Switzerland: International Labour Organization.

Billett, S. (1994). Situated learning: A workplace experience. *Australian Journal of Adult and Community Education, 34*(2), 112–130.

Billett, S. (2001). *Learning in the workplace: Strategies for effective practice.* Crows Nest, Australia: Allen & Unwin.

Engeström, Y. (2001). Expansive learning at work: Towards an activity theoretical reconceptualization. *Journal of Education and Work, 14*(1), 134–156.

Eraut, M., Alderton, J., Cole, G., & Senker, P. (1998). *Development of knowledge and skills in employment.* Brighton: University of Sussex.

Hargreaves, P., & Jarvis, P. (1998). *Human resource development handbook.* London: Kogan Page.

Lee, M. M., Letiche, H., Crawshaw, R., & Thomas, M. (Eds.). (1996). *Management education in the New Europe: Boundaries and complexity.* London: International Thompson Business Press.

Marsick, V. J. (1987). *Learning in the workplace.* New York: Croon Helm.

Marsick, V. J., & Volpe, M. (Eds.). (1999). *Informal learning on the job* (Advances in Developing Human Resources, no. 3). San Francisco: Berrett-Koehler.

Marsick, V. J., & Watkins, K. E. (1990). *Informal and incidental learning in the workplace.* London: Routledge.

Rothwell, W., Sanders, E., & Soper, J. (1999). *ASTD models for workplace learning and performance.* Alexandria, VA: The American Society for Training and Development.

Sadler-Smith, E. (2006). *Learning and development for managers: Perspectives from research and practice.* Malden, MA: Blackwell.

Sambrook, S., & Stewart, J. (Eds.). (2007). *Human resource development in the public sector: The case of health and social care.* London: Routledge.

Stern, E., & Sommerlad, L. (1999). *Workplace learning, culture and performance* (Issues in People Management). London: Institute of Personnel and Development.

Stewart, J., & McGoldrick, J. (1996). *Human resource development: Perspectives, strategies and practice.* London: Pitman.

Stewart J., McGoldrick, J., & Watson, S. (Eds.). (2001). *Understanding human resource development: A research based approach.* London: Routledge.

Swanson, R. A., & Holton, E. F., III (Eds.). (1997). *Human resource development research handbook: Linking research and practice.* San Francisco: Berrett-Koehler.

Van der Krogt, F. J. (1998). Learning network theory: The tension between learning systems and work systems in organizations. *Human Resource Development Quarterly, 9*(2), 157–178.

Walton, J. (1999). *Strategic human resource development.* Harlow: Prentice Hall.

Watkins, K. E. (1991). *Facilitating learning in the workplace.* Geelong, Australia: Deakin University.

Wilson, J. P. (Ed.). (2005). *Human resource development: Learning and training for individuals and organizations* (2nd ed.). London: Kogan Page.

Yorks, L. (2005). *Strategic human resource development.* Mason, OH: Thomson South-Western.

Part I
Workplace Learning Interventions

Chapter 2
Strategies of HRD Practitioners in Different Types of Organization: A Qualitative Study Among 18 South Australian HRD Practitioners

Karen Oostvogel, Marieke Koornneef, and Rob F. Poell

Ever since the term Human Resource Development (HRD) was coined by Nadler (1970), HRD practitioners have been the subject of many studies. The 1990s and 2000s saw a range of studies that focused on the changing role of HRD practitioners. In theory, the role of the HRD practitioner is supposed to change from a more traditional way of delivering and organizing training toward a more modern way of facilitating employee learning (e.g., Slotte, Tynjälä, & Hytönen, 2004; Tjepkema et al., 2000). Modern HRD practitioners are supposed to be concerned mainly with encouraging self-directed learning in the workplace. The empirical research conducted thus far, however, has failed to show such a big shift taking place toward a new focus on employee learning. Most HRD practitioners are still busy designing and providing training instead of supporting employees' workplace learning and development (Buyens, Wouters, & Dewettinck, 2001; Koornneef, Oostvogel, Poell, & Harris, 2002; Nijhof, 2004).

In 1998, Poell and Chivers (1999, 2003) conducted a qualitative study among 19 HRD practitioners in the United Kingdom. Results showed that HRD practitioners at the time experienced a strong lack of recognition for training issues in their organizations. Managers and workers resisted changes in the way training and learning should take place in the organization. A 2002 follow-up study among 20 Dutch HRD practitioners (Poell, Pluijmen, & Van der Krogt, 2003) showed that many of these practitioners wanted to focus on facilitating self-directed employee learning. However, often this strategy was not supported by management and/or employees. The results of these two studies were in accordance with the qualitative study conducted in Finland by Hytönen (2002; see also Hytönen, Poell, & Chivers, 2002). Finnish HRD practitioners also felt resistance in their organization when they attempted to put their ideals into practice.

The earlier studies conducted in the United Kingdom and the Netherlands looked also at the relationship between HRD strategies and the type of work carried out in the organization. Differences in strategies among HRD practitioners were expected to depend on the type of work performed by the employees. The Learning-Network

R.F. Poell (✉)
Department of Human Resource Studies, Tilburg University, Tilburg, The Netherlands
e-mail: r.poell@uvt.nl

R.F. Poell, M. van Woerkom (eds.), *Supporting Workplace Learning*, Professional
and Practice-based Learning 5, DOI 10.1007/978-90-481-9109-3_2,
© Springer Science+Business Media B.V. 2011

Theory (Van der Krogt, 1998) assumes that different work types in organizations call for different approaches to organizing learning and training. Therefore, different work types could ask also for different strategies of HRD practitioners in the organization (Koornneef et al., 2002).

Two research questions will be investigated in this chapter:
1. Which strategies do HRD practitioners use in their role?
2. To what extent are differences in strategies among HRD practitioners related to the type of work in their organizations?

Theoretical Framework

Action Domains of HRD Practitioners

The main role played by HRD practitioners, which is to operationalize organizational development goals and individual learning goals, can be implemented in practice in many different ways. Through interaction with management and employees, the HRD practitioner organizes various types of learning program. This can be done in processes of negotiation, collaboration, participation, and conflict, according to Poell and Chivers (1999). To define HRD practitioners, many different descriptions have been used. In their literature study, Koornneef et al. (2002) used the definition of an HRD practitioner postulated by Hytönen et al. (2002): *those who have full-time responsibility in their organisations for a wide range of HRD activities, from training to education, from organisation development to career development.* An important aspect of this description is that their commitment to HRD rather than their diplomas or educational background define them as a group. For the present study this definition was used.

HRD strategies are the actions undertaken by HRD practitioners to implement their roles, tasks, and responsibilities in practice. HRD practitioners have in their job description various responsibilities and tasks that they need to realize. The ways in which this is done can be seen as the strategies used by these HRD practitioners.

In their study about the roles of workplace trainers in increasing learning opportunities, Poell, Van der Krogt, Vermulst, Harris, and Simons (2006) distinguished among several action domains of HRD practitioners. Action domains are the job areas on which HRD practitioners focus their strategies. The present study analyzed the job areas related to how HRD practitioners conduct their roles, how they create learning activities, how they influence the organizational structure and culture, how they cope with problems, and how they handle changes in society, education, and in their organization (Poell et al., 2006).

The Learning-Network Theory

The Learning-Network Theory (Van der Krogt, 1998) was used as a theoretical framework. It assumes that there are four different ideal types of learning

Table 2.1 Four theoretical types of learning network and their corresponding work types. Reprinted from Poell and Chivers (1999)

	Liberal	Horizontal	Vertical	External
Content structure (Profile)	Unstructured, individually oriented	Thematically structured, problem-oriented	Heavily pre-structured, task-oriented	Methodically structured, profession-oriented
Organizational structure (Relations)	Loosely coupled, contractual	Egalitarian, group-based	Centralized, formalized	Externally inspired, professional
Development of learning processes	Individuals create own learning program to solve their problems	Group learning program develops incrementally while being undertaken	HRD staff make management policy into training program	Employees adapt work to innovations from professional association
Role of HRD consultant	Facilitating individual learning arrangements	Facilitating group learning arrangements	Designing and delivering training programs	Help professionals adapt work to external innovation
Corresponding type of work	Entrepreneurial work	Autonomous teamwork	Machine-bureaucratic work	Professional work

network. The interactions between management, HRD department, and employees when organizing learning programs, result in one of these four learning networks. In practice actual learning networks take hybrid forms. The theory by Van der Krogt also hypothesizes that the type of learning network is related to the type of work in the organization. Table 2.1 gives an overview of the four theoretical types of learning network that are distinguished in the Learning-Network Theory.

The liberal learning network expects individual workers to create their own learning programs; they are responsible for their own learning. This means that there is little structure from above and that the learning programs are unstructured beyond individual self-direction. HRD practitioners facilitate the individual learning process.

In a horizontal learning network, there is group facilitation by HRD practitioners and learning programs are developed at the same time they are being delivered. An important aspect of this learning network is that decisions are made by the group, not by management or HRD practitioners. In this way, the experiences of all the participants and their ideas are crucial for the end results of the program. In this learning network there is a very strong focus on on-the-job learning and on learning by doing.

The vertical learning network is more or less the opposite of the liberal and horizontal learning networks, because there is linear planning from above and learning programs are very structured and pre-designed, based on the learning policies set by management. HRD practitioners have to translate these policies into learning activities and control the delivery of the programs.

The external learning network is governed by professional associations outside the organization, who introduce research-based innovations and new occupational procedures to participants from the same profession. The learning activities focus on adapting their work repertoire to the newly developed scientific work methods.

As Table 2.1 shows, according to the Learning-Network Theory (and based on Mintzberg, 1989), liberal learning networks are expected to be related to entrepreneurial work. Entrepreneurial work is characterized as broad and relatively simple work, for instance, a job in sales. A horizontal learning network is likely to be found in (semi) autonomous teamwork, where work is broad and complex, for example, website development. A vertical learning network is expected in machine bureaucratic work, which is narrow and relatively simple in nature (e.g., manufacturing jobs). Finally, the external learning network can likely be found in professional work, as conducted by, for example, medical doctors and lawyers, whose work is both narrow and complex (Poell & Chivers, 1999; Van der Krogt, 1998; Koornneef et al., 2002).

Method

Design

Qualitative methods were used to gather and analyze the data, in accordance with the two previous studies conducted in the United Kingdom (Poell & Chivers, 1999, 2003) and the Netherlands (Poell et al., 2003). Semi-structured interviews were held with 18 South Australian HRD practitioners working in different types of organization, in order to investigate which strategies they used in shaping their HRD roles.

Sample

Respondents were collected using the snowball method. 'Interest forms' were first sent to potential respondents (alumni from the University of South Australia degree program in Training and Development) in order to get an impression of their organization as well as their roles and tasks. Topics like age, gender, role description, and organizational characteristics were covered on this small questionnaire. The initial set of respondents with an interest in participating was asked for other possible HRD practitioners to include in the study. A total of 18 respondents were selected with the intention to get as broad a range of roles and organizational types represented as possible. In two cases, two people from the same (larger) organization were interviewed, which means that there were 18 visits to 16 different organizations, ranging from private consultancy firms to manufacturing organizations and government institutions. In most cases, and certainly in the small- to medium-sized companies, respondents were the only HRD practitioners employed by the organization.

There were eight male respondents and ten female respondents. The ages of the respondents ranged from 38 to 63 years old, with an average age of 46. Most of the respondents had an operational background rather than an educational (or HRD) background. In some cases respondents had been working in the same company for a very long time and had rolled into the job of HRD practitioner, with the advantage of knowing the history and structure of the organization. Although most of them had an operational background, they had also taken several programs in the area of HRD, for example, training courses in adult education.

Instrument

Semi-structured interviews were held using a topic list containing the following elements:

- General information about the respondent: especially their educational background and work experience.
- Type of organization in which the respondent worked: its mission, history, structure, culture, clients.
- Respondent's role in the organization: their responsibilities, tasks, roles, position within the organization.
- HRD strategies: their ways of doing needs analysis, developing HRD programs, engaging different actors, and evaluating effectiveness.
- Case story: an in-depth account of one of their recent learning programs.

The case story was included in the interview to make sure the respondents did not only speak about their espoused theories but also about their theories in use (Argyris & Schön, 1996). They were asked to tell in detail about a specific learning program they had recently organized and/or delivered in their organization. At the end of the case story, respondents were asked whether they could provide the researchers with written materials from the courses (e.g., program outlines and evaluation forms). During data analysis, the interview transcript was compared to these materials in order to see whether respondents had talked about their actual way of working (rather than their preferred modus operandi).

Data Analysis

All 18 interviews were fully transcribed on the basis of a tape recording. Both primary researchers transcribed nine interviews each. To ensure everything had been reproduced correctly, the researchers checked each other's transcription. Next, the fully transcribed interviews were sent back to the respondents for their feedback and/or additions. Ten participants responded to this request with additional information.

The transcriptions were then divided into episodes and coded by both researchers independently. Through constant comparison and iterative discussion among all three researchers, the final codes to be used for the analysis of the interviews were determined. These codes were administered using a qualitative data analysis program called *Kwalitan* (Peters, Wester, & Richardson, 1989; Peters & Wester, 1990). Using this software program, topics emerging from the data were structured. Five cycles of comparison were needed to structure all 921 episodes in the interviews. By the end of this process there were 94 different codes, which amounts to one third of the total number of codes attributed in the first cycle. In total 1471 codes were attributed, leading to an average of 1.6 codes for each episode.

Coding resulted in five main categories, each divided into sub-categories, which were sometimes divided into sub-categories again. Pluijmen et al. (2001) found very similar categories in their empirical study. The following are the five main categories:

1. 'Context,' which refers to organizational characteristics (e.g., culture).
2. 'Changes,' which refers to changes in learning, society, and the organization.
3. 'Learning activities,' which refers to the ways in which learning programs were developed and taken by the respondents.
4. 'HRD roles,' which refers to the tasks and roles of the respondents.
5. 'Problems, success factors, and challenges,' which refers to the ways in which the respondents dealt with problems as well as to the problems and success factors they experienced in doing their job.

To answer the first research question, all strategies employed by the respondents were listed. The five categories named earlier were used to group these strategies into action domains. In this way the job areas on which HRD practitioners focused their strategies were established. The action domains in this study do not indicate objective sets of activities, for example, job descriptions; rather, they refer to those areas in their work that HRD practitioners emphasize as a core concern in how they shape their role. For an analysis of the strategies according to the Learning-Network Theory, the relevant quotes of each respondent were coded deductively using categories of this theory. Characteristics of each ideal type of the Learning-Network Theory (see Table 2.1) were compared with the information given by the respondents. In doing so, strategies that the respondents named in the interviews could be put into the framework of the theory. Not all strategies that were mentioned clearly made a match with one of the ideal types of the Learning-Network Theory. Sometimes, the strategies were too general to link them to this theory.

To answer the second research question, the different strategies of the respondents were cross-tabulated with the type of work in their organization. For an analysis of the dominant work type according to the Learning-Network Theory, the relevant quotes of each respondent were coded deductively using categories of this theory. All 16 organizations were found to be falling within one dominant type of work.

Results

Table 2.2 provides an overview of the characteristics of the respondents as well as some of the results that will be explained below.

Table 2.2 Dominant work type and action domains of the respondents, in terms of strategies and according to the LNT ($n = 18$)

Respondent	Type of work	Action domains	Dominant action domain (Strategies)	Dominant action domain (LNT)
R1	Entrepreneurial	Material	Material	Horizontal
R2	Bureaucratic	Informal style/material/learning culture	Informal style	Horizontal
R3	Entrepreneurial	Learning culture/material	Material	Horizontal
R4	Teamwork	Material/informal style	Informal style	–
R5	Bureaucratic	Participants/informal style	Informal style	Horizontal
R6	Bureaucratic	Learning culture/informal style	Learning culture	–
R7	Professional	Learning culture/participants/informal style	Informal style	Horizontal/liberal
R8	Teamwork	Material/informal style	Material	Horizontal
R9	Teamwork	Learning culture/material/informal style	Informal style	Horizontal
R10	Entrepreneurial	Learning culture/material	Material	–
R11	Teamwork	Material	Material	Liberal
R12	Entrepreneurial	Learning culture/informal style	Learning culture	Liberal
R13	Entrepreneurial	Learning culture/participants/informal style	Informal style	Liberal
R14	Professional	Learning culture/material/Informal style	Material	Liberal
R15	Entrepreneurial	Learning culture/participants/informal style	Participants	Horizontal/liberal
R16	Teamwork	Material/informal style	Material	Vertical/horizontal
R17	Teamwork	Participants	Participants	–
R18	Bureaucratic	Learning culture/participants	Participants	Liberal

Note: R5 and R6 are two respondents from the same organization, as are R12 and R13.

Strategies Employed by HRD Practitioners

The third column of Table 2.2 presents all action domains of HRD practitioners found in the interviews; those areas in their work that HRD practitioners emphasize as a core concern in how they shape their role. Three action domains emerged, namely strategies focused on learning activities, strategies focused on the context, and strategies focused on the HRD role. This means that the two other action domains (i.e., strategies focused on handling changes and problems) were not found among the Australian respondents. Because within the action domain 'learning activities' there was still diversity among the respondents, this domain was split up into two different sub-domains, namely 'participants' and 'material.' Within the action domain 'HRD role' all respondents focused their strategies especially on their informal operating style; therefore, this action domain was re-labeled 'informal style.' A similar thing occurred in the action domain 'context': as respondents focused mainly on the learning culture of their organization, this action domain was re-labeled 'learning culture.'

The fourth column of Table 2.2 contains the dominant action domains in which the respondents employed their strategies, as determined by the frequency of strategies within each action domain. The dominant action domain shows the job area on which each respondent focused their strategies the most. As Table 2.2 shows, none of the respondents employed strategies in all four action domains: 'learning culture,' 'material,' 'participants,' and 'informal style' (illustrated below). Some respondents focused on one action domain only, while others focused on three action domains. Strategies in 'learning activities' were dominant, in that 16 respondents used some of their strategies in the action domains 'participants' or 'material.' The only two respondents who did not have any of their strategies in one of these two action domains were two HR managers (interviewed alongside the HRD practitioner working in their organization). The HR managers were focused on the context and learning culture in the organization rather than on designing and delivering training and learning programs.

In the remainder of this section, the four action domains on which the respondents focused their strategies are illustrated in more detail.

Strategies in the Action Domain 'Material'

Ten of the 18 respondents used strategies within the action domain 'material.' These strategies are all concerned with the learning and training material. They can range from how the material relates to business goals to how the HRD practitioners develop and tailor existing materials and so on.

Six of these ten respondents used mainly these strategies, so in their case the strategies in this action domain were dominant. This means that although these six HRD practitioners also employed strategies within other action domains, they concentrated their strategies above all on the learning material. Some of these practitioners tried to relate their training materials to work as well as to life outside the organization. By using examples from sports (e.g., to explain the role of a coach), these practitioners (often trainers) created interactive material that lies close to the participants' experiences. The involvement of the participants is crucial in developing this material.

R8: I don't use overheads, I don't use videos, I only use whiteboard and sometimes paper. And we work it all up, so the material they're using is the material they have developed. And so if we're looking at overheads, it's because they have developed overheads. They have to take away what they were doing in the group and try and work out what it means back at their place, for them, for their management.

Strategies in the Action Domain 'Participants'

Six respondents of the 18 used strategies within the action domain 'participants.' In this action domain, the strategies are focused on the ways in which the participants are mixed into groups. Three of the six respondents employed this action domain as the main focus of their strategies. They deemed group interaction very important, therefore they often created active groups. Through a mixture of participants from different levels in the organization, most of these HRD practitioners attempted to stimulate group learning and collaboration.

R15: Where, if you monitor them while they're working in a group you get more idea of what they can do. So it's easier if they're in a group situation; so most of our training is group work, most of it.

Strategies in the Action Domain 'Informal Style'

Twelve of the 18 respondents used strategies within the action domain that deals with their operating style as HRD practitioner. Six of these 12 respondents had this domain as the main focus of their strategies. This does not mean that these six did nothing else than wonder about their style of working; rather, it indicates that amidst all their HRD-related activities they spent a lot of energy on consciously influencing the way they were going to be perceived by employees (and managers). As a result, most of these HRD practitioners tended to espouse a very informal attitude toward the employees and the participants in the courses. They saw themselves as coaches and they did not want to work in a hierarchical manner. One of the respondents emphasized not wearing any ties or suits so as to avoid creating a gap between himself/herself and the employees. Some of the respondents tried to be a link between management and employees by being on site any time and by trying to meet everyone's needs. By employing such strategies, these HRD practitioners attempted to gain more influence in the organization.

R9: And so I often am a bridge to make sure that they're talking to each other and we know that this is going to work at the same time. And we're meeting everybody's needs, because they have different operational concerns.

Strategies in the Action Domain 'Learning Culture'

More than half (11 of the 18) respondents used strategies within the action domain 'learning culture'; however, only for two respondents this was their dominant action domain. Remarkably, the two latter respondents were the only two HR managers who were interviewed. Apparently, they were more concerned with organizational aspects (e.g., culture) than with actual learning activities and their operating style. Mostly the strategies in the 'learning culture' action domain were concerned with the ways in which the respondents attempted to influence the learning culture of the organization, for instance, by encouraging employees to participate in training and learning activities. Through active encouragement, the respondents motivated employees to participate in training sessions, knowing that this would ultimately benefit the organization itself as well.

> R6: We encourage people to multi skill, up to our highest pay group, because obviously there's a benefit for the employee because they get more wage, but also a benefit for the company because we have a more flexible workforce. So we actually encourage it, but ultimately it's their choice.

Strategies Categorized According to the Learning-Network Theory

The strategies employed by the 18 respondents were divided according to the four ideal types of the Learning-Network Theory. As Table 2.3 shows, most of the strategies reflected the liberal or horizontal types. No external strategies emerged in the data set. Horizontal strategies were obvious, for example, from respondents talking about material that was developed with a great deal of input from the participants, about capitalizing on the advantage of group learning, about encouraging collaboration among the participants, and so on. Liberal strategies emerged, for instance, where respondents encouraged one-on-one coaching of the employee by the HRD practitioner, and where they motivated employees to take their own professional development into their own hands.

Strategies of Respondents Related to Type of Work in the Organization

In order to answer the second research question, respondents were clustered into three groups: those with strategies in only one action domain (narrow range), those with strategies in two action domains (medium range), and those with strategies in three action domains (broad range). Respondents with strategies in four action domains were not found (see Table 2.2).

The three respondents who focused on only one action domain (R1, R11, and R17) restricted their strategies to either 'material' or 'participants.' These HRD practitioners are mainly concerned with learning activities and can be said to employ a narrow range of strategies.

The nine respondents who used strategies within two action domains (R3, R4, R5, R6, R8, R10, R12, R16, and R18) also focused mainly on learning activities (with more than half combining 'participants' with 'material'). All other combinations of two action domains were found in the data as well; therefore, no clear pattern emerged other than the focus on learning activities.

Table 2.3 Dominant action domains in relation to type of work ($n = 18$)

	Dominant action domain in terms of strategies				Dominant action domain according to the LNT			
	Material	Participants	Informal style	Learning culture	Liberal	Vertical	Horizontal	External
Entrepreneurial	3	1	1	1	3	–	3	–
Bureaucratic	–	1	2	1	1	–	2	–
Teamwork	3	1	2	–	1	1	3	–
Professional	1	–	1	–	2	–	1	–
Total	7	3	6	2	7	1	9	0
	(Total: 18)				(Total: 17)			

Note: The total of 17 for 'dominant action domain according to the Learning-Network Theory' can be explained by the fact that not all strategies, undertaken by the respondents, could be coded according to this theory. This led to the situation that not all respondents had strategies that could be categorized in one of the four categories of the theory, namely R4, R6, R10, and R17 (see also Table 2.3). Since some respondents had a combination of two categories, the total of this table sums up to 17. The total of the most dominant action domain is 18, since it was possible to categorize the strategies in one or more action domains.

The six respondents who employed strategies in three action domains (R2, R7, R9, R13, R14, and R15) can be said to use a broad repertoire of strategies. The majority had 'informal style' as their dominant action domain, that is, they devoted a lot of energy to consciously influencing the way they were perceived in the wider organization. This suggests that HRD practitioners with a broad set of strategies are very much concerned with their position in the organization and operating style. As in the middle group, no specific dominant combination of three action domains emerged. All respondents in the broad-repertoire group focused their strategies on context, material, as well as learning activities (participants or material).

Next, in order to answer the second research question, it was tested whether any differences in the number of action domains covered by the respondents were related to the type of work in their organization. No clear-cut relationships emerged from the data. In all four types of work, HRD practitioners used strategies in two or three action domains. Notable was that two of the three respondents who used strategies in one action domain only (learning activities) were employed in team-based organizations (R11 and R17), as Table 2.3 shows. Reasoning the other way around, HRD practitioners employed in entrepreneurial and team-based organizations used more strategies in the action domain 'material,' whereas respondents in machine bureaucratic and professional organizations employed more strategies in the action domain 'informal style.'

Conclusions and Implications

The main aim of this study was to investigate the HRD strategies employed by HRD practitioners working for South Australian organizations. A total of 18 semi-structured interviews were held with HRD practitioners from 16 different organizations. Many different strategies were found, which were categorized into four distinct groups referred to as action domains: 'material,' 'participants,' 'informal style,' and 'learning culture.'

Most respondents used strategies in more than one domain. A small minority of the respondents used strategies in only one action domain (either 'participants' or 'material'); these HRD practitioners are mainly concerned with organizing learning activities. They might have a narrow perception of their role as HRD practitioners or perhaps their position prevents them from using more different strategies (cf. Poell et al., 2006). Similarly, the respondents with a broader repertoire of strategies (spanning two or even three domains) may have a broader role conception or their position in the organizations may grant them more leeway. No specific combinations of action domains used by the respondents were found to be more dominant than other combinations.

Most respondents focused their strategies on the action domain 'participants' and/or 'material,' both of which deal with learning activities. This suggests that organizing learning and training programs for employees is still a major part of the role of HRD practitioners (cf. Buyens et al., 2001; Nijhof, 2004). The two HR managers who were interviewed besides the 16 HRD practitioners came up with a somewhat different picture, in that they were the only two respondents who did not mention strategies associated with learning activities ('participants' or 'material'), focusing their dominant strategies on the action domain 'learning culture' instead. Perhaps this had something to do with their difficult position in the organization, between management and employees. Attempting to influence the learning culture in the organization (e.g., the ways in which organizational members think about learning and development) may be a prominent way to have an impact in such positions.

In terms of the Learning-Network Theory, especially horizontal (team-based) and liberal (individual-based) HRD strategies were found among the South Australian HRD practitioners. In line with two earlier studies conducted in the United Kingdom (Poell & Chivers, 1999, 2003) and the Netherlands (Poell et al., 2003), no external (profession-based) strategies were found. Apparently, HRD professionals are more concerned with learning and development that have meaning primarily within the organization than they are with continuing professional development (which transcends the boundaries of the organization and crosses into the domain of professional associations). It is possible that this finding emerged by not having external HRD practitioners included in the sample.

There were some indications in the data that HRD practitioners employed in entrepreneurial and adhocratic organizations used different strategies than those from machine bureaucratic and professional organizations. The former were most active in the action domains 'material' and 'participants,' which have a highly horizontal character. The latter focused their strategies more on their HRD role ('informal style') than on learning activities ('material' and 'participants'). It may be that in bureaucratic organizations more standardized learning programs are developed, which makes it more difficult for HRD practitioners to have an impact on them. The only way they could influence the learning that occurs is through their personal role and operating style in delivering these programs.

A more detailed comparison of the present findings with the two earlier studies (Poell & Chivers, 1999, 2003; Poell et al., 2003) reveals that our results are more similar to the results of the Dutch study (Poell & Chivers, 1999, 2003). The British study (Poell et al., 2003) found more vertical strategies among the HRD practitioners, whereas a tendency to more liberal and horizontal strategies emerged in the Netherlands. Perhaps this is due to the fact that the Dutch and Australian studies were conducted a few years later than the British study. Another explanation could be that in the two previous studies, all HRD practitioners graduated from the same University in England (Sheffield) and in the Netherlands (Nijmegen). In the present study, many respondents were gathered through the snowball method, therefore all respondents had different backgrounds.

Despite the emphasis still being placed on organizing programs, all respondents in the present study spoke about the importance of 'adult learning,' stressing the fact that there must be enough flexibility in the program as well as input from the participants. Delivering lectures in the more traditional way seems to be no longer accepted among HRD practitioners. All respondents tried to create (open) learning atmospheres. It can be discussed whether this tendency is desirable, always and everywhere. There may still be plenty of situations where lecturing and pre-designed training programs are very effective means of knowledge transfer (e.g., memorizing legislative texts, practicing safety regulations). Perhaps the trend toward wanting to create liberal and horizontal learning programs prevents HRD practitioners from taking into account all possibly effective strategies?

Some limitations of the present study should be taken into account when interpreting the conclusions. First, using semi-structured interviews can lead to not all potentially relevant issues being discussed; however, this decision was made to enable a comparison with the two earlier studies in other countries. Second, for practical reasons (and comparison), only HRD practitioners were interviewed; adding information from employees and management would provide a richer picture of the ways in which learning programs are developed and delivered. In most cases only one HRD practitioner per company was interviewed (usually because they were the only one employed by the company); perhaps if they would have HRD colleagues we would have heard about different strategies in an interview. Third, it is possible that using a different theoretical framework would result in more and different types of strategies and action domains; perhaps the four categories of the Learning-Network Theory are too limited in this respect. Fourth, it needs to be taken into account that, in practice, there may be considerable overlap among strategies from different action domains ('material,' 'participants,' 'learning culture,' and 'informal style'). Many respondents stressed the importance of collaboration, interaction, and team activities, which seem to have ramifications for all four action domains.

Despite the limitations of the present study, we think our conclusions still provide a useful contribution to the discussion about dominant HRD strategies, bringing an Australian dimension to it. The four action domains that emerged from this study are new constructs, which may be used in further research on this topic. Future studies should specifically attempt to include professional organizations, where it seems more likely to find HRD strategies associated with the external dimension (according to the Learning-Network Theory).

References

Anderson, G., & Johnston, R. (1997). *Human resource development: Developing the developers in a changing field.* Paper presented at the Fifth Annual International Conference on Post-Compulsory Education and Training, Gold Coast, Queensland, Australia, 26–28 November.

Argyris, C., & Schön, D. A. (1996). *Organizational learning II.* Reading, MA: Addison-Wesley.

Buyens, D., Wouters, K., & Dewettinck, K. (2001). Future challenges for human resource development professionals in European learning-oriented organisations. *Journal of European Industrial Training, 9*, 442–453.

Hytönen, T. (2002). *Exploring the practice of human resource development as a field of professional expertise.* PhD thesis, University of Jyväskylä, Finland.

Hytönen, T., Poell, R. F., & Chivers, G. E. (2002). HRD as a professional career: Perspectives from Finland, The Netherlands and the United Kingdom. In W. Nijhof, A. Heikkinen, & L. Nieuwenhuis (Eds.), *Shaping flexibility in vocational education and training: Institutional, curricular and professional conditions* (pp. 227–242). Dordrecht, The Netherlands: Kluwer.

Koornneef, M., Oostvogel, K., Harris, R., & Poell, R. F. (2002). Strategies of HRD practition-
ers in stimulating learning: An overview of theory and comparative empirical research. In
J. Searle & D. Roebuck (Eds.), *Envisioning practice, implementing change* (pp. 166–174).
Brisbane: Australian Academic Press.

Nijhof, W. J. (2004). Is the HRD profession in the Netherlands changing? *Human Resource
Development International, 1*, 57–72.

Peters, V., & Wester, F. (1990). *Qualitative analysis in practice: Including user's guide Kwalitan
version 2*. Nijmegen, The Netherlands: University of Nijmegen, Department of Research
Methodology.

Peters, V., Wester, F., & Richardson, R. (1989). *Kwalitatieve analyse in praktijk en handleiding
bij Kwalitan, versie 2* [Qualitative analysis in practice: Guide to using Kwalitan, version 2].
Nijmegen, The Netherlands: ITS.

Pluijmen, R., Poell, R. F., & Van der Krogt, F. J. (2001). *Strategieën van HRD professionals
bij het organiseren van leertrajecten* [Strategies of HRD professionals in organizing learning programs]. Internal research report. Nijmegen, The Netherlands: University of Nijmegen,
Department of Educational Sciences.

Poell, R. F., & Chivers, G. E. (1999). *New roles of HRD consultants in different organizational
types*. Paper presented at the VET Forum meeting on 'learning in learning organizations,' held
in Evora, Portugal, November.

Poell, R. F., & Chivers, G. E. (2003). Experiences of HRD consultants in supporting organisational
learning. In B. Nyhan, P. Cressey, M. Kelleher, & R. F. Poell (Eds.), *Facing up to the learning
organisation challenge: Selected European writings* (pp. 247–264). Luxembourg: Office for
Official Publications of the European Communities.

Poell, R. F., Pluijmen, R., & Van der Krogt, F. J. (2003). Strategies of HRD professionals in organising learning programmes: A qualitative study among 20 Dutch HRD professionals. *Journal
of European Industrial Training, 27*, 125–136.

Poell, R. F., Van der Krogt, F. J., Vermulst, A. A., Harris, R., & Simons, M. (2006). Roles of informal workplace trainers in different organizational contexts: Empirical evidence from Australian
companies. *Human Resource Development Quarterly, 17*, 175–198.

Slotte, V., Tynjälä, P., & Hytönen, T. (2004). How do HRD practitioners describe learning at work?
Human Resource Development International, 4, 481–499.

Tjepkema, S., Stewart, J., Sambrook, S., Mulder, M., Ter Horst, H., & Scheerens, J. (2002). *HRD
and learning organisations in Europe*. London: Routledge.

Van der Krogt, F. J. (1998). Learning-Network Theory: The tension between learning systems and
work systems in organisations. *Human Resource Development Quarterly, 9*, 157–177.

Walton, J. (1999). *Strategic human resource development*. Harlow: Pearson Education.

Chapter 3
Conceptualising Participation in Formal Training and Development Activities: A Planned Behaviour Approach

Ronan Carbery and Thomas N. Garavan

An increasing number of organisations make use of training and development activities in order to deal with immediate staffing problems, to replace expensive selection procedures, to ensure that employees are sufficiently skilled, to meet strategic challenges and contribute to competitive advantage (Day, Harrison, & Halpin, 2009). Employees are expected to take ownership for the development of their generic competencies and, as a result, are more likely to participate in training and development on a continuous basis (Antonacopoulou, 2000). The requirement to be self-directed in the context of training and development has given rise to the need to further understand the factors that explain self-directed behaviour and what factors predict participation in training and development. The theory of planned behaviour (TPB) is considered one such theory (Ajzen, 1991). The theory of reasoned action (TRA; Ajzen & Fishbein, 1970) and its extension, TPB, are considered two of the more pervasive of the attitude-behaviour models.

The TPB arose to address the limitations of the TRA in dealing with behaviours over which individuals do not have complete volitional control. TPB argues that human action is guided by three kinds of beliefs: beliefs regarding the likely outcomes of the behaviour and the evaluation of these outcomes (behavioural beliefs); beliefs about the normative expectations of others and motivation to comply with these expectations (normative beliefs); and beliefs regarding the presence of factors that may facilitate or impede performance of the behaviour and the perceived power of these factors (control beliefs). Where individuals have a sufficient degree of actual control over the behaviour, they will be expected to carry out their intentions when the opportunity arises. TPB assumes that intention is an immediate antecedent of actual behaviour. The extent to which an individual intends to perform behaviours depends in part on the availability of resources and the control they have over their own behaviour. The perceived behavioural control of an individual in a decision-making situation will affect his/her behavioural intentions. While the

R. Carbery (✉)
Department of Personnel & Employment Relations, Kemmy Business School, University of Limerick, Ireland
e-mail: Ronan.Carbery@ul.ie

R.F. Poell, M. van Woerkom (eds.), *Supporting Workplace Learning*, Professional and Practice-based Learning 5, DOI 10.1007/978-90-481-9109-3_3,
© Springer Science+Business Media B.V. 2011

TPB is a widely used and well-supported theoretical framework, its operation in the context of participation in training and development is not yet fully understood. Therefore, the first purpose of this chapter is to explore the issues that need to be considered in understanding the value of TPB in explaining participation in training and development. Second, we discuss the research and practice implications of our proposed model.

The Theoretical Context

Figure 3.1 displays the TPB as applied to participation in training and development. Specifically, training participation behaviour is predicted by individuals' intention to participate in training and development (Intention to Participate). Intentions to participate are predicted by individuals' attitudes towards training and development (Participation Attitudes), by the perceived social pressures to participate in training and development (Subjective Norms) and by Perceived Behavioural Control. Participation Attitudes in the context of training and development focus on personal and career growth expectancies, work-related expectancies, achievement expectancies and training system expectancies. Subjective Norms focus on perceptions that significant referents desire the individual to perform or not perform a behaviour (Taylor & Tood, 1995). The most salient subjective norms in the context of participation in training and development are development norms, perceptions of the transfer environment, contribution expectations of the organisation culture, achievement norms and norms related to staffing. Perceived Behavioural Control focuses on how individuals deal with situations where they have certain intentions but cannot act upon those due to resource or other limitations. We highlight four dimensions of perceived control: self-directedness for learning, self-efficacy beliefs, confidence to use particular learning strategies and task/organisational constraints. We first address general-person characteristics given their influence on the abovementioned three key aspects of the theory of planned behaviour.

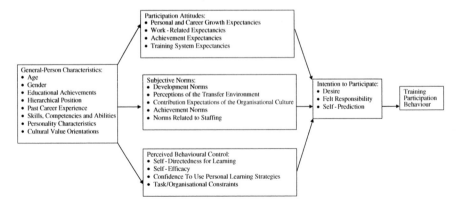

Fig. 3.1 Conceptualising participation in training and development: a planned behaviour model

The Role of General-Person Characteristics

The TPB makes an important distinction between general-person characteristics and behaviour-specific characteristics. General-person characteristics are typically identified as including age, gender, personality characteristics, human capital characteristics and personality characteristics and cultural value expectations. Our model postulates that general-person characteristics influence participation in training and development through their influence on participation attitudes, subjective norms and perceived behavioural control, which in turn influence intentions to participate. This is the general stance of the TPB, however, a number of studies in other contexts have found that age and gender directly contributed to the prediction of intentions (Lawton, Parker, Stradling, & Manstead, 1997).

Age

We postulate that age is related to participation attitudes, subjective norms and perceived behavioural control. Age has been shown to explain achievement expectancies [participation attitudes] (Mannheim, Baruch, & Tal, 1997) and to be positively related to self-directedness in learning [perceived behavioural control] (Stockdale, 2003) while Woodley and McIntosh (1979) found evidence that mature learners were more likely to engage in self-directed learning activities. Older employees may, however, have stronger self-efficacy and have more confidence to use personal learning strategies [perceived behavioural control] (Judge, Cable, Boudreau, & Bretz, 1995). Older employees may find it more difficult to secure resources for training and development due to age stereotypes and discriminatory organisational training and development participation practices. Age, therefore, can impact on the attitudes of employees towards intention to participate. It is also important in explaining psychological dimensions of control such as self-efficacy.

Gender

We postulate that gender is related to participation attitudes, perceptions of subjective norms and perceived behavioural control. Gender will likely influence achievement expectancies [participation attitudes] (Leuven, 1997). Mannheim et al. (1997) found that females were more self-directed and were better planners. Gender may also explain self-efficacy. Carbery and Garavan (2007) suggest that females have lower self-efficacy for particular types of training, e.g. management training. We suggest that gender may also influence issues such as management sponsorship, participation in decisions concerning training and development and the existence of facilitating factors in the wider organisation. Women are frequently disadvantaged when resources are allocated for participation in training and development (Cleveland & Shore, 1992).

Educational Achievements

Participation in education activities in the past is related to a number of participation attitudes, perceptions of subjective norms and aspects of perceived behavioural control (Belanger & Tuijnman, 1997). Individuals who have participated in the past are more likely to be self-directed (Bryan & Schultz, 1995). Levels of education may directly impact subjective norms and how an employee perceives development norms (Belanger & Tuijnman, 1997). Employees with high level of educational attainment are likely to possess greater self-efficacy and to have greater confidence in the use of personal learning strategies (Kuijpers & Scheerens, 2006). Level of education attainment may explain the availability of training and development opportunities within organisations. Garavan and Carbery (2003) found that individuals with lower levels of education attainment had fewer opportunities to participate in training and development.

Hierarchical Position

The hierarchical position of the employee will be related to many of the variables specified in the model associated with participation attitudes, subjective norms and perceived behavioural control. Self-directedness in learning processes is positively correlated with hierarchical position, e.g. manager versus operator (Owen, 2002). Managers show higher levels of self-directedness (Stockdale, 2003) and the extent of job responsibilities are related to self-directedness (Bromsfield-Day, 2002). Claes and Ruiz-Quintanilla (1998) found that lower level occupations are relatively less self-directed. Managers also have higher achievement expectations (Garavan, Hogan, & Cahir-O'Donnell, 2009). Employees in these senior positions are also likely to have a greater number of training and development opportunities (Bosley, Arnold, & Cohen, 2007). Noe (1986, p. 793) has pointed out that "it is important that the trainees believe that programme participation and mastery of content are related to the attainment of desired outcomes such as prestige, horizontal and vertical career movement, enhancement of self-confidence and salary increases". Giangreco, Sebastiano, and Peccei (2009) found that more senior level employees were more likely to have these expectations than junior employees.

Past Career Experience

Past career experiences are related to three dimensions of the TPB specified in our model. Past career experience can be defined as past career success, employment and mobility experiences. These experiences, and the way they are perceived, can affect self-directedness, self-efficacy and confidence to use learning strategies. It is also related to career growth expectancies, work achievement and training system expectancies (Maurer, Weiss, & Barbeite, 2003). Employment and mobility experiences can also influence expectancies, self-confidence and self-directedness. Slocum, Cron, Hansen, and Rawlings (1985) argued that remaining employed in the same position for some time influences career expectancies and level of self-directedness. Mobility experiences are likely to impact a range of expectancies (Claes & Ruiz-Quintanilla, 1998), and aspects of perceived behavioural control such as self-directedness, self-efficacy and knowledge for control beliefs (Landau, Shamir, & Arthur, 1992).

Skills, Competencies and Abilities

An individual's skills, competencies and abilities are likely to impact the self-confidence and expectations of an employee in respect of participation in training and development. Garofano and Salas (2005) proposed that competencies will impact confidence to learn. Competency strength and ability impact beliefs concerning the value of learning and training system expectancies. Implicit beliefs will be framed based on developmental learning and perceptions of competencies. It is therefore not simply the level of ability or competence; it also focuses on perceptions of how valuable that ability or competence was in the past (Fossum, Arvey, Paradise, & Robbins, 1986).

Personality Characteristics

Personality characteristics are likely to be important in predicting various attitudes towards participation, subjective norms and perceived behavioural control. Seibert, Kraimer, and Crant (2001) highlight that proactive personality is a key antecedent of a range of attitudes and aspects of perceived behavioural control. Hurtz and Williams (2009) emphasise four specific personality traits: work centrality; job involvement; learning goal orientation; and conscientiousness. Work centrality is defined as the degree of importance that work plays in an individual's life (Paullay, Alliger, & Stone-Romero, 1994). Garafano and Salas (2005) argue that work centrality has value in explaining the utility that individuals attach to participation in training and development. Job involvement is defined as the degree to which an individual is cognitively concerned and focused on his/her current job. Mathieu and Martineau (1997) suggested that job involvement may predict various work and training expectancies, especially where the skills to be learned are considered central to a person's job. Learning goal orientation as a personality trait is proposed by Dweck (2000) as potentially relevant in explaining motivation to learn. It appears to be particularly relevant in explaining an individual's beliefs regarding the extent to which he/she can improve. Hurtz and Williams (2009) found that learning goal orientation was important in explaining participation attitudes, with individuals more likely to value opportunities to learn and develop job-related skills. Conscientiousness is highlighted as an important in explaining achievement expectations (Colquitt et al., 2000).

Cultural Value Orientations

Cultural value orientations are relevant in explaining a range of attitudes, perceptions and subjective norms. A number of studies suggest that individualism–collectivism may influence subjective norms and attitudes to participation. Markus and Kitoyama (1991) argue that individuals have independents constructions of the self whereas collectivists are more interdependent. Applied to the TPB, individuals will likely have higher expectancies, more self-directedness and self-efficacy for and a stronger intention to participate. Individualists and collectivists will likely perceive subjective norms differently. Lee (2004) found a significant relationship between nationality and self-directedness.

Participation Attitudes

An individual's attitudes and beliefs regarding training and development activities are important determinants of intention to participate (Noe, Wilk, Mullen, & Wanek, 1997). Bates (2001) highlights that attitudes can be particularly salient. Where, for example, individuals see a relationship between work, training or personal skills, they are likely to be more interested in learning, more willing to attend training and more likely to use that learning. It is possible to specify a number of motivational concepts that have relevance to participation in training and development. The concept of expectancy beliefs has value in explaining these motivation dimensions. Expectancy theory advocates a decision theory of motivation and choice (Vancouver, 2008; Ryan & Deci, 2000). Motivational behavioural choices rest on an individual's belief that particular behaviours will lead to valued outcomes (value and instrumentality) and that the attainment of these outcomes is possible (expectancy). Intention to participate in training is viewed as a function of an employee's belief concerning the value of training outcomes, that efforts diverted to training will lead to other outcomes and that the outcome as a result of training participation can be attained. Four particular expectancies are relevant in the context of our model: personal and career growth related, work related, and achievement expectations and training system expectancies.

Personal and Career Growth Expectancies

For a significant number of individuals, participation in training and development may provide interesting and challenging learning opportunities. Therefore, the individual's growth need strength plays a role in determining intention to participate in training and development. Hackman and Oldham (1976) highlighted that growth need strength has an important role to play in explaining how individuals respond to various job characteristics. This suggests that where particular learning opportunities are personally interesting or challenging or provide a significant growth experience for the individual, the learner will have stronger participation intentions. Where individuals emphasise personal development and consider that participation will result in significant personal or professional growth experiences, this will likely result in stronger intentions to participate in training and development.

Work-Related Expectancies

Many individuals participate in training and development for reasons specifically related to work performance and work skill needs. It may be possible for employees to achieve financial rewards for skill acquisition and certification. Individuals with a strong desire for pay and promotion will likely have a stronger intention to participate in training and development. Where individuals perceive that participation

in training and development will be of benefit to work, they wil
attitudes and a stronger intention to participate in skill developr

The development of new skills resulting from participation ii
opment may lead to both positive and negative changes in the
the employee. Individuals may expect to be given more comple:
work variety and take on more responsibility and authority. Indi'
view that skill acquisition could result in greater control of the v ....., ...g.. ..
enhanced role or a greater understanding of the current job role. These will likely
result in stronger intentions to participate in training and development (Vancouver,
2008). It may also lead to greater physical and mental demands, increased stress and
role ambiguity. These negative perceptions may be related to a variety of general-
person characteristics and trainee perceptions of past training and development
opportunities. Such negative perceptions may result in an intention not to participate
in training and development.

Achievement Expectancies

Employees differ in their achievement expectancies. These differences will influence their intentions to participate in training and development and the types of
training and development opportunities that they engage in. (Chiaburu & Marinova,
2005; Colquitt et al., 2000). Goulet and Singh (2002), for example, found that
individuals with high achievement expectations expressed a strong desire to get
ahead. Participation in training and development may be viewed as a challenging
experience with opportunities for significant success or failure. Opportunities for
certification may be viewed as an indicator of achievement. Likewise, where individuals possess a strong drive for professional credibility, they will have stronger
intentions to participate in training and development. Where individuals have strong
achievement expectancies, they will place more value on learning and are more
likely to apply that learning in the workplace. Individuals may possess the belief that
effective transfer will enhance their professional status. If this is the case, they are
more likely to exhibit increased intentions to participate in training and development
(Bates & Holton, 1999; Seyler, Holton, Bates, Burnett, & Carvalho, 1998).

Training System Expectancies

Individuals may have particular attitudes towards training experiences in an organisation. They may also have previous reinforcements concerning participation in
training and development. Individuals may have formulated beliefs concerning the
extent to which the training provided would be of value in achieving the ultimate
goal of learning. These expectancies may be influenced by previous experience with
the training programme and/or the trainer, knowledge required concerning the reputation and quality of the training and development event and the general quality of
the training function in the organisation (Switzer, Nagy, & Mullins, 2005).

Individuals may attend training and development for affective or hedonic reasons (Kraiger, Ford, & Salas, 1993). These affective responses will likely relate to
past training experiences, the process of enrolling for training or the organisation's

rnation processes. These attitudes are likely to influence future intention to participate. Particular post-training experiences may have the effect of enhancing an individual's self-esteem, providing affirming feedback or are simply entertaining. However, they may also have been negative, boring, extremely difficult, demoralising or humiliating. Depending on the nature of previous training experiences, these will influence intention to participate in the future.

Previous training transfer success is also important. Campbell (1989) suggested that an individual's previous success in applying new learning on the job can affect intentions to participate in training and development. Where an individual has had success in mastering training content, applying ideas on the job and receiving rewards for application, this will foster stronger intentions to participate. The training-related histories of individuals have the effect of creating attitudes, values and behaviour that influences participation intentions. It is well established that past learning transfer success will enhance positive expectations about the outcomes of training, increase training-related motivation and lead to stronger intentions to participation in training and development (Noe, 1986).

Subjective Norms About Participation in Training and Development

Norms and culture within organisations influence intentions to participate in training and development (Benson, Finegold, and Mohrman, 2004; Holton, 2005). These include the role of developmental norms (Klein, Noe, & Wang, 2006) and the general transfer environment (Kozlowski & Salas, 1997; Kraiger, McLinden, & Casper, 2004). We focus on five subjective norms here: development norms, transfer environment, contribution expectations, achievement norms and norms related to staffing. Individuals perceive these norms in different ways.

Development Norms

Development norms refer to perceptions of the organisation's learning culture. A continuous learning culture may emerge to reflect an organisation's belief system that considers training and development as a key responsibility for all employees. Continuous learning cultures value and support learning activities and the application of learning outcomes on the job. Farr and Middlebrooks (1990) found that when these values are widely shared within an organisation they will positively influence intentions to participate in training.

Development norms are influenced by trainee perceptions of past training and development opportunities. Where positive perceptions exist, individuals will expect strong approval for participating in training and development. This approval will come from both managers and co-workers. The perceived presence of supports or constraints is highlighted as a particular characteristic of development norms. Social supports are particularly important. Social support is characterised as a positive social environment where participation in training and development is encouraged, regular feedback is provided regarding development needs or where employees are encouraged to implement newly acquired skills and knowledge by both supervisors and peers. Alternatively, the support of peers or co-workers may not be forthcoming. The organisation may have developed a norm of non-compliance with management initiatives. There may also be a strong culture of underperformance. This suggests that where employees decide to participate in training and development, this behaviour will be considered undesirable. A planned behaviour approach suggests that employees who have opportunities to participate in training and development will make an assessment of the level of approval or disapproval from peers, co-workers and managers, and use this to decide whether to participate in training and development. Hurtz and Williams (2009) conceptualise the development norms of the organisation along three dimensions: perceptions of general support for development; co-worker support for development; and supervisory support. Noe and Wilk (1993) suggest that the assessments made by employees will explain intention to develop new skills and participate in formal training and development activities.

Cohen (1990) found that where trainees had more supportive supervisors, they entered training with stronger beliefs that the training would be useful. Supervisors demonstrated their support through discussion of the training with employees, the establishment of training goals, provision of release time to prepare for the training and the provision of general encouragement to the employees. Cohen (1990) also found that where trainees set developmental goals prior to participation they had stronger intentions to participate.

Perceptions of the Transfer Environment

Perceptions of the transfer environment can influence intentions to participate (Kontoghiorghes, 2004; Holton et al., 2001). Transfer of training is generally defined as the extent to which trainees effectively apply the knowledge, skill and attitudes gained in a training context back to the job. The more recent literature has focused on examining the transfer environment. Earlier studies by Rouillier and Goldstein (1991) and Ford, Quinones, Sego, and Sorra (1992) found that the transfer environment was enhanced by strong supervisory support. These studies emphasise the importance of situational, goals and task and structural cues. Where employees have opportunities to apply what they have learned this will influence both intentions to participate.

Kontoghiorghes (2004) studied the impact of both the transfer climate and the work environment on intentions to participate. Dimensions of transfer climate found to be significant included accountability for training, opportunities to practice, opportunities to use new skills and knowledge and the rewards available to employees who use these new skills. Saks and Belcourt (2006) found that the amount of transfer declines significantly with time post-training. The overall decline was explained by poor trainee input and involvement, training attendance policies, and supervisory involvement both before and after training.

Contribution Expectations of the Organisation Culture

Contribution expectations focus on the extent to which an organisation's cultures supports employee contribution. Contribution expectations focus on the extent to which the employee believes it is possible to influence decisions, contribute ideas and implement changes in work practices. Organisations may, for example, implement work systems that demand a lot from individuals. Strong contribution expectation cultures are generally supported by a variety of initiatives such as employee involvement and participation programmes, quality circles, continuous improvement teams, self-managed team and empowerment activities. Positive contributions will influence both intentions to participate and participation behaviours. Employees are most likely to value training and development activities that facilitate involvement in self-managed activities. Foucher and Brezot (1997) concluded that more opportunities to contribute in a decentralised management style stimulated stronger intentions to participate.

Achievement Norms

Some organisation cultures are characterised by competitive behaviours. These behaviours have a collective character and differ from the achievement expectations of individuals. Culture may promote achievement norms such as achieving exceptional performance, high potential employee labels and fast track career progression. Achievement-focused cultures tap into the autonomy orientation of individuals. High achievement-oriented individuals will attend to cues in the culture that suggest "free choice" and norms that highlight exceptional achievement. Organisations increasingly mandate that employees include stretch goals in their performance and development plans. The organisation's culture will base its rewards on how well these stretch goals are achieved. Similarly, Drach-Zahavy and Erez (2002) found that performance will decrease when goals are framed in terms of avoiding a negative outcome rather than a positive one. In the context of training, the primary achievement-related activity focuses on skill development, certification and enhancement of opportunities for job and career advancement. Where achievement norms within the culture are strong, this will have a positive impact on individual decisions to participate in training and development.

Norms Related to Staffing

How individuals perceive the organisation's staffing strategies will influence their intention to participate in training and development. Collins and Kehoe (2009) make a distinction between a commitment staffing model and a professional staffing model. Commitment staffing places a strong emphasis on an employee's ability to adopt and grow with the organisation. There is a strong emphasis on employee development and extended tenure. In contrast, Baron, Hannan, and Burton (2001) argue that a professional model places emphasis on specific task abilities and employment attachment through challenging work. Organisations that follow a professional model do not invest substantially in generic competency development.

Employees are more likely to place greater value on opportunities to acquire generic competencies. These provide greater portability and have greater value in the internal and external labour market. Specific competencies are of greater value to the organisation, however they have less portability. Noe and Wilk (1993) have suggested that intentions to participate in training and development will be influenced by employees' perceptions of these approaches.

Perceived Behavioural Control

The concept of perceived behavioural control was proposed in order to deal with situations where intentions could not be acted upon due to resource or control limitations. In our model we postulate that perceived behavioural control influences both intention to participate and, thereby, training participation behaviour.

Perceived behavioural control may relate to perceptions of both personal and organisational resources. It includes four dimensions of control: self-directedness for learning; self-efficacy beliefs (Bandura, 1977); confidence to use personal learning strategies; and task/organisational constraints. This latter category includes task characteristics, management sponsorship, participation in training and development decisions and resource constraints imposed on training and development.

Self-Directedness for Learning

Self-directedness is a key aspect of perceived behavioural control in the context of intention to participate in training and development (Brockett & Hiemstra, 1991). High self-directedness is related to both intention to participate and participation behaviour (Lankhuijzen, 2002). Individuals who are high on self-directedness are more likely to take on more difficult tasks and to be more goal-focused. Abele and Wiese (2008) found that self-directedness was relevant in explaining subjective career success. Self-directedness results in the setting of more specific goals and in the selection of more appropriate strategies to implement them.

Self-Efficacy

Self-efficacy refers to an individual's confidence to cope with challenging situations (Bandura, 1977). Self-efficacy can be conceptualised as a potential antecedent to participation in training and development. While self-efficacy may be viewed as a general-person characteristic, the evidence suggests that it is best measured specific to a given task setting (Maurer, 2001). Individuals who possess the belief that they are capable of mastering particular training content are more likely to display stronger intentions to participate in training. Self-efficacy influences intention to participate in training. Colquitt and Simmering (2000) summarised 20 years of research in factors affecting intention to participate and self-efficacy emerged as a particularly important individual characteristic.

Our model acknowledges relationships between perceived behavioural control and participation attitudes. Self-efficacy, for example, will be influenced by various expectations related to work, career and personal growth. Expectations regarding rewards, for example, will not impact behaviour if performance self-efficacy is low. However, self-efficacy will not affect intention and behaviour if an individual's expectations are not perceived as positive. In the context of training and development participation, the extent to which individuals mobilise their efforts will be determined by the outcomes and their self-efficacy that they can master the training content (Napier & Latham, 1986).

Confidence to Use Personal Learning Strategies

We propose that the extent to which individuals perceive that they can use personal learning strategies is relevant in explaining their intention to participate in training and development. It is an important dimension of perceived behavioural control. Warr and Allen (1998) suggest that individuals may use a variety of personal learning strategies which may be cognitive, behavioural or self-regulatory in nature. The notion of confidence to use personal learning strategies taps into the strong desire which employees may have for self-determination. Self-determination is a sense of choice in initiating and regulating one's actions (Deci, Connell, & Ryan, 1989). In the context of intention to participate in training and development it reflects a sense of autonomy of choice over the initiation or continuation of learning behaviour and processes.

Task/Organisational Constraints

Various dimensions of the task or the organisation can set limits or present constraints on both intention to participate and participation behaviour. We focus on a number of these characteristics here.

Task Constraints. Jobs may contain differing degrees of autonomy, complexity, task variation and growth potential (Kohn & Schooler, 1982). Low-task variety will likely weaken intention to participate in training and development and jobs that possess less learning potential will weaken intention to participate and participation behaviour.

Management Sponsorship. We propose that management sponsorship in the form of support for training or giving permission to attend is important (Arthur, Bennett, Edens, & Bell, 2003). Participation in training may involve pay and promotion issues. Where individuals perceive that management are not supportive and are not likely to sponsor training activities that involve attendance off-site, this will likely have a negative impact on intentions to participate in training and development. Where senior organisational members actually encourage skill development and provide employees with resources in visible ways, it will increase intention to participate in training and development.

Knowledge for Control Beliefs. Individuals will use various forms of knowledge to assess or determine their control beliefs in the context of intentions to participate in training and development. Knowledge is used by employees to self-assess readiness to participate in training to develop new skills and knowledge. Blanchard and Thacker (2007) highlight that organisations may formally do this via a thorough needs assessment before training activities are designed and delivered. Learners can use the needs identification process to enhance knowledge of their learning needs, the necessary prerequisites for training and development, and whether the learning activity is appropriate. Knowledge of both self-readiness and of personal learning needs will lead to increased intention to participate in training and development and participation behaviour (Fowlkes, Salas, Baker, Cannon-Bowers, & Stout, 2000).

Another dimension of knowledge for control beliefs concerns knowledge of organisational and career skill requirements. Management influence the amount and type of information that is available and the format in which it is available (Leisink & Greenwood, 2007). Management use various devices and strategies to communicate the skills that are valued by the organisation, the desirability to acquire particular competencies and the rewards available to employees who acquire skills and competencies (Bates, 2001; Baldwin, Magjuka, & Loher, 1991). Management communicate important requirements concerning the value of certification and the regulatory and institutional requirements on the organisation (Garavan, Shanahan, & Carbery, 2008). Individuals likewise play an important role in terms of knowledge flow. They focus on aspects of information that are important to the job, the role and/or the career. Individuals will attend to issues related to the steps required to get access to training and development and what it takes to succeed in training. The attention given by the individual will determine the accuracy and completeness of the information that will be used to make decisions concerning participation. Where individuals have greater knowledge, this will strengthen their intention to participate in training and development.

Participation in Training and Development Decisions. Wlodkowski (1985) argued that the involvement of employees in decisions about the training process could influence their intention to participate in training and development. In the pre-training context, participation may span a spectrum of activities such as informing the employee regarding the training content, finding out about training content, finding out the trainees preferences for learning content and methods and provide the trainee with scope to make decisions concerning whether to attend or not.

It may also involve situations where an individual has scope to influence the design of training and development activities. Kessels and Plomp (1999) introduce the concept of external consistency to refer to the level of congruence in how the training agenda is understood by various stakeholders, to what extent is there homogeneity of ideas and perceptions of the learning needs and the type of training situation desired. Greater involvement of the individual in the design process will lead to greater levels of external consistency.

The research on participation in training design and strategy selection decisions presents a mixed picture concerning it's importance. Participation enables individuals to develop familiarity with the workings and content of the training. However, the depth and nature of pre-training information tends to vary. Baldwin et al. (1991) found that where trainees received information concerning the training, they were more likely to participate. Hicks and Klimoski (1987) found that where trainees were provided with a realistic description of the training, they reported more a stronger intention to participate. Participation in decisions concerning training choices may enhance feelings of involvement, create more realistic training expectations, provide signals as to the importance of the training and provide the learner with sufficient time to align personal goals with the goals of the training.

Resource Constraints on Training and Development. Organisations differ in terms of the resources they allocate to training and development. The first dimension of resources focuses on the financial allocation given to training and development on a yearly basis (Garavan et al., 2008). This resource is likely to vary depending upon economic conditions, the size of the organisation and whether the organisation is an independent subsidiary or part of a multinational organisation (Matlay, 2002). The second dimension concerns time off to participate, appropriate scheduling of training, appropriate and sufficient equipment, and the anticipated availability of training and development opportunities. Where the individual has positive perceptions of these resource dimensions, it will likely enhance both intention to participate and training and participation behaviour.

Intention to Participate and Training Participation Behaviour

The TPB makes an important distinction between intentions and behaviour. Ajzen (1991) describes intentions as the extent to which people are willing to try hard to perform a behaviour or exert effort. Hurtz and Williams (2009) suggest that intention to participate can be operationalised by desire, felt responsibility and self-prediction. Desire is the individual's perception that he or she wants to participate in future development activities; felt responsibility refers to the feeling that he or she is obligated to participate in future development activities; and self-prediction is the expectation that he or she will participate in future training and development activities.

Participation can be conceptualised as actual participation in voluntary or mandatory formal training and development activities. Carbery and Garavan (2007) suggested that actual participation means formal commitment which includes enrolling and participating in organisationally provided formal learning and development programmes. What constitutes attendance may include a variety of behaviours such as attendance at formal training classes, attendance at conferences, completion of a project or it may focus on the amount of time spent on each activity. Research suggests a strong relationship between intention and actual behaviour (Van Hooft & De Jong, 2009).

Conclusions and Implications for Research and Practice

The TPB has theoretical value in explaining people's intentions and behaviours in the context of training and development. We confined our discussion to formal training and development activities; however, the TPB has application to informal training activities. The study of participation in training and development is important from both theoretical and practical perspectives. At a theoretical level, the TPB highlights a number of constructs that are relevant in conceptualising both intention to participate and participation behaviours. General-person characteristics are postulated to have an indirect effect on intention to participate through their influence on participation attitudes, subjective norms and perceived behavioural control.

It is assumed that there is a strong relationship between intention to participate and participation behaviour, however, this assertion is not yet fully understood in the training and development literature. This link may differ for various types of training and development activities. We suggest that the concept of perceived behavioural control is particularly relevant in the context of training and development. The process through which individuals interpret different aspects of behavioural control requires more empirical investigation from this perspective. Five dimensions of behavioural control are highlighted, of which four relate to the characteristics of individuals that enable them to form an intention to participate or actually participate. The fifth variable captures a range of organisational constraints that may influence intention to participate or constrain actual participation. This suggests that organisations have scope for influence some dimensions of behavioural control over others. The TPB suggests that opportunities to participate in decisions regarding participation, the provisions of support and advice, resources to facilitate participation and the provision of knowledge for control beliefs should be particularly beneficial.

Training and development specialists should adopt support and guidance strategies that reflect the unique needs of individuals and in raising their self-efficacy, self-directedness and confidence to use learning strategy beliefs. These beliefs are strongly associated with intention to participate and they are particularly proximal to actual participation in training and development.

References

Abele, A. E., & Wiese, B. S. (2008). The nomological network of self-management strategies and career success. *Journal of Occupational and Organizational Psychology, 81*, 733–749.

Ajzen, I., & Fishbein, M. (1970). The prediction of behavioural intentions in a choice situation. *Journal of Experimental Social Psychology, 5*, 400–416.

Ajzen, I. (1991). The theory of planned behaviour. *Organizational Behaviour and Human Decision Processes, 50*, 179–211.

Antonacopoulou, E. P. (2000). Employee development through self-development in three retail banks. *Personnel Review, 29*, 491–508.

Arthur, W. Jr., Bennett, W. Jr., Edens, P. S., & Bell, S. T. (2003). Effectiveness of training and organizations: A meta-analysis of design and evaluation features. *Journal of Applied Psychology, 88*(2), 234–245.

Baldwin, T T., Magjuka, R. J., & Loher, B. T. (1991). The perils of participation: Effects of choice of training on trainee motivation and learning. *Personnel Psychology, 44*, 51–66.

Bandura, A. (1977). *Social learning theory.* Englewood Cliffs, NJ: Prentice-Hall.

Baron, J. N., Hannan, M. T., & Burton, M. D. (2001). Labor pains: Organizational change and employee turnover in young, high-tech firms. *The American Journal of Sociology, 106*, 960–1012.

Bates, R. A. (2001). Public sector training participation: An empirical investigation. *Journal of Training and Development, 5*(2), 136–152.

Bates, R. A., & Holton, E. F. (1999). *Learning transfer in a social service agency: Test of an expectancy model of motivation.* Paper presented at the academy of human resource development, Arlington, VA.

Belanger, P., & Tuijnman, A. (1997). The "silent explosion" of adult learning. In P. Belanger & A. Tuijnman (Eds.), *New patterns of adult learning: A six-country comparative study* (pp. 1–16). Oxford: Pergamon.

Benson, G., Finegold, D., & Mohrman, S. (2004). You paid for the skills, now keep them: Tuition-reimbursement and voluntary turnover. *Academy of Management Journal, 47*(3), 315–333.

Blanchard, P. N., & Thacker, J. W. (2007). *Effective training: Systems, strategies, and practices* (3rd ed.). Upper Saddle River, NJ: Pearson Education.

Bosley, S., Arnold, J., & Cohen, L. (2007). The anatomy of credibility: A conceptual framework of valued career helper attributes. *Journal of Vocational Behaviour, 70*, 116–134.

Brockett, R. G., & Hiemstra, R. (1991). *Self-direction in adult learning: Perspectives on theory, research and practice.* London: Routledge.

Bromsfield-Day, D. (2000). *Employee readiness for self-directed learning and selected organisational variables as predictors of job performance*, UMI No. 3000231.

Bryan, V., & Schulz, S. F. (1995). Self-directed learning in distance education: The relationship between self-directed learning readiness scores and success in completing distance education programmes through home-study training. In H. B. Long & Associates (Eds.), *New dimensions in self-directed learning* (pp. 135–158). College of Education: University of Oklahoma.

Campbell, J. (1989). The agenda for training theory and research. In I. L. Goldstein (Ed.), *Training and development in organizations* (pp. 469–486). San Francisco: Jossey-Bass.

Carbery, R., & Garavan, T. N. (2007). Conceptualising the participation of managers in career-focused learning and development: A framework. *Human Resource Development Review, 6*(4), 394–418.

Chiaburu, D. S., & Marinova, S. V. (2005). What predicts skill transfer? An exploratory study of goal orientation, training self-efficacy and organizational supports. *International Journal of Training and Development, 9*, 110–23.

Claes, R., & Ruiz-Quintanilla, S. A. (1998). Influences of early career experiences occupational group, and national culture on proactive career behaviour. *Journal of Vocational Behaviour, 52*, 359–378.

Cleveland, J. N., & Shore, L. M. (1992). Self- and supervisory perspectives on age and work attitudes and performance. *Journal of Applied Psychology, 77*(4), 469–484.

Cohen, D. J. (1990, November) What motivates trainees? *Training and Development Journal, 44*, 91–93.

Collins, C. J., & Kehoe, R. R. (2009). Recruitment and selection. In J. Storey, P. M. Wright, & D. Ulrich (Eds.), *The Routledge companion to strategic human resource management* (pp. 209–223). London: Taylor and Francis Group.

Colquitt, J. A., & Simmering, M. J. (1998). Conscientiousness, goal orientation, and motivation to learn during the learning process: A longitudinal study. *Journal of Applied Psychology, 85*, 654–665.

Colquitt, J. A., LePine, J. A., & Noe, R. A. (2000). Toward an integrative theory of training motivation: A meta-analytic path analysis of 20 years of research. *Journal of Applied Psychology, 83*, 678–707.

Day, D. V., Harrison, M. M., & Halpin, S. M. (2009). *An integrative approach to leader development.* New York: Routledge.

Deci, E. L., Connell, J. P., & Ryan, R. M. (1989). Self-determination in a work organization. *Journal of Applied Psychology, 74*, 580–590.

Drach-Zahavy, A., & Erez, M. (2002). Challenge versus threat effects on the goal-performance relationship. *Journal of Organizational Behavior, 88*, 667–682.

Dweck, C. S. (2000). *Self-theories: Their role in motivation, personality, and development.* Lillington: NC: Psychology Press.

Farr, J. L., & Middlebrooks, C. L (1990). Enhancing motivation to participate in professional development. In S. L. Willis & S. S. Dubin (Eds.), *Maintaining professional competence* (pp. 195–213). San Francisco: Jossey-Bass.

Ford, J. K., Quinones, M. A., Sego, D. J., & Sorra, J. S. (1992). Factors affecting the opportunity to perform trained tasks on the job. *Personnel Psychology, 45*(3), 511–524.

Fossum, J. A., Arvey, R. D., Paradise, C. A., & Robbins, N. E. (1986). Modeling the skills obsolescence process: A psychological/economic integration. *Academy of Management Review, 11*(2), 362–374.

Foucher, R., & Brezot, F. (1997). Self-directed learning in health care institutions: An analysis of policies and practices. In H. B. Long & Associates (Eds.), *Expanding horizons in self-directed learning* (pp. 101–116). Norman, OK: Public Managers Center, College of Education, University of Oklahoma.

Fowlkes, J., Salas, E., Baker, D., Cannon-Bowers, J., & Stout, R. (2000). The utility of event-based knowledge elicitation. *Human Factors, 42*, 24–35.

Garafano, C. M., & Salas, E. (2005). What influences continuous employee development decisions? *Human Resource Management Review, 15*, 281–304.

Garavan, T. N., Hogan, C., & Cahir-O'Donnell, A. (2009). *Developing managers and leaders: Concepts, perspectives and debates,* Dublin: Gill and MacMillan.

Garavan, T. N., Shanahan, V., & Carbery, R. (2008). *Training and development: National employer survey of benchmarks 2007.* Dublin: CIPD.

Goulet, L. R., & Singh, P. (2002). Career commitment: A reexamination and an extension. *Journal of Vocational Behavior, 61*, 73–91.

Giangreco, A., Sebastiano, A., & Peccei, R. (2009). Trainees' reactions to training: An analysis of the factors affecting overall satisfaction with training. *International Journal of Human Resource Management, 20*(1), 96–111.

Hackman, J. R., & Oldham, G. R. (1976). Motivation through the design of work: Test of a theory. *Organizational Behavior and Human Performance, 16*, 250–279.

Hicks, W. D., & Klimoski, R. J. (1987). Entry into training programs and its effects on training outcomes: A field experiment.*Academy of Management Journal, 30*, 542–552.

Holton, E. F., III. (2005). Holton's evaluation model: New evidence and construct elaborations. *Advances in Developing Human Resources, 7*(1), 37–54.

Hurtz, G. M., & Williams, K. J. (2009). Attitudinal and motivational antecedents of participation in voluntary employee development activities. *Journal of Applied Psychology, 94*(3), 635–653.

Judge, T. A., Cable, D. M., Boudreau, J. W., & Bretz, R. D. (1995). An Empirical Investigation of the Predictors of Executive Career Success. *Personnel Psychology, 48*, 485–519.

Kessels, J., & Plomp, T (1999). A systematic and relational approach to obtaining curriculum consistency in corporate education. *Journal of Curriculum Studies, 31*(6), 679–709.

Kohn, M. L., & Schooler, C. (1982). Job Conditions and Personality: A Longitudinal Assessment of Their Reciprocal Effects. *American Journal of Sociology, 87*, 1257–86.

Klein, H. J., Noe, R. A., & Wang, C. (2006). Motivation to learn and course outcomes: The impact of delivery mode, learning goal orientation, and perceived barriers and enablers. *Personnel Psychology, 59*, 665–702.

Kontoghiorghes, C. (2004). Reconceptualizing the learning transfer conceptual framework: Empirical validation of a new systemic model. *International Journal of Training and Development, 8*(3), 210–221.

Kozlowski, S. W. J., & Salas, E. (1997). An organizational systems approach for the implementation and transfer of training. In J. K. Ford & Associates (Eds.), *Improving training effectiveness in work organizations* (pp. 247–290). Hillsdale, NJ: LEA.

Kraiger, K., Ford, K. J., & Salas, E. (1993). Application of cognitive, skill-based, and affective theories of learning outcomes to new methods of training evaluation. *Journal of Applied Psychology, 78*, 311–328.

Kraiger, K., McLinden, D., & Casper, W. J. (2004). Collaborative planning for training impact. *Human Resources Management, 43*(4), 337–351.

Kuijpers, M. A. C. T., & Scheerens, J. (2006). Career competencies for the modern career. *Journal of Career Development, 32*, 303–319.

Landau, J. C., Shamir, B., & Arthur, M. B. (1992). Predictors of willingness to relocate for managerial and professional employees. *Journal of Organisational Behaviour, 13*, 667–680.

Lankhuijzen, E. (2002). Learning in a self-managed management career: The relation between managers' HRD-patterns, psychological career contracts and mobility perspectives. Utrecht: The University of Utrecht.

Lawton, R., Parker, D., Stradling, S. G., & Manstead, A. S. R. (1997). Self-reported attitude towards speeding and its possible consequences in five different road contexts. *Journal of Community and Applied Social Psychology, 7*(2), 153–165.

Lee, I. H. (2004). *Readiness for self-directed learning and the cultural values of individualism/collectivism among American and South Korean college students seeking teacher certification in agriculture.* Thesis submitted to the Office of Graduate Studies of Texas A&M University.

Leisink, P., & Greenwood, I. (2007). Company-level strategies for raising basic skills: A comparison of Corus Netherlands and UK. *European Journal of Industrial Relations, 13*, 341–360.

Leuven, E. (1997). Gender differences in work-related training. In P. Belanger & A. Tuijnman (Eds.), *New patterns of adult learning: A six-country comparative study* (pp. 189–207). Oxford: Pergamon.

Mannheim, B., Baruch, Y., & Tal, J. (1997). Alternative models for antecedents and outcomes of work centrality and job satisfaction of high-tech personnel. *Human Relations, 50*(12), 1537–1562.

Markus, H. R., & Kitayama, S. (1991). Culture and the self: Implications for cognition, emotion, and motivation. *Psychological Review, 98*, 224–253.

Mathieu, J. E., & Martineau, J. W. (1997). Individual and situational influences on training motivation. In J. K. Ford, S. W. J. Kozlowski, K. Kraiger, E. Salas, & M. S. Teachout (Eds.), *Improving training effectiveness in work organizations* (pp. 193–221). Hillsdale, NJ: Erlbaum.

Matlay, H. (2002). Training and HRD strategies in family and non-family owned small businesses: A comparative approach. *Education and Training, 44*(8/9), 357–369.

Maurer, T. J. (2001). Career-relevant learning and development, worker age, and beliefs about self-efficacy for development. *Journal of Management, 27*, 123–142.

Maurer, T. J., Weiss, E. W., & Barbeite, F. G. (2003). A model of involvement in work-related learning and development activity: The effects of individual, situational, motivational, and age variables. *Journal of Applied Psychology, 88*, 707–724.

Napier, N., & Latham, G. (1986). Outcome expectancies of people who conduct performance appraisals. *Personnel Psychology, 39*, 827–837.

Noe, R. A. (1986). Training attributes and attitudes: Neglected influences of training effectiveness. *Academy of Management Review, 11*, 736–49.

Noe, R. A., & Wilk, S. A. (1993). Investigation of the factors that influence employees' participation in development activities. *Journal of Applied Psychology, 78*, 291–302.

Noe, R. A., Wilk, S. L., Mullen, E. J., & Wanek, J. E. (1997). Employee development: Issues in construct definition and investigation antecedents. In J. K. Ford, S. W. Kozolowski, K. Kraiger, E. Salas, & M. S. Teachout (Eds.), *Improving training effectiveness in work organizations* (pp. 153–189). Mahwah, NJ: Lawrence Erlbaum.

Owen, T. R. (2002). *Self-directed learning in adulthood: A literature review.* (ERIC Document Reproduction Services No. ED461050).

Paullay, I. M., Alliger, G. M., & Stone-Romero, E. F. (1994). Construct validation of two instruments designed to measure job involvement and work centrality. *Journal of Applied Psychology, 79*(2), 224–228.

Rouillier, J. Z., & Goldstein, I. L. (1991). *Determinants of the climate of transfer of training, Montreal.* Paper presented at the meeting of the society of industrial and organizational psychologists.

Ryan, R. M., & Deci, E. L. (2000). Self-determination theory and the facilitation of intrinsic motivation, social development, and well-being. *American Psychologist, 55*(1), 68–78.

Saks, A. M., & Belcourt, M. (2006). An investigation of training activities and transfer of training in organizations. *Human Resource Management, 45*(4), 236–264.

Seibert, S., Kraimer, J., & Crant, M. (2001). What do proactive people do? A longitudinal model linking proactive personality and career success. *Personnel Psychology, 54*, 845–874.

Seyler, D. L., Holton, E. F. III, Bates, R. A., Burnett, M. F., & Carvalho, M. A. (1998). Factors affecting motivation to use training. *International Journal of Training and Development, 2*, 2–16.

Slocum, J., Cron, W. M., Hansen, R., & Rawlings, S. (1985). Business Strategy and The management of the platitude Performer. *Academy of Management Journal, 28*, 133–154.

Stockdale, S. (2003). Development of an instrument to measure self-directedness. *Dissertation Abstracts International, 59*(6A), 1969 (UMI No. 3092836).

Switzer, K. C., Nagy, M. S., & Mullins, M. E. (2005). The influence of training reputation, managerial support, and self-efficacy on pre-training motivation and perceived training transfer. *Applied HRM Research, 10*, 21–34.

Taylor, S., & Todd, P. A. (1995). Understanding information technology usage: A test of competing models. *Information Systems Research, 6*(2), 144–176.

Vancouver, J. B. (2008). Integrating self-regulation theories of work motivation into a dynamic process theory. *Human Resource Management Review, 18*, 1–18.

Van Hooft, E., & De Jong, M. (2009). Predicting job seeking for temporary employment using the theory of planned behaviour: The moderating role of individualism and collectivism. *Journal of Occupational and Organizational Psychology, 82*(2), 295–316.

Warr, P., & Allen, C. (1998). Learning strategies and occupational training. *International Review of Industrial and Organizational Psychology, 13*, 83–121.

Wlodkowski, R. J. (1985). *Enhancing adult motivation to learn.* San Francisco: Jossey-Bass.

Woodley, A., & McIntosh, N. E. (1979). *Age as a factor in performance at the Open University.* Paper presented at the 5th international conference on improving University Teaching, London, City University.

Chapter 4
Experiences of E-Learning and Its Delivery Among Learners Who Work: A Systematic Review

Christopher Carroll, Andrew Booth, Diana Papaioannou, and Anthea Sutton

Workplace-based learning is increasingly recognised as an important mechanism in transferring skills and knowledge from the academic environment and embedding them within working practice. In the past, workplace-based learning occurred as a discrete activity (e.g. day release, sandwich courses, clinical attachments, etc.). E-learning offers the potential for synergies, and indeed synchronicities, between academic content and workplace context. It covers the spectrum from a technology-supported "blended" approach (combining traditional and e-learning approaches) to learning that is delivered entirely online. E-learning is not universally accepted as a potential learning method for all, but it does provide a potential route by which to counter the twin barriers of lack of time and geographical isolation encountered by many learners (Childs et al., 2005; Wutoh, Boren, & Balas, 2004). Online learning has been found to be effective for learners in formal employment (Coultas, Luckin, & du Boulay, 2003; Lain & Aston, 2005), but this effectiveness has also been found to be mediated by their experience of this form of delivery, i.e. where a learner considers their experience to be rewarding and productive, they learn more effectively (Lain & Aston, 2005). It is also not known which techniques most enhance work-based students' experience of online learning. Indeed, a survey of universities found that the "pedagogical response" to the needs of work-based students is "not well developed" and progress is slow (Collis & van der Wende, 2002). The aim of this review therefore is to evaluate the views and attitudes of work-based students towards the delivery of e-learning, i.e. those techniques, both technologies and pedagogic approaches, that are used to deliver e-learning. The aim is to identify those techniques that most enhance the learning experience. The findings may then be used to inform the development and delivery of online courses to learners in formal employment.

C. Carroll (✉)
University of Sheffield, School of Health and Related Research (ScHARR), Sheffield, S1 4DA, UK
e-mail: c.carroll@shef.ac.uk

R.F. Poell, M. van Woerkom (eds.), *Supporting Workplace Learning*, Professional and Practice-based Learning 5, DOI 10.1007/978-90-481-9109-3_4,
© Springer Science+Business Media B.V. 2011

Theoretical Background

A previous systematic review of e-learning for health professionals and students reviewed 57 studies and identified eight different issues relating to delivery of successful e-learning programmes: organisational, economics, hardware, software, support, pedagogical, psychological and skills (Childs et al., 2005). For example, organisational barriers and solutions included allotting time to study, provision of facilities and institutional commitment and accreditation; and psychological barriers and solutions included managers' resistance to change, technophobia and motivation. This review by Childs et al. offers a useful backdrop to the present work, especially in terms of the structural prerequisites for delivery of e-learning, but paid little attention to the particular components of e-learning and their impact on the student experience. Once issues such as hardware and software availability and the economics of engagement are resolved, it is necessary to consider more specifically the methods used to deliver e-learning. Consequently, this review aims to address the following question: What factors affect experiences of e-learning among students in employment, with a particular focus on the United Kingdom (UK) context? In other words, what factors moderate the relationship between the course and learners' reported experiences of the course? For the purposes of this review e-learning is defined as "Learning facilitated and supported through the use of information and communications technology [which] can cover a spectrum of activities from the use of technology to support learning as part of a 'blended' approach (a combination of traditional and e-learning approaches), to learning that is delivered entirely online" (JISC, 2007). As a variety of contextual, educational and environmental factors may mediate the learner experience, and the UK Higher Education Academy who commissioned this review is most concerned with applicability of findings to the higher education community in the UK, this review focused on this specific context to facilitate and enhance the meaningful synthesis of research findings. A global review would potentially have achieved greater generalisability only at the expense of specificity and contextual detail.

Method

Systematic reviews offer an explicit and reproducible methodology for the identification, appraisal and synthesis of the best available evidence (NHS Centre for Reviews and Dissemination, 2009). To be included in this systematic review, primary research studies had to satisfy the following criteria: the study sample had to consist of a majority (more than half) of adults in formal employment (full or part time), undertaking a course that was delivered either purely or primarily by e-learning; courses also had to be delivered by a UK Higher Education institution, a professional body (e.g. a Royal College) or other relevant organisation. In addition, the specific techniques being used in course delivery had to be specified, e.g. discussion forums, email, group work (i.e. the studies should contain sufficient "thickness" of detail [Popay, Rogers, & Williams, 1998]); and student experience had to be recorded as an outcome (e.g. satisfaction, enjoyment, perspectives, etc.).

Other limitations applied were to include English language publications only, and a date limit of 1992 onwards (a date marking increased use of the internet by Higher Education following roll-out of the Super JANET network). Studies were excluded if they did not satisfy the above criteria.

A search strategy was constructed to identify relevant studies using free-text and, where available, database thesaurus terms, representing e-learning (such as "online learning", "virtual learning") and all work sectors (such as "staff" or "profession") in order to capture any potentially relevant study (search strategies are available from the authors). This strategy was modified as appropriate for each database searched. The following databases were searched for both published and unpublished studies: Applied Social Sciences Index and Abstracts (ASSIA), Australian Education Index, British Education Index, Cumulative Index in Nursing and Allied Health Literature (CINAHL), CSA Abstracts (Social Services, Sociology, Information Technology Case Studies), Dissertation Abstracts, Emerald, ERIC, the International Bibliography of the Social Sciences (IBSS), Index to Theses, LISA (Library and Information Science Abstracts), MEDLINE, PsycINFO and the Social Science Citation Index. In addition, the references of all included studies were screened and citations for all included studies were tracked using CINAHL and Web of Science.

All citations were downloaded into a Reference Manager database and duplicates removed. Four members of the project team (AB, CC, DP, AS) each screened a sample of 100 titles and abstracts using the inclusion and exclusion criteria listed above, and a satisfactory inter-rater reliability score was achieved and recorded (0.8). The titles and abstracts of all citations retrieved were then divided equally between the four reviewers (AB, CC, DP, AS), who screened them for relevance. In cases where a decision could not be made about inclusion, citations were checked by a second reviewer and disagreements were either resolved by discussion or the full paper was retrieved in order to make a definitive judgement.

Full papers of all potentially relevant citations were retrieved, divided equally among the reviewers, screened against the inclusion criteria by each reviewer and their decision verified by a second reviewer. The resulting studies for inclusion were then extracted using a form developed specifically for this review, and piloted on a sample of two papers by three reviewers (CC, DP, AS); the consistency of this extraction was checked by a fourth reviewer (AB). Three reviewers then extracted all the data for analysis. Given that quality assessment of qualitative studies is considered to be a difficult and, in the view of some, an impossible process (Dixon-Woods et al., 2007, 2004), no study was excluded based on quality. However, each included study was independently assessed by a reviewer using criteria derived from relevant quality assessment checklists, principally for qualitative studies and surveys, the most dominant study designs (Tong et al., 2007; Boynton, 2004). The aim of this assessment was to comment very generally on the relative quality of the included studies, based on the following criteria: the reporting of their sampling strategies, and the reporting and conduct of methods of data collection and analysis. Good or very good studies provided details on all or most of these criteria, and the least good studies only one or none. In this way, the reviewers were able to explore quality as an explanation for any differences in the results of otherwise similar studies, and to consider its impact on the internal validity of the review. This is an accepted approach for quality assessment in the systematic review of qualitative data (NHS Centre for Reviews and Dissemination, 2009).

The data for analysis provided by the included studies consisted of either verbatim quotations from study participants or findings reported by study authors that were clearly supported by study data. Thematic analysis was performed on these data (Miles & Huberman, 1984). The first stage of this method is data reduction: i.e. reducing the data in the included studies to a small number of themes that reflect or capture the essence of those data, i.e. they are a valid interpretation of the data. The aim was to classify into themes learners' experiences relating to the ways in which e-learning was delivered. The primary analysis of the data was carried out by one reviewer (CC). Three other reviewers (AB, DP, AS) then validated or challenged this thematic analysis by examining whether the lead reviewer's interpretations of the data were plausible and by offering competing interpretations where appropriate. The second stage of the analysis method was data presentation. In doing this, the team drew up a refined and mutually agreed framework that captured thematically the experiences of e-learning and its delivery among students who work.

Results

The search of electronic databases generated 3,476 unique citations. After the screening of titles and abstracts, 107 potentially relevant full papers were retrieved and examined to determine whether they satisfied the inclusion criteria. The principal reasons for the exclusion of studies were that: the study was not UK-based; the students were full time, i.e. not students in employment; student experience was not an outcome. Thirty of the 107 studies assessed were found to be relevant. Four additional studies were identified from the references of the included papers (Conole et al., 2002; Cahill, Cook, & Jenkins, 2003; Jenkins et al., 2001; Thorpe & Godwin, 2006), four from non-systematic, unstructured searching around the topic (Allan & Lewis, 2006; Bacigalupo et al., 2003; Morgan et al., 2006; Sutton et al., 2005), and three were located by citation searching of the included studies (Thorley et al., 2007; Hall et al., 2004; Bury et al., 2006). For full results, see the accompanying flowchart which follows the QUOROM standards for reporting of review methods (Moher, 1999) (Fig. 4.1).

Forty-one studies in total are therefore included in this review (brief details of all included studies are given in Table 4.1).

Most studies examined online courses delivered by UK Higher Education organisations to health professionals and the health sector, i.e. health professionals, and other health sector staff, e.g. managers, librarians, scientists (29 studies). The other groups of employees covered were in education (6 studies), industry and commerce (4 studies), the public sector generally (1 study) and a variety of different professions (1 study). The 41 studies covered courses delivered by more than 30 different universities from throughout the UK, as well as different levels and types of courses: fewer of the evaluated courses were accredited (i.e. counting towards a degree, diploma or other formal certification; 15 studies), than were non-accredited (i.e. stand-alone courses, often developed for continuing professional development (CPD) programmes; 26 studies). Although many of the studies had at least one

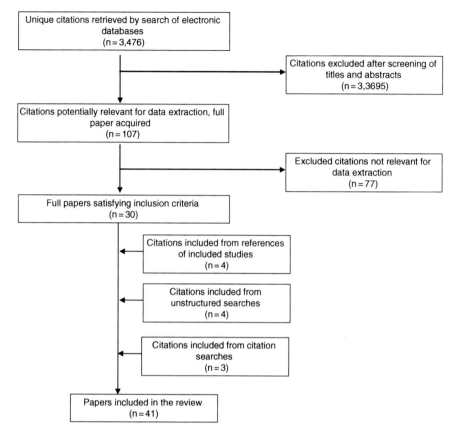

Fig. 4.1 QUOROM flow diagram

important methodological limitation, principally inadequate details of the sample
population, or unclear or non-explicit forms of data collection and analysis, the
remainder were found to be of good or very good reported methodological quality
(Allan & Lewis, 2006; Bosely & Young, 2006; Bird, 2001; Morgan et al., 2006;
Pegler, 2005; Stephenson & Saxton, 2005; Thorpe & Godwin, 2006; Wilkinson
et al., 2004; Larsen & Jenkins, 2005; Sandars et al., 2007; Whittington et al., 2004;
Gresty et al., 2007; Conole et al., 2002; Cahill et al., 2003; Thorley et al., 2007; Hall
et al., 2004). The resulting synthesis can therefore be considered sufficiently robust
to sustain the subsequent interpretation and analysis.

As described in the methodology, analysis involved the data being reduced to a
number of themes reflecting the data reported in the studies. The resulting themes
were therefore grounded in the data. A further process of data reduction produced
an even smaller number of broader, overarching themes reflecting in a new way
these "sub-themes", and thus the data in the included studies. The resulting thematic
framework therefore offered an original interpretation and representation of the
available data on the experience of e-learning among working students (see Fig. 4.2).
The five broad themes that emerged from the analysis were: *peer communication;
flexibility; support; knowledge validation; and course presentation and design.*

Table 4.1 Included studies

Study	Sample (n)	Type or level of course, provider	Data collection
Allan and Lewis (2006)	Healthcare workers ($n = 16$)	CPD course, Hull University	Survey, analysis of discussion boards and learning logs, VLE tracking system
Anonymous (2001)	Aquaculture workers ($n = 23$)	CPD course, Inverness college	NR
Anthony (2006)	Doctors, nurses, midwives, speech and occupational therapists, physiotherapists, radiographers ($n = $ NR)	Single skills courses, UG and PG courses, NR (a number of UK universities)	Survey
Anthony and Duffy (2003)	Nurses ($n = $ NR)	CPD course, DeMontfort University	Survey, analysis of discussion boards, interviews
Bacigalupo et al. (2003)	Healthcare professionals and managers ($n = $ NR)	PG degree, University of Sheffield	Surveys, group discussion
Bahn et al.(2001)	Nurses ($n = $ NR)	Conversion course, Hull University	NR
Bird (2001)	NR	PG diploma in Management, Coventry University	Discussion boards, focus groups, and interviews
Booth, Ayiku, Sutton, and O'Rourke (2005)	Health librarians ($n = $ NR)	CPD course, University of Sheffield	Survey
Bosley and Young (2006)	Postgraduate learners ($n = 9$)	PG course, University of Derby	NR
Brosnan and Burgess (2003)	Professionals from health, education, pharmacy and social work ($n = 16$)	CPD course, University of Stirling	Tracking facilities, WebCT, telephone interviews, discussion boards
Bury et al. (2006)	Health professionals ($n = $ NR)	CPD course, Edge Hill University	Survey, group discussion
Cahill et al. (2003)	Doctors ($n = 18$)	CPD course, Bristol University	Survey, interviews, analysis of discussion boards

Table 4.1 (continued)

Study	Sample (n)	Type or level of course, provider	Data collection
Chadda (2000)	NHS staff ($n = 8$)	PG degree, University College London	Interview
Clarke et al. (2005)	NHS training managers and e-learning champions ($n = $ NR)	CPD course, Hull University	Survey
Conole et al.(2002)	Doctors ($n = 20$)	CPD course, Southampton University	Survey, analysis of discussion boards
Forsyth (2002)	Academic staff ($n = 28$)	CPD course, Manchester Metropolitan University	NR
Gresty et al. (2007)	Podiatrist, occupational therapist, nurses, midwives, doctors, health visitors, GPs, dietician, other professionals allied to medicine ($n = 193$)	CPD course, Plymouth University	Survey
Hall et al. (2004)	Health scientists ($n = 28$)	CPD course, Greenwich University	Interviews
Hare et al. (2006)	Nurses ($n = 34$)	CPD course, Derby University	Survey
Haynes et al. (2004)	Academic staff ($n = 40$)	CPD course, Brighton University	NR
Hurst (2005)	Nurses ($n = $ NR)	CPD course, City University	Survey
Innes et al. (2006)	Nurses ($n = 25$)	CPD course, Stirling University	Survey
Irving et al. (2007)	Nurses ($n = 1,564$)	CPD course, Nursing Learning, UK Charity	Survey
Jenkins et al. (2001)	Doctors ($n = 14$)	CPD course, Bristol University	Survey, interviews
Kinghorn (2005)	Nurses ($n = 29$)	Accredited MSc module, Newcastle University	Web-based survey, analysis of discussion boards

Table 4.1 (continued)

Study	Sample (n)	Type or level of course, provider	Data collection
Larsen and Jenkins (2005)	Doctors (n = 20)	CPD course, UK Dept. of Work & Pensions	Interviews
Lee and Patterson (2003)	NR (n = NR)	UG degree, University of Glamorgan	NR
Milligan (1998)	Academic, research, administration and support staff in Higher Education (n = 617)	CPD course, Heriot-Watt University	Feedback forms, case study reports, surveys
Morgan et al. (2006)	Health and social care practitioners (n = 25)	UG degree, University of Southampton	Surveys, focus group discussions, discussion boards
Peachey (2004)	Academic, research and administration staff (n = 22)	CPD course, University of Glamorgan	Interviews, surveys, focus groups
Pegler (2005)	Academic staff, library staff, production staff, student support staff, research students (n = 76)	CPD course, Open University	Surveys, discussion board messages, feedback emails
Sandars et al. (2007)	Doctors, GPs, Public health specialists (n = 73)	CPD course, Manchester University. Leeds University	Semi-structured telephone interviews, analysis of discussion boards
Stephenson and Saxton (2005)	Management, administrative, education and training, and technical staff; self-employed; engineers; health and social care staff (n = NR)	UG and PG diplomas and degrees, Ufl Learndirect partnership with Derby University and others	Survey, interviews
Sutton et al. (2005)	Health librarians (n = NR)	CPD course, University of Sheffield	Survey
Terrell et al. (2004)	Student support staff; teaching assistants; ICT technicians (n = 300)	UG degree, Anglia Polytechnic University	Survey, discussion groups, interviews
Thompson and Homer (2000)	NR (n = NR)	Accredited module, University of Wolverhampton	Survey

Table 4.1 (continued)

Study	Sample (n)	Type or level of course, provider	Data collection
Thorley et al. (2007)	Doctors ($n = 213$)	CPD course, Manchester University	Survey
Thorpe and Godwin (2006)	Students on 36 UG courses ($n = 4512$)	UG degree, Open University	Survey
Treharne and McClelland (2004)	NHS Managers and leaders ($n = NR$)	CPD course, Leadership Wales	Surveys, focus groups
Whittington et al. (2004)	Doctors, nurses, midwives, health scientists ($n = 20$)	PG degree, Bristol University	Web-based survey
Wilkinson et al. (2004)	Nurses ($n = 39$)	UG (and 1 Diploma) level modules, King's College London	Survey, Group interviews

NR = Not reported; CPD: Continuing Professional Development; UG = Undergraduate; PG = Postgraduate; NHS = UK National Health Service

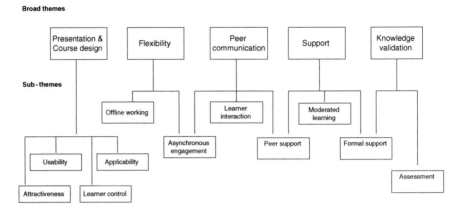

Fig. 4.2 Thematic framework representing work-based learners' experience of online learning

Peer Communication

For many students the nature and quality of interaction between learners constitutes a major consideration in their experience of an online course. Learners felt
a sense of belonging (*peer support*) when they engaged in discussions or other
forms of peer-group interaction (Kinghorn, 2005; Conole et al., 2002). Some students found confidence in the new medium, embracing the anonymity of e-learning
and its scope for reflection, having the time to contribute more measured comments
to discussions (Kinghorn, 2005; Innes et al., 2006). However, some doctors within
one study reported that they felt exposed and vulnerable and unable to contribute to
public discussions as they did not wish to risk looking foolish in front of their peers
(Cahill et al., 2003). Studies frequently reported non-participation, i.e. what Cahill
(2003) describes as passive "lurking", as opposed to active involvement (Anthony &
Duffy, 2003; Larsen & Jenkins, 2005; Sandars et al., 2007; Whittington et al., 2004;
Anthony, 2006; Gresty et al., 2007; Cahill et al., 2003; Chadda, 2000). This failure
of some students to contribute was a source of frustration and criticism for those
who did (Anthony, 2006; Chadda, 2000). Some learners, however, felt that viewing
others' contributions was an effective means of learning even though this could not
be construed as active participation (Anthony, 2006).

Ten of the studies contributed to the theme of information sharing (Kinghorn,
2005; Innes et al., 2006; Sandars et al., 2007; Whittington et al., 2004; Anthony,
2006; Cahill et al., 2003; Hall et al., 2004; Chadda, 2000; Bird, 2001; Terrell et al.,
2004), across many professions and types of course. Findings were universally positive about this aspect of peer interaction: students felt that they learned a great deal
from one another on discussion boards and in group work. Reciprocal learning was
seen as a major benefit of student interaction. Information sharing was reportedly
promoted by such techniques as discussion groups, chat rooms and group-working.

Another aspect of *learner interaction*, group-working, also prompted positive
comments (Innes et al., 2006; Wilkinson et al., 2004; Hall et al., 2004, Bacigalupo

et al., 2003; Sutton et al., 2005), especially in terms of mutual motivation. In such instances it was important for scheduling to accommodate asynchronous methods (*asynchronous engagement*), as learners could not always guarantee to be available at specific times, due to work demands (Hall et al., 2004; Bacigalupo et al., 2003). Also, many learners were happy to interact with fellow learners once they had been introduced online; it was not always felt necessary to have interacted via face-to-face day schools (Bahn et al., 2001; Conole et al., 2002; Cahill et al., 2003).

Flexibility

Five studies reported that students' experience of e-learning was enhanced by facilities that enabled flexible, *asynchronous engagement* with both fellow learners and tutors (Wilkinson et al., 2004; Whittington et al., 2004; Anthony, 2006; Innes et al., 2006; Hall et al., 2004). However, it was another type of flexibility, the ability to work offline (*offline working*), without being at a PC or connected to the internet, that emerged as a theme in seven studies (Irving et al., 2007; Kinghorn, 2005; Innes et al., 2006; Wilkinson et al., 2004; Jenkins et al., 2001; Hall et al., 2004; Larsen & Jenkins, 2005). This required materials and resources to be provided in downloadable or printable formats (Larsen & Jenkins, 2005; Hall et al., 2004) or the provision of CD-ROMs (Wilkinson et al., 2004).

Support

Three sub-themes informed the broader theme of support. First, the informal support and encouragement provided by fellow students (*peer support*) was identified as important in six studies (Peachey, 2004; Terrell et al., 2004; Kinghorn, 2005; Anthony & Duffy, 2003; Anthony, 2006; Conole et al., 2002), but the *formal support* offered by the course provider was considered essential. This might take the form of prompt and instructive help provided by email correspondence with lecturers, which was frequently viewed positively (Stephenson & Saxton, 2005; Wilkinson et al., 2004; Conole et al., 2002; Hall et al., 2004). Additionally, technical help (another type of *formal support*) from the host institution, such as facilities or services explaining how to use the discussion boards, download materials and find information, was considered valuable (Haynes et al., 2004; Clarke et al., 2005; Innes et al., 2006; Conole et al., 2002). Studies often reported mixed views about the quality of such help facilities (Innes et al., 2006; Conole et al., 2002).

Finally, in eight studies learners cited tutors' input or moderation as a vital element in the delivery or completion of courses and their tasks (*moderated learning*) (Peachey, 2004; Bahn et al., 2001; Kinghorn, 2005; Hurst, 2005; Sandars et al., 2007; Conole et al., 2002; Cahill et al., 2003; Hall et al., 2004). Comments usually related to the failure of course providers or tutors to moderate adequately, e.g. too much information (Peachey, 2004; Bahn et al., 2001), an absence of direction for group activities or tasks (Kinghorn, 2005; Sandars et al., 2007), or discussion groups that required moderation both to precipitate and to facilitate discussions among learners (Cahill et al., 2003; Hall et al., 2004). However, tutors could not always precipitate discussions between learners successfully, even if they made great efforts to do so (Cahill et al., 2003).

Knowledge Validation

Eight studies, all focusing on health professionals, found that such students enjoyed being tested on what they had learned (Irving et al., 2007; Wilkinson et al., 2004; Larsen & Jenkins, 2005; Whittington et al., 2004; Anthony, 2006; Gresty et al., 2007; Conole et al., 2002; Hall et al., 2004). Learners derived confidence from successfully completing tests and quizzes, which were seen as a good way to consolidate taught material. *Assessment* also provided students with an incentive to study (Hall et al., 2004). However, one family doctor pointed out that, while being useful in itself, simple testing also removed the opportunity for potentially valuable debate (Larsen & Jenkins, 2005).

Presentation and Course Design

Real-world case studies or scenarios, or tasks that were immediately relevant and applicable to learners' jobs, were generally well received (*applicability*) (Kinghorn, 2005; Larsen & Jenkins, 2005; Pegler, 2005; Haynes et al., 2004; Jenkins et al., 2001; Thorley et al., 2007). In one study, most interviewees mentioned that using real-life scenarios was one of the best ways to learn, and made facts more digestible (Larsen & Jenkins, 2005). In a study of nurses, the section of the website that responders rated the most interesting was that containing the interactive case studies (Bahn et al., 2001). Online resources or materials could not simply be presented without effort or thought, as in one case when documents appeared to be little more "than a typed piece of paper, placed on the Internet" (Larsen & Jenkins, 2005). Instead they had to engage learners visually or to exploit the interactivity offered by electronic and online delivery (*attractiveness*) (Clarke et al., 2005; Hare et al., 2006; Larsen & Jenkins, 2005; Gresty et al., 2007).

In the same way, web-based learning environments that are confusing and difficult to navigate (Hare et al., 2006; Clarke et al., 2005; Milligan, 1998), or lacking in necessary help or search facilities (Clarke et al., 2005; Whittington et al., 2004; Anthony, 2006; Hall et al., 2004), were found to be detrimental to the student experience. However, when *usability* of the virtual learning environment was good, learners' experience was enhanced (Wilkinson et al., 2004). Finally, a small number of studies evaluated continuing professional development courses in which learners exercised a higher than normal degree of control over both the course content and the pace of learning (*learner control*) (Stephenson & Saxton, 2005; Pegler, 2005; Terrell et al., 2004). Although only one study commented on the pedagogic qualities of this particular type of course delivery in relation to the student experience

(Stephenson & Saxton, 2005), the response to the sense of ownership and control felt by students was universally positive.

Discussion

The focus of this review is specifically on work-based students' experiences of and views about the ways in which online courses are delivered. The themes represent a number of factors that appear to moderate the relationship between the course and learners' reported experiences of the course, e.g. the usability, applicability and attractiveness of the course and its materials, all influence positively or negatively learner's experience of course. Other related topics such as students' experience of e-learning in general, for example regarding issues surrounding access, motivation, confidence with information technology, time pressures, flexibility and student isolation (Childs et al., 2005; Schweizer, 2004; Williams et al., 2005), and the relative experiences of students taking online and face-to-face courses (Allen et al., 2002), are well covered elsewhere. Furthermore, only two of the themes that emerged from this review specifically related to a particular professional group or type of course (knowledge validation among health professionals, and learner control among students in industry), and both may, at least theoretically, be applicable to other groups, so the findings may be considered to be fairly generalisable. Also, no theme was only reported by studies of lower quality. Rather, each theme was supported by different types and quality levels of study, increasing confidence in the internal validity of the findings. The techniques reported by the included studies as enhancing the learner's experience of e-learning are also considered here, both to add context to the findings and to highlight how they may be applied in practice by course providers.

Communication between students was most frequently reported across the included studies. Discussion forums and related media, such as group-working and prior socialisation through induction programmes, are the techniques most prominent in the research. It is perhaps not surprising that the various elements of peer communication, especially *information sharing*, were such a frequent target for comment within the included studies. The idea that learning is a social activity, in which learners enter into a community of practice, of shared beliefs, behaviours and knowledge, i.e. they learn from one another, is well founded (Lave & Wenger, 1991; Wenger 1998). This is especially the case for working students engaged in forms of continuing professional development where they are already likely to share professional beliefs and experiences.

The findings of this review strongly support the social nature of learning, espoused in the situated learning theory of Lave (1991) and Wenger (1998), especially in the themes of socialisation, learner confidence and information sharing. However, social learning is not simply about knowledge sharing or the existence of an online community. It must also take account of learning styles. Learners who perform less well in traditional face-to-face learning environments may gain confidence from the time for reflection offered by techniques such as asynchronous discussion groups and online group work. It has been noted that effective participation in such online communities requires motivation, time and effort, all of which may be in short supply for learners in formal employment as a result of the demands of work and home life (Macpherson et al., 2005, Jones & McCann, 2005). This review confirms that not everyone feels willing or able to engage in such social learning, and as such may risk feeling isolated or being marginalised by other members of the community, who may be frustrated by their peers' lack of engagement (Hodgson & Reynolds, 2005; Kear, 2004). These learners may also feel uncomfortable and exposed when making contributions, possibly explaining their reluctance to do so. When students are *lurking* in this way, they may not be considered part of the community, although, as the findings of this review make clear, some students feel that they can learn by "viewing" alone, so a form of passive rather than active social learning may still be taking place. Despite this ambiguity of feeling towards discussion forums, learners' experience, on the whole, was extremely positive about techniques of online socialisation and discussion.

Many students advocated course induction programmes, both online and face-to-face, as the most effective technique by which to create the appropriate level of *socialisation* and comfort for learners to begin to engage with one another. These findings run counter to views that face-to-face inductions programmes alone are capable of generating learner interaction (Brosnan & Burgess, 2002). Group work is also seen to perform this role. The on-going *moderating* and *supporting* role of the tutor in encouraging and facilitating such online discussions was also recognised in the findings. A function of the tutor is both to offer formal support to students, including encouraging and facilitating discussions, and to act as a moderator in debates and discussions, thus enhancing information sharing and reciprocal learning. The fact that tutors have such a vital role to play in the creation of online dialogues between students has been noted previously (Salmon, 2003). Such a role encompasses several of the themes that emerged from this review: a function of the tutor is both to offer *formal support* to students and to facilitate and *moderate* debates and discussions. In this way, tutors foster a so-called culture of inquiry among students (Littleton & Whitelock, 2004).

As the review makes clear it is not sufficient simply to make discussion boards or email contact with lecturers available; these facilities need to be *managed* and *supported* by tutors. Tutors also need to use other methods to encourage communication, such as induction programmes. Peer communication and social learning will not necessarily occur without the help of tutors applying both technological and pedagogic techniques. However, it is also clear that tutors cannot be expected simply to provide such support; rather the tutors themselves need to be adequately and appropriately trained in providing such online techniques (Salmon, 2003).

Flexibility is a widely reported advantage of e-learning, especially relating to when and where someone chooses to access course facilities and materials (Childs et al., 2005; Anthony & Duffy, 2003; Carroll-Barefield & Murdoch, 2004). In this review, however, it was the flexibility offered by being able to work offline, using technologies such as CD-ROMs and printable materials, which was enjoyed by students. The ability to engage asynchronously with tutors and fellow learners, and to work offline as an individual, offers work-based learners this necessary, flexible, independent element. Not all learning is social.

Responses to regular formal assessment of what has been learned were universally positive in those studies that reported on learners' experience of this technique. All learners in these studies were health professionals, a group for whom *knowledge acquisition and validation* is a key outcome of the learning process. There is no reason, however, why this pedagogic technique of on-going assessment should not also enhance the learning experience of those working in other fields. Certainly, learners increase in confidence as they begin to recognise the extent and nature of their personal achievements (Morgan et al., 2006).

Techniques such as discussion forums, email and different forms of feedback and assessment do not simply provide means of accessing materials online, but rather offer interactivity. Such variety is also likely to accommodate the range of learning styles among students (Lu et al., 2003). For example, the technique of *assessment* focused on giving learners confidence in their practical knowledge, and thus their ability to do their jobs. The use of techniques such as case studies and scenarios makes coursework relevant to learners' professional lives, thus offering "authentic learning" (Bruner, 1982), by which the learning experience is inseparable from the learner's professional reality.

Few included studies reported *learner control* over what is learned and the pace at which it is learned. Only one of these studies explicitly evaluated learner control, but the evaluation was overwhelmingly positive (Stephenson & Saxton, 2005). This perspective of open-ended tasks and greater *learner control* is advocated by Stephenson (2003) in his paradigm on e-learning pedagogy, based on work-based online learning generally, principally from research in the private sector.

Finally, it should be recognised that gaining a more in-depth understanding of techniques impacting on the student experience, and the application of these lessons in practice, is not without its challenges. The delivery of e-learning to those in the workplace is frequently constrained by the demands of the academic setting. The demand for flexibility, even beyond that currently offered by e-learning providers, may be limited by academic deadlines and the course timetable. Similarly, while the framework suggests that in theory it is desirable to offer students certain opportunities, such as group-working, this can be at the expense of other potential benefits, such as either flexibility or control enjoyed by learners as a result of offline working or asynchronous engagement.

The opportunity to interact through problem-based group work may also require additional time for completion of shared tasks and may create critical dependencies upon inputs from other students. In the same way, learner interaction, an apparently vital element of online learning, may compromise non-social forms of learning, such as "lurking" or, once again, working offline. Such "forced" interaction may also decrease the sense of learner control while undoubtedly achieving against other desirable aspects of the framework. In addition to these logistic challenges there are associated pedagogic tensions. For example, the desire for students to be able to validate their learning through self-assessment quizzes suggests a more objective sense of what is correct and what is not than the relativistic view of learning accommodated by group problem-solving using real-life scenarios. Nevertheless through the adroit labelling of feedback as "sample answers" rather than "model answers", it may be possible to reconcile such tensions. The picture is therefore more complex than it may appear at first sight.

Implications and Recommendations for Practice

This review offers a conceptual framework for describing and understanding the experience of e-learning among learners in formal employment. It indicates that this experience will be enhanced by techniques that:

- promote *interaction between learners*
- provide learners with *control* over their learning
- offer learners *attractive, relevant*, easily *useable* course materials
- promote *flexibility*
- offer learners timely and effective *support* by tutors and course providers
- *validate* and reinforce what learners have actually learned

Flexibility, learner control, the support of "proactive, attentive and sensitive online supervisors", and relevance to work were also among the elements identified by Stephenson (2003) as likely to enhance the experience of students in general online programmes delivered in the workplace. Other elements identified in the Stephenson (2003) model, but not found by this review, include accreditation, in-house support, alignment of learner and employer needs, and the facility of "successful withdrawal". The thematic framework constructed for the current review, derived from a synthesis of the experiences of work-based learners, both reinforces and builds on Stephenson's approach, offering greater substance, depth and detail to its foundations. The evidence synthesised here may be used to inform the development and delivery of online courses to learners in formal employment. The results outlined above also refer to those techniques, both pedagogic approaches and technologies, demonstrated by the evidence to enhance student experience in the ways described above:

- Online and face-to-face induction programmes
- Discussion forums
- Online group work
- Personalised learning
- High quality, carefully constructed course content
- Case studies and scenarios
- CD-ROMs (or contemporary equivalents, such as USB/memory sticks) and printable materials
- Email and discussion group support by tutors
- Regular assessment of knowledge acquisition (formal and informal)

Some techniques may garner better responses from some students than from others, simply because of the variety of learning styles among individuals. However, the techniques listed above were all found in studies identified for this review to enhance the e-learning experience of students in formal employment. This was only the case, however, if they were delivered with care, actively compensating for the potential limitations of each technique, e.g. discussion forums need to be developed and nurtured by course providers and tutors if the substantial benefits of social learning are to be realised. In this way, the present review not only validates and reaches beyond existing models but, through consideration of techniques, offers the means for applying the new conceptual framework to the delivery of e-learning to work-based students. Given the tensions between some of the themes identified here, however, the challenge for developers of workplace-based e-learning is to optimise and appropriately target the elements of this framework rather than to slavishly pursue all aspects simultaneously and with equal vigour.

Recommendations for Future Research

Future research should consider the experiences of work-based learners outside the UK. The thematic framework presented by this review could be augmented by a broader dataset to identify commonalities and differences between UK and non-UK learners. This would be a literature-oriented variant on "respondent validation" and could be used to inform the external validity of both previous and future research on students engaged in online learning. Research might also consider longitudinal evaluations of experience in association with effectiveness, to demonstrate that the use of effective techniques, identified by this review, enhance the learning experience and result in improved learning outcomes.

Conclusion

Where online courses seek to enhance working students' experience of e-learning, and consequently to improve the effectiveness of online delivery, course providers need to take careful account of presentation and course design, they must provide flexibility, offer means of both support and rapid assessment and develop effective and efficient means of communication, especially between the students themselves. While focusing on the delivery of courses to UK learners, this review has identified many techniques that may enhance the learning experience of work-based students more universally. By offering an evidence-based framework for designing and providing potentially successful e-learning for working students, this review not only highlights issues that online courses should seek to address, but also outlines techniques, both technologies and pedagogic approaches, that have been demonstrated by the evidence to enhance the learning experience. These include online and face-to-face induction programmes; discussion forums; group work; high quality, carefully constructed course content; case studies and scenarios; CD-ROMs and printable materials; email and discussion group support by tutors together with regular assessments.

Acknowledgements This review draws on data collected for a project funded by the UK Higher Education Academy.

References

Allan, B., & Lewis, D. (2006). Virtual learning communities as a vehicle for workforce development: A case study. *Journal of Workplace Learning, 18*(6), 367–383.

Allen, M., Bourhis, J., Burrell, N., & Mabry, E. (2002). Comparing student satisfaction with distance education to traditional classrooms in higher education: A meta-analysis. *American Journal of Distance Education, 16*(2), 83–97.

Anonymous (2001). Inverness College: Innovations in aquaculture training. Report from ED467205.7.

Anthony, D. (2006). Online courses in nursing and midwifery: Comparisons with allied healthcare professions. *British Journal of Healthcare Computing and Information Management, 20*(1), 28–30.

Anthony, D., & Duffy, K. (2003). An evaluation of a tissue viability online course. *ITIN 15*(4), 20–28.

Bacigalupo, R., Bath, P., Booth, A., Eaglestone, B., Levy, P., & Procter, P. (2003). Studying health informatics from a distance: The impact of a multimedia case study, *Health Informatics Journal, 9*(1), 5–15.

Bahn, D., Needham, Y., & Marsh, D. (2001). Using the web to develop an EN conversion course. *Nursing Standard, 15*(26), 37–40.

Bird, L. (2001). Virtual Learning in the workplace: The power of communities of practice". Report from ED467924.9.

Booth, A., Ayiku, L., Sutton, A., & O'Rourke, A. (2005). Fulfilling a yearning for e-learning? Fun, collaborative courses for NHS support staff. *Library & Information Update, 4*(10), 27–29.

Bosley, S., & Young, S. (2006). On line learning dialogues in learning through work. *Journal of Workplace Learning, 18*(6), 355–366.

Boynton, P. (2004). Hands-on guide to questionnaire research: Selecting, designing, and developing your questionnaire. *British Medical Journal, 328*(7451), 1312.

Brosnan, K., & Burgess, R. (2003). Web based continuing professional development – A learning architecture approach. *Journal of Workplace Learning, 15*(1), 24–33.

Bruner, J. (1982). *The relevance of education.* New York: Norton.

Bury, R., Martin, L., & Roberts, S. (2006). Achieving change through mutual development: Supported online learning and evolving roles of health and information professionals. *Health Information and Libraries Journal, 23*(S1), 22–31.

Cahill, D., Cook, J., & Jenkins, J. (2003). How useful are World Wide Web discussion boards and email in delivering a case study course in reproductive medicine. In C. Ghaoui (Ed.), *Usability evaluation of online learning programs* (pp. 360–370). London: Information Science.

Carroll-Barefield, A., & Murdoch, C. (2004). Using online learning to enhance interdisciplinary education. *Journal of Allied Health, 33*(1), 78–81.

Chadda, D. (2000). Cyberschool days. *Health Service Journal, 24*(3), 5–6.

Childs, S., Blenkinsopp, E., Hall, A., & Walton, G. (2005). Effective e-learning for health professionals and students – barriers and their solutions. A systematic review of the literature—findings from the HeXL project. *Health Information and Libraries Journal, 22*(S2), 20–32.

Clarke, A., Lewis, D., Cole, I., & Ringrose, L. (2005). A strategic approach to developing e-learning capability for healthcare. *Health Information and Libraries Journal, 22*(S2), 33–41.

Collis, B., & van der Wende, M. (Eds.). (2002). ICT and the internationalisation of higher education: Models of change. *Special Issue of the Journal for Studies in International Education.*

Conole, G., Hall, M., & Smith, S. (2002). An evaluation of an online course for medical practitioners. *Education, Technology and Society, 5*, 66–75.

Coultas, J., Luckin, R., & du Boulay, B. (2003). How compelling is the evidence for the effectiveness of e-Learning in the post-16 sector? Retrieved May 28, 2009, from http://www.reveel.sussex.ac.uk/files/ConsultES204.pdf

Dixon-Woods, M., Shaw, R., Agarwal, S., Smith, J. (2004). The problem of appraising qualitative research. *Quality and Safety in Health Care, 13*(3), 223–225.

Dixon-Woods, M., Sutton, A., Shaw, R., Miller, T., Smith, Young., B et al. (2007). Appraising qualitative research for inclusion in systematic reviews: A quantitative and qualitative comparison of three methods. *Journal of Health Services Research and Policy, 12*, 42–47.

Forsyth, R. (2002). Making professional development flexible: A case study. *Open Learning, 17*(3), 251–258.

Gresty, K., Skirton, H., & Evenden, A. (2007). Addressing the issue of e-learning and online genetics for health professionals. *Nursing and Health Sciences, 9*(1), 14–22.

Hall, N., Harvey, P., Meerabeau, L., & Muggleston, D. (2004). *An evaluation of online training in the NHS workplace.* London: University of Greenwich.

Hare, C., Davies, C., & Shepherd, M. (2006). Safer medicine administration through the use of e-learning. *Nursing Times, 102*(16), 25–27.

Haynes, P., Ip, K., Saintas, P., Stanier, S., Palmer, H., Thomas, N., et al. (2004). Responding to technological change: IT skills and the academic teaching profession. *Active Learning in Higher Education, 5*, 152–165

Hodgson, V., & Reynolds P. (2005). Consensus, difference and multiple communities in networked learning, *Studies in Higher Education, 30*(1), 11–24.

Hurst, J. (2005). Evaluating staff and student experiences of multidisciplinary continuous professional development via distance-learning. *EDINA/ERCA Journal, 31*, 160–163.

Innes, A., Mackay, K., & McCabe, L. (2006). Dementia studies online: Reflections on the opportunities and drawbacks of eLearning. *Journal of Vocational Education and Training, 58*(3), 303–317.

Irving, M., Irving, R., & Sutherland, S. (2007). Graseby MS16A and MS26 syringe drivers: Reported effectiveness of an online learning programme. *International Journal of Palliative Nursing, 13*(2), 56–62.

Jenkins, J., Cook, J., Edwards, J., Draycott, T., & Cahill, D. (2001). A pilot internet training programme in reproductive medicine. *British Journal of Obstetrics and Gynaecology, 108*, 114–116.

JISC (2007). *E-learning.* Retrieved May 28, 2009, from http://www.jisc.ac.uk/whatwedo/themes/elearning.aspx

Jones, S., & McCann, J. (2005). Virtual learning environments for time-stressed and peripatetic managers. *Journal of Workplace Learning, 17*(5/6), 359–369.

Kear, K. (2004). Peer learning using asynchronous discussion systems in distance education. *Open Learning, 19*(2), 151–164.

Kinghorn, S. (2005). Electronic learning. Delivering multiprofessional web-based psychosocial education: The lessons learnt. *International Journal of Palliative Nursing, 11*(8), 432–437.

Lain, D., & Aston, J. (2005). *Literature review of evidence on e-Learning in the workplace. IES occasional paper.* Retrieved May 28, 2009, from http://www.employment-studies.co.uk/pdflibrary/01580.pdf

Larsen, T., Jenkins, L. (2005). *Evaluation of online learning module about sickness certification for general practitioners.* Leeds: Department of Work and Pensions.

Lave, J., & Wenger, E. (1991). *Situated learning: Legitimate, peripheral participation.* Cambridge: Cambridge University Press.

Lee, S., & Patterson, L. (2003). Supporting e-learners 24x7 throughout Wales and beyond. *SCONUL Newsletter, 29*, 48–53.

Littleton, K., & Whitelock, D. (2004). Guiding the creation of knowledge and understanding in a virtual learning environment. *CyberPsychology & Behavior, 7*(2), 173–181.

Lu, J., Yu, C.-S., & Liu, C. (2003). Learning style, learning patterns, and learning performance in a WebCT-based MIS course. *Information & Management, 40*(6), 497–507.

Macpherson, A., Homan, G., & Wilkinson, K. (2005). The implementation and use of e-learning in the corporate university. *Journal of Workplace Learning, 17*(2), 33–48.

Miles, J., & Huberman, L. (1984). *Qualitative data analysis: A source book of new methods.* Beverly Hills, CA: Sage.

Milligan, C. (1998) *The role of virtual learning environments in the online delivery of staff development.* Report 1: Review of experiences of delivering TALi SMAN online courses. Joint information systems committees technology applications programme, 39.

Moher, D., Cook, D., Eastwood, S., Olkin, I., Rennie, D., Stroup, D. (1999). Improving the quality of reports of meta-analyses of randomised controlled trials: The QUOROM statement. *The Lancet, 854,* 1896–1900.

Morgan, J., Rawlinson, M., & Weaver, M. (2006). Facilitating online reflective learning for health and social care professionals. *Open Learning, 21*(2), 167–176.

NHS Centre for Reviews and Dissemination (2009). *Systematic reviews. CRD's guidance for undertaking reviews in health care.* York: University of York.

Peachey, P. (2004). *An addictive property of the discussion forums of the VLE as perceived by students undertaking a web-based course.* Paper presented at the British Educational Research Association Annual Conference, University of Manchester, 16–18 September.

Pegler, C. (2005) Objects and issues – A Sunday supplement view of continuing professional development in higher education. *Open Learning, 20*(1), 51–64.

Popay, J., Rogers, A., & Williams, G. (1998). Rationale and standards for the systematic review of qualitative literature in health services research. *Qualitative Health Research, 8,* 341–51.

Salmon, G. (2003). *E-moderating: The key to teaching and learning online* (2nd ed.). London: Kogan Page Limited.

Sandars, J., Langlois, M., & Waterman, H. (2007). Online collaborative learning for healthcare continuing professional development: A cross-case analysis of three case studies. *Medical Teacher, 29*(1), E9–E17.

Schweizer, H. (2004) E-Learning in business. *Journal of Management Education, 28*(6), 674–692.

Stephenson, J. (2003). A review of research and practice in e-learning in the workplace and proposals for its effective use. *American Education Research Association.* Retrieved May 9, 2009, from http://www.iclml.co.uk

Stephenson, J., & Saxton, J. (2005). Using the internet to gain personalized degrees from learning through work: Some experience from Ufi. *Industry and Higher Education, 19*(3), 249–258.

Sutton, A., Booth, A., Ayiku, L., & O'Rourke, A. (2005). e-FOLIO: Using elearning to learn about e-learning. *Health Information and Libraries Journal, 22*(S2), 84–88.

Terrell, I., Revill, G., & Down, J. (2004). *Developing the role and effectiveness of teacher support staff through an innovative online graduate programme.* Paper presented at the British Educational Research Association's Annual Conference, University of Manchester. 16–18 September.

Thompson, D., & Homer, G. (2000). Delivering web based IT training in a rural environment. *Information Services & Use, 20,* 139–143.

Thorley, K., Turner, S., Hussey, L., Zarin, N., & Agius, R. (2007). CPD for GPs using the THOR-GP website. *Occupational Medicine, 57,* 575–580.

Thorpe, M., & Godwin, S. (2006). Interaction and e-learning: The student experience. *Studies in Continuing Education, 28*(3), 203–221.

Tong, A., Sainsbury, P., & Craig, J. (2007) Consolidated criteria for reporting qualitative research (COREQ): A 32-item checklist for interviews and focus groups. *International Journal for Quality in Health Care, 19*(6), 349–357.

Treharne, R., & McClelland, S. (2004). Findings from a venture into elearning in NHS Wales. *British Journal of Healthcare Computing & Information Management, 21*(1), 33–35.

Wenger, E. (1998). *Communities of practice: Learning, meaning, identity.* Cambridge: Cambridge University Press.

Whittington, K., Cook, J., Barratt, C., Jenkins, J., Whittington, K., Cook, J., et al. (2004). Can the internet widen participation in reproductive medicine education for professionals? *Human Reproduction, 19*(8), 1800–1805.

Wilkinson, A., Forbes, A., Bloomfield, J., Fincham, G., Wilkinson, A., Forbes, A., et al. (2004). An exploration of four web-based open and flexible learning modules in post-registration nurse education. *International Journal of Nursing Studies, 41*(4), 411–424.

Williams, P., Nicholas, D., & Gunter, B. (2005). E-learning: What the literature tells us about distance education. An overview. *Aslib Proceedings: New Information Perspectives, 57*(2), 109–122.

Wutoh, R., Boren, S., & Balas, E. (2004). eLearning: A review of Internet-based continuing medical education. *Journal of Continuing Education in the Health Professions, 24*(1), 20–30.

Part II
The Role of Social Support

Chapter 5
Managerial Coaching as a Workplace Learning Strategy

Andrea D. Ellinger, Robert G. Hamlin, Rona S. Beattie,
Yu-Lin Wang, and Orla McVicar

The workplace has always been conceived as a place where adults learn and the learning itself has often been described as a daily ongoing process that is interwoven in and inseparably connected to the daily processes of work (Antonacopoulou, 2006; Boud & Middleton, 2003; Dirkx, 1999; Ellinger & Cseh, 2007). Scholars have differentiated workplace learning from formal educational learning as 'experience-based learning in complex authentic environments' (Bauer, Festner, Gruber, Harteis, & Reid, 2004, p. 284). Similarly, Billett (2004) has emphasized the socially situated and social learning perspective of learning within the workplace, highlighting that 'engaging in workplace activities interdependently links individuals' thinking and acting and their learning to social sources...[including] interactions with human partners...that contribute to individuals' capacity to perform and to the learning that arises from their performance' (p. 316). More recently, research has been focused on exploring how learners interact with other learning partners (Doornbos, Bolhuis, & Denessen, 2004; Eraut, Alderton, Cole, & Senker, 2002; Koopmans, Doornbos, & van Eekelen, 2006; Neilsen & Kvale, 2006; Poell, van der Krogt, Vermulst, Harris, & Simons, 2006). Some of this work has examined the notion of learning facilitators, facilitating agents (Salomon & Perkins, 1998), interaction partners (Koopmans et al., 2006), and informal workplace trainers (Poell et al., 2006). Billett (2004) has also drawn attention to the work of Rogoff (1995) who emphasized the need for guidance for acquiring knowledge (and skills) in areas that would be difficult to learn without the support of a more knowledgeable human partner. It is argued in this chapter that an important 'human partner' in workplace learning is the managerial coach or mentor.

The concept of managers serving as coaches or mentors is not new (Bartlett & Goshal, 1997; Beattie, 2006, 2007; Coetzer, 2007; Ellinger & Bostrom, 1999; Evered & Selman, 1989; Marquardt & Loan, 2006; Marsh, 1992; McGill & Slocum, 1998; Orth, Wilkinson, & Benfari, 1987). The scholarly literature has suggested that frontline supervisors and managers are becoming increasingly held responsible for performing many human resource management (HRM) and human resource

A.D. Ellinger (✉)
University of Texas, Tyler, USA
e-mail: aellinger@uttyler.edu

R.F. Poell, M. van Woerkom (eds.), *Supporting Workplace Learning*, Professional
and Practice-based Learning 5, DOI 10.1007/978-90-481-9109-3_5,
© Springer Science+Business Media B.V. 2011

development (HRD) practices, such as developing their employees and facilitating their learning (de Jong, Leenders, & Thijssen, 1999; Gilley, 2000; Hankins & Kleiner, 1995; Larsen, 1997; McGovern, Gratton, Hope-Hailey, Stiles, & Truss, 1997; Mindell, 1995; Schuler, 1990; Thornhill & Saunders, 1998; Yarnall, 1998). This perspective has been supported by the Chartered Institute of Personnel and Development's (CIPD) (2003) change agenda, which identified coaching by line managers as one of three key activities to drive the shift from training to learning in workplaces. This CIPD study found a strong link between learning and knowledge development, and coaching and mentoring. A more recent CIPD (2007) survey of learning and development reported significant activity being undertaken to build internal coaching capability (CIPD) (2006) & (CIPD) (2007).

There is growing recognition that the need 'to foster learning at and through work has far-reaching consequences for managers, who are expected to manage the workplace as a place fit for learning' (Coetzer, 2007, p. 417) through coaching and facilitating employee learning. An additional benefit of managerial involvement in supporting employee learning is that they too can benefit from 'the reciprocal process of learning … through co-participation at work' (Billett, 2004, p. 316). However, despite the increasing attention that is being given to managers as coaches and mentors, Peterson and Little (2005) have indicated that 'there has been a relative paucity of resources aimed specifically at helping managers to coach people better' (p. 179). Therefore, given the importance of coaching and mentoring by managers in large organizations and small- and medium-sized enterprises (SME's) (Billett, Hernon-Tilling, & Ehrich, 2003; Coetzer, 2007; The Leitch Report, 2006), the purpose of this chapter is to thoroughly examine the empirical research on managerial coaching as an approach to facilitating workplace learning.

In the sections that follow, we begin by differentiating conceptualizations of coaching and mentoring found in the literature. We then focus more exclusively on managerial coaching in terms of how managers can recognize coaching opportunities, the skills and behaviors required to coach, the benefits of coaching, and the contextual factors that may enhance the prospect of managers assuming coaching roles in their organizations. We conclude with some general observations about managerial coaching as a workplace learning approach.

Differentiating Between Mentoring and Coaching

In many organizations, the terms 'mentoring' and 'coaching' are often used interchangeably. However, various scholars and 'professional' mentors and coaches have claimed that these learning facilitation activities are different (Burdett, 1998; Clutterbuck, 2004a, 2004b; Evered & Selman, 1989; Hargrove, 1995; King & Eaton, 1999; Kirk, Howard, Ketting, & Little, 1999; Mink, Owen, & Mink, 1993; Minter & Thomas, 2000; Orth, Wilkinson, & Benfari, 1987; Popper & Lipshitz, 1992). Based upon a recently conducted definitional examination (Beattie, Hamlin, Ellinger, & Sage, 2009) of 11 European and 12 North American definitions of 'mentoring' and of the term, 'mentor,' Beattie et al. (2009) have produced an all-embracing, non-definitive composite conceptualization as follows.

Mentoring is 'a learning *facilitation process* conducted in a trusting and/or caring *one to one relationship* between two individuals, in which typically a more experienced person, the *mentor,* helps and *supports* a less experienced *person, the mentee or protégé,* to (i) develop their skills and career; (ii) make a transition in knowledge, work and thinking; (iii) transition a period of change; (iii) improve performance at the individual, team and organisational level; (iv) achieve their professional goals and full potential; and/or (v) meet personal growth and personal development needs'. The Mentoring Process can involve the mentor in (i) *sharing/passing on* knowledge, experience, and wisdom; (ii) *creating* learning and development *possibilities or opportunities*; (iii) *providing feedback, advice* or *guidance*; (iv) acting as a *sounding board, role model* or *partner*; and (v) *tutoring, teaching, coaching* or *counseling* as required, in every possible permutation.

The results of this examination have provided strong support for Clutterbuck's (2004b) claim that there are two schools of mentoring. The 'Sponsorship' school, which originated in the United States, involves sponsorship, hands-on help, the tapping into the authority, and contacts of the senior partner, and focuses mostly on career development through mentee-focused learning. In contrast, the 'Developmental' school, which originated in Europe, focuses on a two-way learning partnership in which the mentor expects the mentee will do more for himself or herself, and focuses on the development of the mentee's capabilities. The concept of 'sponsorship' mentoring was present in 9 of the 12 North American definitions but in only 3 of the 11 European definitions. However, the concept of 'developmental' mentoring, which was common to all of the European definitions, also featured in 9 of the 12 North American definitions.

A similar definitional examination of 36 definitions of 'coaching' has been conducted by Hamlin, Ellinger, and Beattie (2008, 2009). While many definitions of coaching refer specifically to 'coaching' in general terms, other definitions are more specific and have been labeled as 'executive' coaching, 'business', and 'life' coaching. Based upon these definitions, their analysis revealed four categories or variants of coaching, as identified by the keywords held in common between the respective descriptive labels used by the authors of these definitions. A further examination of the intended purposes and processes of each of the definitions constituting each category or variant resulted in the creation of an all-embracing, but non-definitive composite conceptualization for that particular variant of coaching, as follows:

> 'Coaching' is a *helping* and *facilitative process* that enables individuals, groups/teams and organisations to acquire new skills, to improve existing skills, competence and performance, and to enhance their personal effectiveness or personal development or personal growth.
> 'Executive Coaching' is a *process* that primarily (but not exclusively) takes place within a *one-to one helping* and *facilitative* relationship between a coach and an executive (or manager) that enables the executive (or manager) to achieve personal-, job- or organisational-related goals with an intention to improve organisational performance.
> 'Business Coaching' is a *collaborative process* that *helps* businesses, owner/managers and employees achieve their personal and business related goals to ensure long term success.

'Life Coaching' is a *helping* and *facilitative process* – usually within a *one-to-one rela-tionship* between a coach and a coachee which brings about an enhancement in the quality of life and personal growth of the coachee, and possibly a life changing experience.

As can be seen by comparing these composite conceptualizations developed for mentoring and for the four categories or variants of coaching, there are few differences in the 'intended purposes' of mentoring and of coaching. Although 'career development' is a distinctive feature of 'sponsorship' mentoring, and is not specifically stated in any coaching definition, coaches often become actively involved in 'career development' issues as an aspect of helping coachees meet their personal growth and personal development needs. The only 'intended purpose' that appears 'unique' is the facilitation of 'possibly a life changing experience'—a distinctive feature of 'life coaching,' which is absent from all of the examined European and North American definitions of mentoring. Regarding 'process', virtually all learning facilitation interventions, techniques, and methods specified in the mentoring definitions appear to be identical/near identical to those found in the coaching definitions. The only distinctive mentoring difference appears to be when mentors share or pass on their experience and wisdom, and act as a sounding board or role model. The only distinctive coaching difference appears to be when business coaches establish a collaborative partnership to co-design the coaching intervention. Even so, one of the mentoring definitions implies that an aspect of mentoring is for mentors to partner with their respective mentees.

From this definitional examination, the conceptual differences between mentoring and coaching appear to be minimal, and that those that do exist relate primarily to 'sponsorship' mentoring and 'life coaching' respectively. Essentially, 'developmental mentoring' appears to be much the same as 'coaching', both in terms of their 'intended purpose' and 'processes'. However, we recognize there could be certain significant and distinctive behavioral differences within a 'coach/coachee', as opposed to a 'mentor/mentee' dyadic relationship in practice; but as yet this is theoretical speculation that needs to be demonstrated empirically. Because of the perceptions of sameness outlined above, we intend to focus the remainder of this chapter on the issue of deploying coaching as a strategy for facilitating workplace learning, with a specific focus on managers who are increasingly being challenged to adopt the role of a managerial coach.

The Emergence of Coaching and Managerial Coaching in Business and Management Contexts

According to Evered and Selman (1989), coaching emerged in the management literature as a master–apprentice type of developmental relationship in the 1950s. Several articles then appeared in the 1970s that sought to translate athletic and sports coaching into managerial contexts. A general base of literature exists on coaching from a sports and athletic perspective. However, some scholars argue the use of a sports analogy of coaching is insufficient for business settings, despite the fact that much of the literature about coaching in the context of management has been drawn from sports coaching (Evered & Selman, 1989; McLean & Kuo, 2000; McNutt & Wright, 1995). Some of the coaching literature has attempted to draw upon various fields such as sports behavior and psychology, youth and adult education, counseling, clinical psychology, family therapy, industrial and organizational psychology, and management (McLean, Yang, Kuo, Tolbert, & Larkin, 2005).

Yet within management, coaching has been conceived as a new paradigm or metaphor for management. In particular, Evered and Selman (1989) have argued that coaching is the heart of management, and that creating a culture for coaching is a core managerial activity. Additionally, various other writers have suggested that coaching is an important role for supervisors, managers, and managerial leaders which should be performed as a part of daily management practice (Antonioni, 2000; Bianco-Mathis, Nabors, & Roman, 2002: Burdett, 1998; Flaherty, 1999; Hunt & Weintraub, 2002; Kraines, 2001; Piasecka, 2000; Ragsdale, 2000; Slater & Narver, 1994b, 1995). More recently, Hamlin, Ellinger, and Beattie (2006) have produced strong empirical evidence that supports notions of the 'facilitative leader' (Slater & Narver, 1995), the 'coaching manager' (Hunt & Weintraub, 2002), and the 'coaching leader' (Bianco-Mathis et al., 2002); furthermore, these research findings suggest coaching is at the heart of managerial effectiveness. The increasing number of practitioner-oriented books and articles on coaching and managerial coaching has reinforced a considerable and growing interest in the topic of coaching (Armentrout, 1995; King & Eaton, 1999; McGovern, et. al., 1997; Redshaw, 2000). In fact, a CIPD Learning and Development Survey (2006) indicated that 47% of line managers in the UK were using coaching in their work, and it is currently estimated that $1–$2 billion worldwide are being spent by organizations to provide coaches to their employees. Yet, despite the growing popularity of coaching in general, and managerial coaching in particular, empirical research on this topic is still relatively limited and in its infancy (Ellinger, Ellinger, Hamlin, & Beattie, 2009).

Defining Coaching and Managerial Coaching

Hamlin et al.'s (2008, 2009) research has indicated that coaching, over the years, has been defined and conceptualized in various ways. Traditionally, it has been perceived as a remedy for poor performance, and as an approach that links individual effectiveness with organizational performance (Anonymous, 2001). For some scholars, coaching is defined from a deficit orientation and is conceived as a process for improving problem work performance (Fournies, 1987). Others approach coaching from a more developmental perspective and empowerment paradigm, and conceive coaching accordingly. For example, from a management perspective, Orth, Wilkinson, and Benfari (1987) and Popper and Lipshitz (1992) consider coaching to be a hands-on process of helping employees to recognize opportunities for improving their performance and capabilities. Similarly, Burdett (1998) and Hargrove (1995) conceive coaching as a process of empowering employees to exceed prior levels of performance. From a learning perspective, Redshaw (2000) and Mink et al. (1993) conceptualize coaching as a process of giving guidance, encouragement, and support to the learner, and as a 'process by which one individual, the coach, creates enabling relationships with others that make it easier for them to learn' (Mink et al., 1993, p. 2). In more recent literature, coaching has been conceptualized as facilitation of learning (Beattie, 2002), and research has suggested that coaching and facilitating learning are synonymous terms (Ellinger, 1997; Ellinger & Bostrom, 1999). While coaching can be provided by external consultants (executive coaches) and coaching professionals (professional business coaches, career coaches, and life coaches, for example), we specifically refer to the concept of 'managerial coaching'.

Managerial coaching has been conceptualized as a supervisor or manager serving as a coach, or facilitator of learning, in which he or she enacts specific behaviors that enable his/her employee (coachee) to learn, develop, and improve his/her performance (Beattie, 2002; Ellinger & Bostrom, 1999; Ellinger, Beattie, & Hamlin, 2010; Talarico, 2002). According to Ellinger, Ellinger et al. (2010), managerial coaching refers to managers being coaching resources to their employees within their organizations. Hunt and Weintraub (2002) have suggested that, while managerial coaching can be a structured intervention, it should be 'slipped into' (p. 18) the daily activities of a manager's interaction with his/her employee. This perspective resonates with managerial coaching as a workplace learning strategy, because managers are often in a position to interact frequently with their employees. Managers are typically responsible for evaluating their employee's performance, and therefore can integrate a coaching approach to facilitate learning while helping to improve employee performance. Often coaching between a manager and an employee may be initiated by a coaching dialogue (Hunt & Weintraub, 2002). This dialogue can be generated as a result of several triggers or catalysts for coaching.

Considering Catalysts for Managerial Coaching

Research has suggested that coaching is typically an approach to remedy performance problems. Thus, a common catalyst to leverage and engage in managerial coaching is when a manager observes a gap or discrepancy in performance. However, there are a number of other catalysts that can stimulate managerial coaching opportunities. Within the management development and workplace learning literature, scholars have acknowledged that any managerial activity can stimulate learning, such as a new assignment, a new challenge, a problem, a shock, or crisis/problem solving within a group, or different standards of performance, or an unsuccessful piece of work (Mumford, 1993). These triggers are similar to those identified by Dechant (1989). Research specifically undertaken to examine the catalysts for managerial coaching identified the circumstances, occurrences, and events that served as the triggers for engaging in a managerial coaching intervention (Ellinger, 2003). In support of existing literature, managers in Ellinger's study reported poor performance, inappropriate behaviors, and mistakes as being catalysts for their involvement as coaches. In some cases, employees instigated the coaching intervention with their managers because they lacked a particular skill, knowledge, or experience, and recognized their respective managers' expertise. In contrast to the existing literature, managers also reported feeling compelled to engage in a coaching intervention with an employee when they thought that the consequences would involve visible, critical, and high stakes for the employee, organization, or if they reflected indirectly on the manager. Lastly, managers reported initiating coaching when they assigned projects or tasks to their employees to stretch them. The notion of developmental opportunities that served as catalysts for coaching emerged in the Ellinger study, and emphasized managers' interests in fostering the development of new skills and capabilities to help their employees become better positioned for their futures.

Finally, Hutchinson and Purcell's (2007) research on behalf of the CIPD in the UK across both private and public sectors found that line managers were recognized as a group 'with a distinctive contribution to make to learning and development' (p. 14). The organizations studied emphasized the pivotal role of line managers in workplace learning, through being 'critical conduits of learning from induction…the design of jobs that stretch … the provision of coaching (both for poor, or new, performers and for budding stars), to the assessment of development needs both formally in the annual performance management cycle and informally as is necessary or opportune' (p. 14).

Managerial Coaching Skills and Behaviors

Empirical research on managerial coaching is still relatively sparse. However, considerable attention has been given to the general skills and behaviors required of coaches in the practitioner-oriented literature, and some recent work has been done to better understand the behaviors that managers engage when serving as coaches or learning facilitators.

The skill sets often identified in the practitioner literature for effective coaching often include: listening skills, analytical skills, interviewing skills, effective questioning techniques, and observation skills. A study by McLean et al. (2005) yielded a self-assessment of coaching skills based upon their four dimensional coaching model. In this model, the 'manager as coach' should communicate openly with others, take a team approach instead of an individual approach with tasks, tend to value people over tasks, and accept the ambiguous nature of the work environment. When critiquing the McLean et al. model, Peterson and Little (2005) questioned the team approach as a primary component of coaching since managerial coaching is often considered to be a one-on-one intervention. They also acknowledged that other skills appearing in the literature, such as developing a partnership, listening skills, providing feedback, and facilitating development, should be considered. Park, McLean, and Yang (2008) recently added a component related to facilitating development as suggested by Peterson and Little (2005), and the revised self-assessment instrument appears to have evidence of validity.

In addition to possessing the skills to coach, enacting behaviors that facilitate managerial coaching are critical to the managerial coaching process. In general, coaching behaviors reported in the literature have included: 'giving and receiving performance feedback', 'communicating and setting clear expectations', and 'creating a supportive environment conducive to coaching'. Behaviors more specific to managerial coaching have been researched, and a growing base of literature on managerial coaching behaviors is evolving. For example, a seminal study on sales managers' coaching behaviors revealed evidence which supported the existing coaching literature regarding 'providing feedback', 'setting clear expectations', and 'creating a climate for coaching' (Graham, Wedman, & Garvin-Kester, 1993, 1994). However, research by Ellinger (1997) and Ellinger and Bostrom (1999) resulted in a managerial coaching behavior taxonomy that extended the range of coaching behaviors performed by managers. The taxonomy consisted of 13 coaching behaviors representing two clusters labeled as *facilitating behaviors* and *empowering behaviors*. The *facilitating* cluster consisted of the following behaviors: 'providing feedback to employees', 'soliciting feedback from employees', 'talking through approaches to solving problems', 'creating and promoting a learning environment', 'setting and communicating clear expectations and helping employees better understand how their contributions fit within the unit and organization', 'broadening employee perspectives', 'stepping into another role to help shift employee perspectives', 'using analogies, scenarios and examples', and 'engaging others to facilitate learning'. The *empowering* cluster consisted of the following behaviors: 'question framing to encourage employees to think through issues', 'removing obstacles by being a resource to the employee', 'transferring ownership and accountability to the employee', and 'consciously not providing the answers to employees by holding back on providing solutions to them'. Their research offered support for prior coaching behaviors as articulated in the general coaching literature, but also identified new behaviors associated with question framing, multiple forms of providing feedback, soliciting feedback, removing obstacles, transferring ownership to employees, and behaviors associated with broadening employee perspectives and encouraging employees to step into other roles to broaden and appreciate alternative viewpoints. Subsequent to this research, Beattie's (2002) study of managerial coaching in the context of a social service organization resulted in 22 discrete effective learning facilitation behaviors which were then classified and allocated into nine behavioral categories. Comparative research between the Ellinger and Beattie taxonomies has found considerable similarity between the coaching behaviors identified in both studies. Furthermore, additional comparisons between these studies and Hamlin's (2004, 2005) 'generic model' of managerial and leadership effectiveness behaviors also resulted in a high congruence of findings across all three studies.

Additional studies examining the learning facilitation behaviors of managers and leaders (Amy, 2005; Powell & Doran, 2003) and managerial coaching behaviors (Shaw & Knights, 2005) have offered support for the behavioral findings that emerged in the earlier Ellinger and Beattie studies. A more recent focus group based study by Longenecker and Neubert (2005) examined the practices that junior managers considered to be critical for senior managers to employ when implementing coaching as a performance improvement strategy. Their findings consisted of ten practices, as follows: 'clarify what results/performance outcomes are desired (*the clarification of results and outcomes to enable junior managers to meet organizational expectations and career success)*; provide honest, ongoing balanced performance feedback (*the consistent provision of specific and usable feedback to foster continuous improvement of the junior managers*); impact feedback based upon an accurate assessment of performance (*the provision of timely feedback on actual performance by junior managers based upon detailed information from peers, other employees, and customers*); know the junior manager's strengths and weaknesses; offer expert advice on performance improvement; develop a working relationship based on mutual benefit and trust; understand the context, pressure, and demands of a junior manager's job; support the junior manager in solving work problems; help the junior manager prioritize and stay focused; and, create account-ability for performance improvement' (the provision of 'specific, measurable, attainable, and organizationally-relevant goals, as well as a timetable for their attain-ment)' (p. 498). These practices, derived from 225 managers in 45 focus groups hold promise for more deeply considering coaching skills and potentially effective behaviors. These practices are remarkably similar to those behaviors identified by previous managerial coaching research. Lastly, Noer (2005), and Noer, Leupold, and Valle (2007) have acknowledged that managerial coaching is a dynamic interaction between assessing, challenging, and support behaviors. Overall, the research litera-ture examining managerial coaching behaviors has revealed considerable similarity in terms of behaviors used by managers to effectively coach their employees. While effective coaching behaviors have been the focus of such research, less attention has been given to the ineffective behaviors that inhibit or impede managerial coach-ing. Ellinger and Beattie both captured ineffective managerial coaching behaviors, and a comparative analysis of such behaviors has identified several commonalities (Ellinger, Hamlin, & Beattie, 2008). For more detailed discussions of the effec-tive and ineffective behaviors associated with managerial coaching, see Ellinger, Hamlin, and Beattie (2010) and Ellinger, Beattie et al. (2009).

The Mindset of the Managerial Coach

The existing practitioner-oriented and empirical literature has provided insight regarding the requisite skills that managerial coaches should possess, as well as the behaviors that can be engaged to leverage coachable moments. But such capabilities are insufficient if managers do not possess a belief system or mindset that sug-gests that coaching is a core managerial activity. According to Hunt and Weintraub (2002), managers who become effective coaching managers appear to show most if not all the attitudes, beliefs, and behaviors comprising what these authors describe as the 'Coaching Mind-Set' (p. 42). Such managers have an overriding attitude of helpfulness when trying to coach others; they believe that most employees want to learn, and by helping them to develop everybody comes out ahead; they set high standards, and show empathy in their dealings with others; and also, such managers are open to personal learning, to receiving feedback, and to being coached, even by their employees. The belief systems of managerial coaches have been explored by Ellinger and Bostrom (2002), and their results offer some empirical support for

Hunt and Weintraub's concept of the 'coaching mind-set'. In addition, Ellinger and Bostrom's research has identified the importance of managers' beliefs about their capabilities to coach, their responsibilities to coach, their perspectives about the learning process, about learning in general, and about the coaches themselves. Although more research is needed in this area, the existing literature does suggest that managers' beliefs and mindsets are crucial to the coaching process, and do influence their coaching behaviors.

Creating the Context for Managerial Coaching

It has been argued that context permeates all aspects of workplace learning, but research on organizational contextual factors in relation to such learning has been limited (Ellinger, 2005: Ellinger & Cseh, 2007; Sambrook, 2005; Sambrook & Stewart, 2000; Skule, 2004). Similarly, this deficit also includes a lack of empirical research into the contextual influences that are critical for promoting managerial coaching behaviors. While scholars have acknowledged that creating a culture of coaching is important to promote managerial coaching behaviors, limited attention has been given to this aspect (Evered & Selman, 1989). However, Beattie's (2002) study provides some initial insight into the environmental and organizational factors that influence managerial coaching in the social service sector (see also Beattie, 2006, 2007).

Beattie's research suggested that environmental influences such as political, economic, societal, and technological trends influenced the management framework and learning needs within the two organizations she studied. Her work also identified organizational influences, including history, mission and strategy, structure, and culture as impacting the context for managerial coaching. Specifically, the aspirations to become learning organizations contributed to the desire and commitment of managers to engage as coaches with their employees. In both organizations, corporate and human resource development strategies were highly integrated, and each organization had adopted a systematic approach to learning and development. Most importantly, a positive partnership between the human resource development function and line managers was cultivated, and training was provided to managers to help them undertake developmental responsibilities. Further, HRD professionals worked closely with managers to foster a more explicit client–customer approach in support of managers as coaches. These strategies also influenced the organizational culture and created developmental expectations as well as promoted a culture of coaching.

Similarly, Hutchinson and Purcell (2007) found that there were five key factors which encouraged line managers to take learning and development responsibilities seriously in the organizations they studied. These factors included a focus on key staff possessing critical business skills (which may lead to inequity of opportunity); building a language of learning and development (similar to the organizations Beattie studied); creating a culture of performance where learning and development is valued; designing effective performance management systems; and developing line managers themselves. There was also recognition of the need for line managers to be appropriately supported in their learning roles as they 'need, above all, self-confidence and a strong sense of their own security in their own organization' (p. 14), as not all managers are equally effective in leading and developing their employees. Hutchinson and Purcell (2007) also emphasized 'the need to recognize the pastoral role of the line manager, and for the individual to be willing to take on the job of coach or mentor' (p. 9). In particular, given the challenges line managers have in relation to role conflicts and overload, they in turn need the support of their own managers. Indeed, they acknowledge that the importance of senior management support and action on the development of line managers and the cultivation of a climate of learning and development cannot be over exaggerated. Hutchinson and Purcell particularly highlight the need to develop newly promoted managers, which is consistent with Beattie's findings that managers, understandably, tend to be less confident and more insecure during the first 2 years of their managerial career. They also recognize the need for support from colleagues with expertise in human resources.

Benefits of Managerial Coaching

It is often assumed that managerial coaching is a performance improvement strategy that can provide enormous benefits to individuals, teams, and organizations. Of the benefits identified in the practitioner literature, it has been suggested that coaching can lead to learning, improved motivation, working relationships, job satisfaction, and enhanced performance (Anonymous, 2001; Redshaw, 2000). However, empirical research on the benefits associated with coaching is relatively limited. A growing body of evidence has suggested that managerial coaching, even at moderate levels, is linked to job satisfaction, and improved job performance (Ellinger, Ellinger, & Keller, 2003). Hannah's study (2004) also found improved competency and enhanced provision of customer service when supervisory coaching was implemented in the British Rail context. Similarly, Shaw and Knights (2005) found that enhanced knowledge and potential growth, along with improved communications and interpersonal relationships resulted from coaching as a preferred leadership style in a small- to medium-sized enterprise. Elmadag, Ellinger, and Franke's (2008) research also supported improved commitment to service quality as a result of managerial coaching, and Park et al. (2008) found that there was a positive influence on organizational learning and turnover intentions.

Unfortunately, despite the apparent benefits associated with managerial coaching as a workplace learning strategy, scholars contend that the managerial coach is a relatively rare species (Goleman, 2000; Hunt & Weintraub, 2002; Hutchinson & Purcell, 2007; Mills, 1986). Some of the reasons attributed to this include the lack of training of line managers to successfully coach their employees, the tensions between operational and developmental activities, a lack of understanding of adult and workplace learning, insufficient support from human resources, a lack of monitoring managers regarding their performance as coaches, and a context and culture that does not recognize, reward, or promote managerial coaching (Beattie, 2002; Hunt & Weintraub, 2002; Hutchinson & Purcell, 2007).

Conclusion

The workplace learning literature has identified management support as a compelling factor that influences conditions at work and promotes learning (Ashton, 2004; Sambrook & Stewart, 2000; Skule, 2004). Yet, a better understanding of what constitutes management support and how it can be operationalized to enhance learning, has not been fully established. Vera and Crossan (2004) have indicated that managers and leaders often 'lack guidance on how their actions facilitate or hinder learning.' Ellinger's (2005) study, which examined the factors that influence workplace learning, identified the critical role that learning-committed leadership and management plays. She articulated seven dimensions associated with this core theme: support and making space for learning, creating learning opportunities, encouraging risk-taking and the sharing of knowledge, providing positive recognition, serving as role models and coaches. Serving as coaches and role modeling such coaching behavior can positively impact workplace learning.

Accordingly, this chapter has provided an overview of the important role that managers and frontline supervisors can adopt as coaches, in order to facilitate learning in workplace settings and to enhance employee performance. It has suggested that managers need to recognize the catalysts that might stimulate coaching opportunities in their daily interactions with their employees. While possessing coaching skills and a clear understanding of the importance of deploying effective behaviors, managers need also to recognize that their respective coaching mindset, attitudes, and beliefs considerably influence their manifested coaching behaviors. Further, it must be recognized that managers are contextually situated in their organizational settings; aspects of the context and environment can support the adoption of the coaching role or hinder or prevent managers serving in these developmental capacities, which then can ultimately hinder or prevent learning from occurring. Although still relatively rare in its application, and in its infancy as a domain of research, managerial coaching represents a rich avenue for promoting workplace learning as well as an area where considerable research can be undertaken.

References

Amy, A. H. (2005). *Leaders as facilitators of organizational learning.* Unpublished doctoral dissertation. Regent University, Virginia Beach, VA, USA.
Anonymous. (2001). Mentoring and coaching help employees grow. *HR Focus, 78*(9), 1–5.

Antonacopoulou, E. P. (2006). The relationship between individual and organizational learning: New evidence from managerial learning practices. *Management Learning, 37*(4), 455–473.

Antonioni, D. (2000). Leading, managing and coaching. *Industrial Management, 4*(5), 27–34.

Armentrout, B. W. (1995). Making coaching your management metaphor. *HR Focus, 72*(6), 3.

Ashton, D. N. (2004). The impact of organizational structure and practices on learning in the workplace. *International Journal of Training and Development, 8*(1), 43–53

Bartlett, C. A., & Goshal, S. (1997). The myth of the generic managers: New personal competencies for new management roles. *California Management Review, 40*(1), 92–116.

Bauer, J., Festner, D., Gruber, H., Harteis, C., & Reid, H. (2004). The effects of epistemological beliefs on workplace learning. *Journal of Workplace Learning, 16*(5), 284–292.

Beattie, R. S. (2002). *Developmental managers: Line managers as facilitators of workplace learning in voluntary organisations*. Unpublished Ph.D. Thesis, University of Glasgow, Glasgow.

Beattie, R. S. (2006). Line managers and workplace learning: Learning from the voluntary sector. *Human Resource Development International, 9*(1), 99–119.

Beattie, R. S. (2007). Environmental, organizational and individual influences on managers' roles as developers. In S. Sambrook & J. D. Stewart (Eds.), *Human resource development in the health and social care context*. (pp. 159–186) London: Routledge.

Beattie, R. S., Hamlin, R. G., Ellinger, A. D., & Sage, L. (2009). Leadership and management: Mentoring and coaching, confusion, conflict, clarity….Does it matter? In T. J. Chermack, J. Storberg-Walker., & C. M. Graham (Eds.), *Proceedings of the academy of human resource development conference*, (CD-ROM). Arlington, VA.

Bianco-Mathis, V. E., Nabors, L. K., & Roman, C. H. (2002). *Leading from the inside out: A coaching model*. Thousand Oaks, CA: Sage.

Billett, S. (2004). Workplace participatory practices: Conceptualising workplaces as learning environments. *The Journal of Workplace Learning, 16*(6), 312–324.

Billett, S., Hernon-Tinning, B., & Ehrich, L. (2003). Small business pedagogic practices. *Journal of Vocational Education and Training, 55*(2), 149–167.

Boud, D., & Middleton, H. (2003). Learning from others at work: Communities of practice and informal learning. *Journal of Workplace Learning, 15*(5), 194–202.

Burdett, J. O. (1998). Forty things every manager should know about coaching. *Journal of Management Development, 17*(2), 142–152.

CIPD (2003). *Focus on the learner: The change agenda*. London: Chartered Institute of Personnel and Development.

CIPD (2006). *Learning and development survey*. London: Chartered Institute of Personnel and Development.

CIPD (2007). *Learning and development survey*. London: Chartered Institute of Personnel and Development.

Coetzer, A. (2007). Employee perceptions of their workplaces as learning environments. *Journal of Workplace Learning, 19*(2), 417–434.

Clutterbuck, D. (2004a). *Making coaching work: Creating a coaching culture*. London: Chartered Institute of Personnel and Development.

Clutterbuck, D. (2004b). *Everyone needs a mentor* (4th ed.). London: Chartered Institute of Personnel and Development.

Dechant, K. (1989). *Managerial change in the workplace: Learning strategies of managers*. Unpublished doctoral dissertation, Columbia University Teachers College, New York.

de Jong, J. A., Leenders, F. J., & Thisjssen, J. G. I. (1999). HRD tasks of first-level managers. *Journal of Workplace Learning, 11*(5), 176–183.

Dirkx, J. (1999). Invited reaction: Managers as facilitators of learning in learning organizations. *Human Resource Development Quarterly, 10*(2), 127–134.

Doornbos, A. J., Bolhuis, S., & Denessen, E. (2004). Exploring the relation between work domains and work-related learning: The case of the Dutch police force. *International Journal of Training and Development, 8*(3), 174–190.

Ellinger, A. D. (2003). Antecedents and consequences of coaching behavior. *Performance Improvement Quarterly, 16*(1), 5–28.

Ellinger, A. D. (2005). Contextual factors influencing informal learning in a workplace setting: The case of 'reinventing itself company.' *Human Resource Development Quarterly, 16*(3), 389–415.

Ellinger, A. D., & Bostrom, R. P. (1999). Managerial coaching behaviors in learning organizations. *The Journal of Management Development, 18*(9), 752–771.

Ellinger, A. D., & Bostrom, R. P. (2002). An examination of managers' beliefs about their roles as facilitators of learning. *Management Learning, 33*(2), 147–179.

Ellinger, A. D., & Cseh, M. (2007). Contextual factors influencing the facilitation of others' learning through everyday work experiences. *Journal of Workplace Learning, 19*, 435–452.

Ellinger, A. D., Beattie, R. S., & Hamlin, R. G. (2010). The manager as coach. In E. Cox, T. Bachkirova, & D. Clutterbuck (Eds.), *The complete handbook of coaching* (pp. 257–270). London, England: Sage.

Ellinger, A. D., Ellinger, A. E., Hamlin, R. G., & Beattie, R. S. (2010). Achieving improved performance through managerial coaching. In R. Watkins & D. Leigh (Eds.), *Handbook for the selection and implementation of human performance interventions*. Silver Spring, MD: International Society for Performance Improvement.

Ellinger, A. D., Ellinger, A. E., & Keller, S. B. (2003). Supervisory coaching behavior, employee satisfaction, and warehouse employee performance: A dyadic perspective in the distribution industry. *Human Resource Development Quarterly, 14*(4), 435–458.

Ellinger, A. D., Hamlin, R. G., & Beattie, R. S. (2008). Behavioural indicators of ineffective managerial coaching: A cross-national study. *Journal of European Industrial Training, 32*(4), 240–257.

Ellinger, A. M. (1997). *Managers as facilitators of learning in learning organizations*. Unpublished doctoral dissertation, University of Georgia, Athens.

Elmadag, A. B., Ellinger, A. E., & Franke, G. R. (2008). Antecedents and consequences of frontline service employee commitment to service quality. *Journal of Marketing Theory and Practice, 16*(2), 95–110.

Eraut, M., Alderton, J., Cole, G., & Senker, P. (2002). Learning from other people at work. In R. Harrison, F. Reeve, A. Hanson, & J. Clarke (Eds.), *Supporting lifelong learning: Perspectives on learning* (Vol. 1) (pp. 127–145). London: Routledge Falmer.

Evered, R. D., & Selman, J. C. (1989). Coaching and the art of management. *Organizational Dynamics, 18*, 16–32.

Flaherty, J. (1999). *Coaching: Evoking excellence in others*. Burlington, MA: Butterworth-Heinemann.

Fournies, F. F. (1987). *Coaching for improved work performance*. New York: Liberty Hall Press.

Gilley, J. W. (2000). Manager as learning champion. *Performance Improvement Quarterly, 13*(4), 106–121.

Goleman, D. (2000). Leadership that gets results. *Harvard Business Review, 78*(2), 78–90.

Graham, S., Wedman, J. F., & Garvin-Kester, B. (1993). Manager coaching skills: Development and application. *Performance Improvement Quarterly, 6*(1), 2–13.

Graham, S., Wedman, J. F., & Garvin-Kester, B. (1994). Manager coaching skills: What makes a good coach? *Performance Improvement Quarterly, 7*(2), 81–94.

Hamlin, R. G. (2004). In support of models of universalistic and leadership effectiveness. *Human Resource Development Quarterly, 15*(2), 189–215.

Hamlin, R. G. (2005) Toward universalistic models of managerial leader effectiveness: A comparative study of recent British and American derived models of leadership. *Human Resource Development International, 8*(5), 5–25.

Hamlin, R. G., Ellinger, A. D., & Beattie, R. S. (2006). Coaching at the heart of managerial effectiveness: A cross-cultural study of managerial behaviours. *Human Resource Development International, 9*(3), 305–331.

Hamlin, R. G., Ellinger, A. D., & Beattie, R. S. (2008). The emergent coaching industry: A wake-up call for HRD professionals. *Human Resource Development International, 11*(3), 287–305.

Hamlin, R. G., Ellinger, A. D., & Beattie, R. S. (2009). Towards a profession of coaching? A definitional examination of 'coaching,' 'organization development,' and 'human resource development.' *International Journal of Evidence Based Coaching and Mentoring, 7*(1), 13–38.

Hankins, C., & Kleiner, B. H. (1995). New developments in supervisor training. *Industrial and Commercial Training, 27*(1), 26–32.

Hannah, C. (2004). Improving intermediate skills through workplace coaching: A case study within the UK rail industry. *International Journal of Evidence Based Coaching and Mentoring, 2*(1), 17–45.

Hargrove, R. (1995). *Masterful coaching.* San Diego, CA: Pfeiffer & Company.

Hunt, J. M., & Weintraub, J. R. (2002). *The coaching manager: Developing top talent in business.* Thousand Oaks, CA: Sage.

Hutchinson, S., & Purcell, J. (2007). *Learning and the line: The role of line managers in training, learning and development.* London: CIPD.

King, P., & Eaton, J. (1999). Coaching for results. *Industrial and Commercial Training, 31*(4), 145–148.

Kirk, J., Howard, S., Ketting, I., & Little, C. (1999). Type C workplace interventions. *Journal of Workplace Learning, 11*(3), 105–114.

Koopmans, H., Doornbos, A. J., & van Eekelen, I. M. (2006). Learning in interactive work situations: It takes two to tango: Why not invited both partners to dance? *Human Resource Development Quarterly, 17*(2), 135–158.

Kraines, G. A. (2001). Are you L.E.A.D.ing your troops? *Strategy and Leadership, 29*(2), 29–33.

Larsen, H. H. (1997). Do high-flyer programmes facilitate organizational learning? *Journal of Managerial Psychology, 12*(1), 48–59.

Leitch, R. (2006). *Prosperity for all in the global economy – World class skills.* Norwich: TSO.

Longenecker, C. O., & Neubert, M. J. (2005). The practices of effective managerial coaches. *Business Horizons, 48*, 493–500.

Marquardt, M. J., & Loan, P. (2006). *The manager as mentor.* Westport, CT: Praeger.

Marsh, L. (1992). Good manager: Good coach? What is needed for effective coaching? *Industrial and Commercial Training, 24*(9), 3–8.

McGill, M. E., & Slocum, Jr., J. W. (1998). A *little* leadership please? *Organizational Dynamics*, 39–49.

McGovern, P., Gratton, L., Hope-Hailey, V., Stiles, P., & Truss, C. (1997). Human resource management on the line? *Human Resource Management Journal, 7*(4), 12–29.

McLean, G. N., & Kuo, M. (2000). Coaching in organizations: Self-assessment of competence. In K. P. Kuchinke (Ed.), *Proceedings of the academy of human resource development conference* (pp. 638–645). Raleigh-Durham, NC: Academy of Human Resource Development.

McLean, G. N., Yang, B., Kuo, M. C., Tolbert, A. S., & Larkin, C. (2005). Development and initial validation of an instrument measuring managerial coaching skill. *Human Resource Development Quarterly, 16*(2), 157–178.

McNutt, R., & Wright, P. C. (1995). Coaching your employees: Applying sports analogies to business. *Executive Development, 8*(1), 27–32.

Mills, J. (1986). Subordinate perceptions of managerial coaching practices. *Academy of Management Proceedings*, 113–116.

Mindell, N. (1995). Devolving training and development to line managers. *Management Development Review, 8*(2), 16–21.

Mink, O. G., Owen, K. Q., & Mink, B. P. (1993). *Developing high-performance people: The art of coaching.* Reading, MA: Addison-Wesley.

Minter, R. L., & Thomas, E. G. (2000). Employee development through coaching, mentoring and counseling: A multidimensional approach. *Review of Business, 21*(1/2), 43–47.

Mumford, A. (1993). *How managers can develop managers.* Aldershot, England: Gower Press.

Neilsen, K., & Kvale, S. (2006). The workplace: A landscape of learning. In E. Antonacopoulou, P. Jarvis, V. Andersen, B. Elkjaer, & S. Hoyrup (Eds.), *Learning, working and living: Mapping the terrain of working life learning.* (pp. 119–135) Houndmills, Basingstoke, Hampshire, England: Palgrave Macmillan.

Noer, D. (2005). Behaviorally based coaching: A cross-cultural case study. *International Journal of Coaching in Organizations, 3*, 14–23.

Noer, D. M., Leupold, C. R., & Valle, M. (2007). An analysis of Saudi Arabian and U.S. managerial coaching behaviors. *Journal of Managerial Issues, 19*(2), p. 271–287.

Orth, C. D., Wilkinson, H. E., & Benfari, R. C. (1987). The manager's role as coach and mentor. *Organizational Dynamics, (Spring)*, 66–74.

Park, S., McLean, G. N., & Yang, B. (2008). Revision and validation of an instrument measuring managerial coaching skills in organizations. In T. J. Chermack, J. Storberg-Walker, & C. M. Graham (Eds.), *Proceedings of the academy of human resource development* (CD-ROM). Panama City Beach, FL AHRD, 83–90.

Peterson, D. B., & Little, B. (2005). Invited reaction: Development and initial validation of an instrument measuring managerial coaching skill. *Human Resource Development Quarterly, 16*(2), 179–183.

Piasecka, A. (2000). Not 'leadership' but 'leadership.' *Industrial and Commercial Training, 32*(7), 253–255.

Poell, R. F., Van der Krogt, F. J., Vermulst, A. A., Harris R., & Simons, M. (2006). Roles of informal workplace trainers in different organizational contexts: Empirical evidence from Australian companies. *Human Resource Development Quarterly, 17*(2), 175–198.

Popper, M., & Lipshitz, R. (1992). Coaching on leadership. *Leadership & Organization Development Journal, 13*(7), 15–18.

Powell, T., & Doran, M. (2003). *Managers' perceptions of their role in facilitating employee learning.* Proceedings of 2003 international academy of human resource development conference, Bangkok, Thailand.

Ragsdale, S. (2000). Finding a high speed button: New management paradigm. *Triangle Business Journal, 16*(7), 23.

Redshaw, B. (2000). Do we really understand coaching? How can we make it work better? *Industrial and Commercial Training, 32*(3), 106–108.

Rogoff, B. (1995). Observing sociocultural activities on three planes: Participatory appropriation, guided appropriation, and apprenticeship. In J. V. Wertsch, P. Del Rio, & A. Alvarez (Eds.), *Sociocultural studies of the mind* (pp. 139–164). Cambridge: Cambridge University Press.

Salomon, G., & Perkins, D. N. (1998). Individual and social aspects of learning. *Review of Research in Education, 23*, 1–24.

Sambrook, S. (2005). Factors influencing the context and process of work-related learning: Synthesizing findings from two research projects. *Human Resource Development International, 8*(1), 101–119.

Sambrook, S., & Stewart, J. (2000). Factors influencing learning in European learning-oriented organizations: Issues for management. *Journal of European Industrial Training, 24*(2), 209–221.

Schuler, R. S. (1990). Repositioning the human resource function: Transformation or demise? *Academy of Management Executive, 4*(3), 49–60.

Shaw, S., & Knights, J. (2005). *Coaching in an SME: an investigation into the impact of a managerial coaching style on employees within a small firm.* Proceedings of the sixth international conference on HRD research and practice across Europe. Leeds, UK.

Skule, S. (2004). Learning conditions at work: A framework to understand and assess informal learning in the workplace. *International Journal of Training and Development, 24*(2), 8–17.

Slater, S. F., & Narver, J. C. (1994a). Market oriented isn't enough: Build a learning organization. *Marketing Science Institute Report, Report No. 94–103*, 1–30.

Slater, S. F., & Narver, J. C. (1995). Market orientation and the learning organization. *Journal of Marketing, 59*(3), 63.

Slater, S. F., & Narver, J. C. (1995). Market orientation and the learning organization. *Journal of Marketing, 59*(3), 63.

Talarico, M. (2002). *Manager as coach in a pharmacy benefit management organization: A critical incidents analysis*. Unpublished doctoral dissertation, University of Minnesota, Saint Paul, Minneapolis, MN.

Thornhill, A., & Saunders, M. N. K. (1998). What if line managers don't realize they're responsible for HR? Lessons from an organization experiencing rapid change. *Personnel Review, 27*(6), 460–476.

Vera, D., & Crossan, M. (2004). Strategic leadership and organizational learning. *Academy of Management Review, 29*(2), 222–241.

Yarnall, J. (1998). Line managers as career developers: Rhetoric or reality? *Personnel Review, 27*(5), 378–395.

Chapter 6
Direct and Indirect Effects of Supervisor Support on Transfer of Training

Derk-Jan Nijman and John Gelissen

Support and coaching at the workplace are believed to play a critical role in assuring the effectiveness of developmental employee activities, concerning both (informal) learning and transfer of learning at the workplace (e.g. Ouweneel, Taris, Van Zolingen, & Schreurs, 2009; Cohen, Underwood, & Gottlieb, 2000). Although support at the workplace can be provided by several different people with a variety of functions, support by supervisors is in this respect often believed to be the most influential kind of support. Results of studies on the effects of supervisor support on transfer of training are inconclusive, however. One explanation for these differing results is that social (supervisor) support is usually considered a one-dimensional construct, however, with a wide variety of conceptualisations of its content. Moreover, whereas a direct relationship between supervisor support and transfer is often assumed, some studies provide indications of a merely indirect relationship. To determine the effects of social supervisor support on transfer of training, it is argued here that social supervisor support is to be considered a multi-dimensional construct, which has to be examined in a systemic view of the transfer process – considering both possible direct and indirect effects on transfer. The study described in this chapter specifically aims at providing more insight in this relationship when distinguishing between different kinds of supervisor support, and when considering the influence of trainee motivation to transfer and the transfer climate on transfer outcomes.

Theoretical Background and Problem Statement

Transfer of learning or training concerns the extent to which the learning results from, for example, corporate training programmes lead to intended changes in employee's job performance. Relatively few studies have been conducted on the actual occurrence of transfer of training, but the small amount of available empirical evidence in general suggests transfer of corporate training programmes to be rather

D.-J. Nijman (✉)
Department of Education, Working and Learning, IVA policy research and advice, Tilburg University, Warandelaan 2 PO Box 90153 5000 LE Tilburg, The Netherlands
e-mail: djjmnijman@uvt.nl

R.F. Poell, M. van Woerkom (eds.), *Supporting Workplace Learning*, Professional and Practice-based Learning 5, DOI 10.1007/978-90-481-9109-3_6,
© Springer Science+Business Media B.V. 2011

slight. For example, Saks and Belcourt (2006) report 62% of employees to apply what they learn in training immediately after attending the training programme, but they also indicate this percentage to decline to 34% 1 year after training.

Considering the large investments in corporate training it is important to find out why transfer results are relatively slight. A common assumption is that social support at the workplace has significant influence on attempts to transfer, and especially supervisor support is believed to be essential for transfer to take place. This supposed importance of supervisor support stems both from notions of the effects of social support in general and from the works of industrial and organisational psychologists, who indicated supervisors to be among the most significant sources of feedback for employees on their performance (Van der Klink, Gielen, & Nauta, 2001).

Several studies have been carried out to examine the relationship between supervisor support and transfer of training. Results often indicate a positive relationship, as can be seen in studies by, for example, Lim and Johnson (2002), Xiao (1996) and Kontoghiorghes (1998). Brinkerhoff and Montesino (1995) examined the transfer outcomes of five training programmes on behavioural skills. They had supervisors who conducted pre- and post-training meetings with trainees in an experimental group, and compared these trainees' transfer outcomes to those of trainees who had had no such meetings with their supervisor. The results indicate that the transfer outcomes of the experimental group were significantly higher than those of the control group, with trainees in the experimental group also mentioning fewer transfer-inhibiting and more transfer-facilitating factors in their work environment. In a review of two studies of banking organisations, however, Van der Klink et al. (2001) concluded that there is no entirely convincing evidence of the supposed impact of supervisor behaviour. In some cases no significant regression weight of supervisor support on transfer of training was found (e.g. Velada, Caetano, Michel, Lyons, & Kavanagh, 2007), and, incidentally, studies have even shown a negative correlation between the extent of supervisor support and transfer of training (Fitzgerald, 2002; see also Fitzgerald & Kehrhahn, 2003). Results thus indicate both a positive and a negative relationship, as well as no relationship at all.

Cheng and Hampson (2008) state that these mixed findings imply that the construct validity of supervisor support is questionable. This is confirmed in a review of studies that points to two characteristics of previous research that might have contributed to these mixed findings (Nijman, 2004). First, the large variety in the conceptualisation of supervisor support in different studies indicates that the exact nature or content of effective supervisor support is still unclear. In other words, what constitutes effective supervisor support? Examples of supportive supervisor behaviour consist of creating a climate that is favourable to transfer by articulating how the application of new knowledge and skills relates to personal and organisational goals, by aligning the workplace to the learning goals of the training programme, giving trainees the time needed to practise and apply new knowledge, skills and attitudes, and modelling desired behaviour (Hastings, Sheckley and Nichols, 1995). Russ-Eft (2002), however, states that supervisor support also includes setting goals together with trainees, and offering positive reinforcement of the use of new behaviour. Moreover, whereas Axtell, Maitlis, and Yearta (1997) ask trainees about the supervisor support they experienced at the moment of training completion – thus referring to both periods before and during training – Hoekstra (1998), for example, measures support experienced after training. Thus, with regard to the relationship between supervisor support and transfer outcomes, it is necessary to determine what support to provide and when to provide it.

Secondly, it is not clear in which way supervisor support affects transfer outcomes. Whereas most research looked at the possible direct effects of supervisor support on transfer outcomes, a study by Facteau, Dobbins, Russell, Ladd, and Kudish (1995) shows that other factors may intervene and may even change the direction of a relationship. More specifically, characteristics of the training programme, the trainee or his or her work environment might all relate to supervisor support and/or transfer outcomes, or to their relationship. In addition to a direct effect, supervisors might therefore be able to increase transfer outcomes indirectly. In order to better understand the relationship between supervisor support and transfer of training, it is therefore also considered necessary to take into account direct as well as possible indirect effects.

Based on the above-mentioned characteristics, the problem statement of this study concerns the design of a valid construct of supervisor support, and the determination of the effects of supervisor support on transfer of training when considering direct and indirect effects. The research question is formulated as follows:

- To what extent is supervisor support related to transfer outcomes, and to what extent is this relationship mediated by other variables?

Conceptual Model and Hypotheses

Classifying Social Support

The diversity of conceptualisations of supervisor support with regard to transfer is to a large part related to confusion about what social support is actually comprised of, and which possible aspects of social support should be considered the most important (House, 1981). Similar to findings in other fields of research (Viswesvaran, Sanchez, & Fisher, 1999), relationships between social supervisor support and transfer of training could well depend on, among other things, the type and source of support. Supervisor support thus might consist of different kinds of supportive behaviour, also differing in their effects on transfer of training.

Various classifications of support functions or dimensions have been distinguished and used in research (Stroebe, 2000). However, most of these center around three or four categories that relate to or are derived from a description of social support as given by House (1981). House's description is the most commonly accepted and used categorisation of social support, and actually distinguishes four types of social support: instrumental, informational, emotional and appraisal support.

Instrumental support refers to the provision of instrumental behaviours that directly help a person in need (House, 1981), and has also been described and included in research as tangible support (e.g. Viswesvaran et al., 1999), practical support, behavioural assistance and material aid (Cohen et al., 2000). It consists of the offering of concrete help or facilities in order to solve or handle difficult situations (Den Ouden, 1992). For example, individuals give instrumental support when they provide others with the tools and equipment to do their work, or when they give assistance with childcare and housecleaning. The – theoretical – benefit of instrumental support is that it solves practical problems and allows more time for relaxation or other coping mechanisms (referring to stressful situations) (Cohen et al., 2000).

Informational support refers to the provision of information that someone can use in coping with personal and environmental problems (House, 1981), and consists of offering information that helps someone get a better grip on and/or view of reality (Buunk, 1992; Den Ouden, 1992). Examples of informational support are the provision of information about resources, or suggesting alternative ways to perform certain tasks at the workplace. The difference between informational and instrumental support is that informational support is not in and of itself helpful, but assists others in helping themselves (House, 1981). It is argued that informational support is important with regard to new or unclear situations, in which individuals seek information from others in order to compare or construct their own opinion (Buunk, 1992). It thus helps to reduce, for example, feelings of insecurity. The benefits of informational support consist of an increased amount of useful information available, it helps to obtain the services needed and leads to more effective coping strategies (Cohen et al., 2000).

Emotional support consists of the availability of persons who can listen sympathetically when one is facing difficulties or problems, and who can provide empathy, care, love and trust (Cohen et al., 2000; House, 1981). Examples of emotional support consist of allowing discussions of feelings and indicating sympathy, approval and compassion. Emotional support refers mainly to feelings of psychological proximity and openness and is believed to reduce tension and anxiety (Buunk, 1992). Theoretical benefits of emotional support consist of reducing the perceived threat (or impact) of certain life events, enhancing self-esteem, reducing anxiety/depression and motivating people to cope (better) with situations or events (Cohen et al., 2000).

Appraisal support, finally, involves the provision of information that is relevant to an individual's self-evaluation (Cohen et al., 2000; House, 1981; Stroebe, 2000). Individuals use information about (and from) others to evaluate their own opinions and abilities, appraisal refers to information that provides a positive evaluation. Its main – theoretical – benefits are that it decreases perceived deviancy, allows acceptance of feelings, provides favourable comparisons and increases feelings of being able to handle problems (Cohen et al., 2000). Appraisal support, for example, consists of giving compliments or providing feedback about job performance and giving indications about one's relative status in a population. Buunk (1992) indicates that it is especially supervisor appreciation at the workplace that is important to employees' well-being, and that positive feedback is specifically appreciated when one feels insecure about one's functioning or has low self-esteem.

These four types are derived from several earlier conceptions of social support; they have also been used and referred to most frequently in research (e.g. Buunk, 1992; Den Ouden, 1992; Hoekstra, 1998; Stroebe, 2000). They might also provide a possible solution for the concerns about the construct validity of supervisor support in research on the relationship between supervisor support and transfer of training. As such, the incorporation of these sub-constructs of supervisor support in research might provide a better insight into the relationship between supervisor support and transfer of training. Based on this assumption and the above review of literature, two hypotheses regarding the effect of supervisor support on transfer of training have been formulated.

- *H1. Scores on the scales for informational, instrumental, appraisal and emotional supervisor support can be explained by a one-factor model of supervisor support.*
- *H2: Supervisor support has a direct positive effect on trainees' transfer of training.*

Factors Mediating the Relationship Between Supervisor Support and Transfer of Training: Transfer Climate and Motivation to Transfer

The effects of supervisor support can only be tested to the extent that other relevant – mediating or moderating – variables are taken into account. It has therefore also been argued that factors affecting transfer should be examined in a systemic view of the transfer process (e.g. Salas & Cannon-Bowers, 2001). Literature suggests several specific characteristics of trainees, the training programme and the work environment to influence training outcomes (e.g. Colquitt, LePine, & Noe, 2000), several of which have hardly been examined, however. Two factors which have been empirically shown to affect transfer of training concern the prevailing transfer climate and trainees' motivation to transfer training, and both have also been related to supervisor support. Transfer climate, trainee motivation to transfer and their supposed effects on transfer of training will be further described below.

Transfer Climate

Social support – especially when provided by supervisors – is one element of the work environment that is believed to play an important role in the occurrence of transfer of training, but research has also shown other characteristics of the work environment to have an effect. The transfer climate refers to those (perceived) characteristics of the work environment that may facilitate or inhibit transfer of training (Burke & Baldwin, 1999), differing from the general work environment in that it is specifically and intentionally directed at the transfer. Current knowledge of the composition of the transfer climate draws to a large extent on a study by Rouiller and

Goldstein (1993), who adapted several categories and definitions from a behaviour-modification model in order to examine the effects of transfer climate. This has been followed by the works of Holton, Bates, Seyler, and Carvalho (1997) and Holton, Bates, and Ruona (2000), who subsequently differentiate among seven transfer climate constructs: supervisor support, opportunities to use learning on the job, peer support, sanctioning of transfer (by supervisors), positive personal outcomes when transferring learning, negative personal outcomes when not transferring learning and resistance to change. Ever since, research on the transfer climate has more or less included these constructs (e.g. Colquitt et al., 2000; Donovan, Hannigan, & Crowe, 2001). Empirical evidence confirms the relationship between transfer climate and transfer of training, as can be seen in studies by, for example, Rouiller and Goldstein (1993), Kontoghiorghes (2001, 2004), and in the review of studies by Colquitt et al. (2000). On the basis of these findings hypothesis three is formulated as follows:

- *H3. Transfer climate has a direct positive effect on trainee transfer of training.*

Supervisor support is part of the work environment and often considered a sub-construct of the transfer climate, and for this reason it is also believed that supportive supervisor behaviour contributes to a positive transfer climate. Supervisors might, for example, create opportunities to use new skills on the job (Ford, Quiñones, Sego, & Speer Sorra, 1992) or they might reward the use of new skills after training. In this sense, transfer climate could mediate the relationship between supervisor support and transfer. Smith-Jentsch, Salas, and Brannick (2001) indeed show that perceptions of team transfer climate mediate the effect of team leader support on post-training behaviour. It is therefore hypothesised that:

- *H4. Supervisor support has a direct positive effect on the transfer climate.*
- *H5. Transfer climate mediates the relationship between supervisor support and trainee transfer of training.*

Motivation to Transfer

Trainee motivation is assumed to affect trainees' enthusiasm for training (energising), the direction of participants to learn and master training (directing) and the use of knowledge and skills on the job (maintenance) (Noe, 1986). Motivation to transfer can be described as the trainee's desire to use on the job the knowledge and skills that have been learned in a training programme (e.g. Axtell et al., 1997; Noe, 1986). Trainee motivation to transfer is believed to be a significant predictor of trainees' attempts to transfer training to the job. Studies by Axtell et al. (1997) and Chiaburu and Lindsay (2008), for example, show motivation to transfer to positively predict transfer outcomes. It is therefore hypothesised here that motivation to transfer enhances trainees' transfer outcomes.

- *H6. Trainee motivation to transfer has a direct positive effect on trainee transfer of training.*

Supervisor support and other transfer climate factors have been shown to positively affect trainee motivation to transfer (Cheng & Hampson, 2008), a positive direct effect is therefore expected. Scaduto, Lindsay, and Chiaburu (2008) found general training motivation to mediate the relationship between leader–member exchange and transfer of training. In this sense, motivation to transfer could be expected to mediate the relationship between supervisor support and transfer of training. The hypotheses concerning the mediating role of motivation to transfer are formulated as follows:

- *H7. Supervisor support has a direct positive effect on trainee motivation to transfer.*
- *H8. Trainee motivation to transfer mediates the effect of supervisor support on transfer of training.*

Finally, it is also believed that perceptions of a positive transfer climate enhance trainees' motivation to transfer training. Kontoghiorghes (2004) showed a positive learning transfer climate to be a significant predictor of trainees' motivation to transfer learning back to the job. With regard to specific aspects of the transfer climate it has been shown that trainees' motivation to transfer is affected by their perceptions of opportunities to use learning on the job (Foxon, 1997), while Seyler, Holton, Bates, Burnett, and Carvalho (1998) also found a positive effect of peer support and a negative effect of supervisor sanctions. Hypothesis five refers to the direct effect of transfer climate on motivation to transfer training.

- *H9. Transfer climate has a direct positive effect on trainee motivation to transfer training.*

Method

Design and Instrumentation

To test the hypotheses a quantitative study was set up. The study was conducted by means of survey research in the form of self-assessment questionnaires, administered at least 3 months after training participation in order to provide sufficient time to transfer training to the job. Questionnaires provide the opportunity to gather a large amount of structured information in a relatively short period of time (e.g. Baarda & De Goede, 1995). Multiple-choice questionnaires for trainees were constructed to measure the variables. Scales were based on existing scales wherever possible, and otherwise based on the review of literature. The questionnaires were composed of propositions, in combination with a five-point Likert-type response scale. All scales were discussed with two other researchers, pilot tested and, when necessary, adjusted. Final reliability estimates of the scales can be found in Table 6.1.

Regarding the sub-constructs of supervisor support, several articles and studies were examined that referred to general descriptions of the sub-constructs (e.g.

Table 6.1 Descriptive statistics, reliability estimates (α) and intercorrelations of the variables

Variable	M	SD	1	2	3	4	5	6	7
1 Instrumental supervisor support	2,72	0.65	(0.81)						
2 Informational supervisor support	2,57	0.72	0.73**	(0.80)					
3 Appraisal supervisor support	2,33	0.64	0.79**	0.81**	(0.83)				
4 Emotional supervisor support	2,87	0.77	0.79**	0.80**	0.79**	(0.83)			
5 Motivation to transfer	3.80	0.58	0.15	0.14	0.15	0.14	(0.82)		
6 Transfer climate	3.24	0.42	0.39**	0.46**	0.38**	0.39**	0.52**	(0.87)	
7 Transfer outcomes	3.59	0.57	0.29**	0.31**	0.34**	0.30**	0.73**	0.54**	–

$**p < 0.01$; $N = 151$ (listwise deletion of missing cases)

House, 1981; Stroebe, 2000) or that referred to actual items or descriptions of con-crete supportive behaviours (e.g. Foxon, 1997; Hastings et al. 1995; Russ-Eft, 2002; Den Ouden, 1992; Hoekstra, 1998). Each of the sub-constructs was defined, and subsequent items were newly formulated or derived from existing scales or descrip-tions in other studies. In general, items referred to the moment of administration of the questionnaire. However, in each of the scales reflecting supervisor support some items retrospectively assessed perceived supervisor support before training participation.

Instrumental supervisor support refers to the extent to which supervisors pro-vide trainees with instrumental help before and after training, in order to enhance the application of what was learned. Eight items were formulated; an exam-ple of one referring to perceived supervisor support before training is "Before I took part in this training programme, my supervisor involved me in planning the programme." An item reflecting perceived supervisor support after training partici-pation is "Since I completed this training programme, my supervisor has provided me with opportunities to apply what I have learned."

Informational supervisor support refers to the extent to which supervisors provide trainees with information related to the training programme itself, the rela-tionship of training to the job and the application of new knowledge, skills and attitudes. For measurement, six items were determined, one of which reads "Since I completed this training programme, my supervisor has made sure I get information about how to apply what I have learned (e.g. suggestions, exemplary others)."

Appraisal support by supervisor refers to the extent to which supervisors indi-cate appraisal (or forthcoming appraisal) to trainees before and after training, if new knowledge, skills and attitudes are applied on the job. Ten items were subsequently formulated, one of which is "Since I completed this training programme, my super-visor has given me specific advantages/rewards if I apply on my job what I have learned (e.g. promotion, salary increase)."

Emotional supervisor support refers to the extent to which trainees receive emotional support from supervisors before and after training, with emotional support regarding the learning and application of what has been learned. Six items were defined, an example of which is "Since I completed this training programme, my supervisor has made it clear he/she would always help in case of problems/difficulties."

Trainees' *motivation to transfer* reflects their current desire to use knowledge, skills and attitudes that have been learned in the training programme on the job. To construct a scale reflecting trainee's motivation to transfer, the works of Hoekstra (1998), Holton (1996) and Noe (1986) were reviewed. Four items were subsequently formulated, an example of which is "Since I completed this training programme, I really feel like applying what I have learned in my job."

Regarding the *transfer climate*, items were developed for all identified components: opportunities to use learning on the job, peer support, sanctioning of transfer by others, positive personal outcomes for using new knowledge and skills after training, negative personal outcomes when not using new knowledge and skills after training, and (team) resistance to change. Among others, studies by Rouiller and Goldstein (1993), Burke and Baldwin (1999), Holton et al. (1997) and Russ-Eft (2002) were consulted to determine the content of items. Twenty-three items remained, one of which is "Since I completed this training programme, I have had ample opportunities in my job to use what I have learned."

Scales measuring *transfer outcomes* were based on the objectives of the training programmes. An example of a proposition measuring transfer outcomes is "Since I completed this training programme, I have motivated subordinate employees considerably better than before the programme."

Sample

Three organisations participated,[1] all of which provide products and services in the fields of advanced technology. Four comparable off-the-job training programmes on the development of social and/or managerial skills were included, selected employees had taken part in one of these training programmes between 3 months and 2 years before sending the questionnaires. E-mails containing a personalised link to a digital questionnaire were sent to 281 employees. A final response of 200 former trainees was obtained, 169 respondents actually completed the questionnaire.

---

[1] As employees are nested within organisations, scores on transfer climate, motivation to transfer and transfer outcomes – endogenous variables in the analysis – were compared to test for possible differences between organizations. An analysis of variance revealed no significant differences, however. In addition, a path model with dummy variables as control variables was estimated for organizational differences. Effects of these control variables were also not significant and the effects of other variables changed only marginally. On the basis of these results and for matters of parsimony, the results are reported from a pooled analysis.

Analyses

To test the research model, structural equation modelling (SEM) was applied. This statistical methodology allows the quantification and testing of substantive theories by combining confirmatory factor analysis and regression analysis. It explicitly takes into account measurement error in the observed variables and can be used to develop, estimate and test complex multivariable models, as well as to study both direct and indirect effects involved in a given model (Raykov & Marcoulides, 2006). Maximum likelihood estimation of the models was done with AMOS 18 (Arbuckle, 2009). To evaluate the fit of the models to the data, we report the model Chi-square, the RMSEA index (Brown & Cudeck, 1993), with its related PClose test for testing the null hypothesis that the population RMSEA is no greater than 0.05, and the comparative fit index (CFI). A value of the RMSEA of 0.05 or less is indicative of the model being good approximation to the analysed data, and CFI values greater than 0.95 are often indicative of good fitting models. The CFI is normed to the 0–1 range and performs well in estimating model fit even in small samples (Hu & Bentler, 1999).

The analyses consisted of two separate stages. First, a measurement model pertaining to supervisor support and its sub-constructs was estimated. The second stage consisted of the evaluation of the structural relationships between the latent exogenous variable supervisor support that resulted from the first stage and the observed endogenous variables transfer climate, transfer motivation and transfer outcomes. Direct, indirect and total effects of supervisor support, transfer climate and transfer motivation on transfer outcomes are reported, allowing to evaluate the degree to which the effect of supervisor support on transfer outcomes is mediated by transfer climate and transfer motivation. In addition, the relative importance of each of these predictors of transfer outcomes was determined.

Results

Descriptive Statistics

Means, standard deviations, intercorrelations and reliability estimates of the variables are presented in Table 6.1.

Table 6.1 shows all scales to have sufficient internal consistency ($\alpha > 0.80$). Scales reflecting the sub-constructs of supervisor support intercorrelate strongly, but are not related to trainees' motivation to transfer. Transfer climate and transfer outcomes correlate significantly to all other variables.

All mean scores in Table 6.1 differ significantly from scale mean 3.00. The mean scores indicate trainees to rate the extent to which they receive support from their supervisors as somewhat to rather negative. They are rather motivated to transfer learned content to their work, however, while considering the transfer climate at the workplace as somewhat positive. Finally, trainees rate their extent of transfer of training (transfer outcomes) as rather positive as well.

In order to inspect for multicollinearity, the variance inflation factors (VIF) included in the collinearity diagnostics in each of the separate regression analyses were examined (see Cohen & Cohen, 1975). The results reveal that no VIF of the independent variables was greater than value 4, whereas, in general, multicollinearity is assumed when VIF values exceed 10. It is therefore concluded that no multicollinearity between the different types of supervisor support exists in this study.

Results of SEM Analyses

Figure 6.1 shows the results of testing hypothesis 1 (H1), which states that supervisor support is a one-factor structure, with sub-dimensions instrumental, informational, appraisal and emotional supervisor support. For matters of comparison, all reported coefficients are standardised. The results indicate that this one-factor model fits the sample data well: the overall Chi-square value = 5.459 with $df = 2$, $p = 0.065$. Although the value of RMSEA is 0.092 – which is larger than the recommended upper bound value of 0.08 for concluding that there is at least a sufficient fit of the model to the data (Browne & Cudeck, 1993) – the p-value of the test of close fit is 0.160.[2] This indicates that the null hypothesis that the population RMSEA is no greater than 0.05 need not be rejected. Note that the loadings

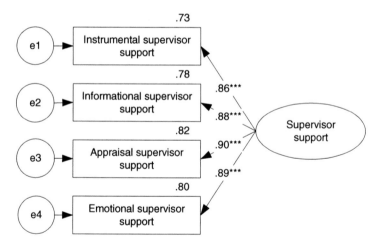

Fig. 6.1 Measurement model for supervisor support ($N = 151$, listwise deletion of missing cases) *Note*: Model Chi-square = 5.459, df = 2, p-value = 0.065. RMSEA = 0.092, p-value of close fit = 0.160; CFI = 0.994. Numbers above scales for instrumental, informational, appraisal and emotional supervisor support are squared multiple correlations

---

[2]This seemingly contradictory finding can be the result of a limited sample size. Hu and Bentler (1993) found that in small samples the RMSEA overrejected the true model, or, in other words, that its value was too large, suggesting a seemingly inadequate fit of the model to the data.

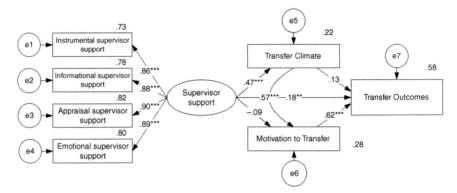

Fig. 6.2 Measurement model for direct and indirect effects of supervisor support on transfer outcomes ($N = 151$, listwise deletion of missing cases)
Note: Model Chi-square $= 13.455$, $df = 11$, p-value $= 0.265$. RMSEA $= 0.033$, p-value of close
fit $= 0.638$; CFI $= 0.997$. R^2 transfer climate $= 0.217$; R^2 transfer motivation $= 0.282$; R^2 transfer
outcomes $= 0.582$. Numbers above scales for transfer climate and transfer outcomes, and next to
motivation to transfer are squared multiple correlations

of the dimensions of supervisor support are all relatively high and of about the same
size, which suggests that all four dimensions of supervisor support play an equally
important role in the structure of this latent variable.

In the second stage of the analyses hypotheses 2–9 were tested. The empirical
model pertaining to these hypotheses is presented in Fig. 6.2.

The model in Fig. 6.2 shows a close fit to the data, with the overall Chi-square
value being 13.455 and 11 degrees of freedom. Furthermore, the null hypothesis of
close fit for the population RMSEA does not have to be rejected, and the CFI is very
close to 1, which all indicate a good fitting model.

The results of this model also indicate positive evidence for hypotheses 2, 4, 6
and 9. That is, supervisor support has a slight direct positive effect on transfer outcomes ($\beta = 0.18$, $p < 0.001$), while motivation to transfer actually has a strong
direct effect on transfer outcomes ($\beta = 0.62$, $p < 0.001$). The transfer climate positively affects trainees' motivation to transfer ($\beta = 0.57$, $p < 0.001$); however, the
hypothesised direct effect of transfer climate on transfer outcomes is not significant
– hypothesis 3 is therefore rejected. As a direct result the assumption that transfer
climate mediates the relationship between supervisor support and transfer outcomes
(H5) is also rejected. In the same way hypotheses 7 and 8 are rejected: the lack
of a significant regression weight of supervisor support on trainees' motivation to
transfer implies that this study provides no empirical evidence for this effect, nor
for motivation to transfers mediating role between supervisor support and transfer
outcomes.

Although hypotheses 3 and 7 have not been confirmed, the model does indicate
an indirect effect of supervisor support on transfer outcomes by means of both transfer climate and motivation to transfer. More specifically, supervisor support leads
to a more positive transfer climate, while this transfer climate enhances trainees'
motivation to transfer. Motivation to transfer positively affects transfer outcomes.

Table 6.2   Direct, indirect and total effects on transfer outcomes

Variables	Effects on transfer outcomes		
	Direct effect	Indirect effect	Total effect
Supervisor support	0.18	0.17	0.35
Transfer climate	0.13	0.35	0.48
Motivation to transfer	0.62	0.00	0.62

Together, the three-predictor variables in this model explain almost 60% of the variance of transfer outcomes.

To investigate the relative importance of each of the predictors of transfer outcomes, total effects of supervisor support, transfer climate and motivation to transfer on transfer outcomes have been calculated. These calculations are based on the model estimates as shown in Fig. 6.2, the effects are reported in Table 6.2.

The results of the effect sizes indicate that motivation to transfer has the largest total effect on transfer outcomes, entirely resulting from a direct effect. Although the regression weight of transfer climate on transfer outcomes is slight and non-significant, its total effect is relatively large. This is a result of transfer climate's strong positive effect on trainees' motivation to transfer, which in turn promotes transfer outcomes. Finally, supervisor support has a direct effect on transfer outcomes, when controlling for transfer climate and transfer motivation ($\beta = 0.18$). In addition, supervisor support has an indirect effect of about the same strength as the direct effect ($\beta = 0.17$), via transfer climate and transfer motivation. The latter provides confirmation of a mediational explanation, different from what was hypothesised; the effect of supervisor support on transfer outcomes can be explained by including both transfer climate and transfer motivation. The effect of supervisor support on transfer outcomes is, however, only *partially* mediated by these variables.

Conclusions and Implications

Conclusions and Discussion

This study tested a model of the direct effect of supervisor support on transfer of training, as well as its indirect effects on transfer of training by means of the transfer climate and trainees' motivation to transfer. Supervisor support was conceptualised by four separate sub-components: instrumental, informational, appraisal and emotional supervisor support. Results indicated these four to be well predicted by one latent construct of supervisor support, and they are therefore believed to provide a more construct valid conceptualisation of supervisor support with regard to its effect on transfer of training. Results of this study thus suggest that research on the relationship between supervisor support and transfer of training should best incorporate each of these elements in the conceptualisation of supervisor support.

A main result of the study is that supervisor support is shown to have a slight direct positive effect on transfer outcomes. In line with several other studies (e.g. Gumuseli & Ergin, 2002), this study thus indicates that supervisor support directly contributes to the use of learned knowledge, skills and attitudes at the workplace. It also indicates supervisor support to contribute indirectly to transfer of training, by means of the transfer climate and trainees' motivation to transfer. More specifically, supervisors are shown to be able to exert considerable influence on the transfer climate. As transfer climate strongly affects trainees' motivation to transfer and motivation to transfer enhances transfer outcomes, the results point to an indirect effect of supervisor support on transfer outcomes.

Instead of what was expected, supervisor support was not found to affect trainees' motivation to transfer directly. As a consequence, motivation to transfer does not mediate the relationship between supervisor support and transfer of training. Seyler et al. (1998) showed similar results, as supervisor support in their study did not have a significant effect on motivation to transfer when controlling for effects of several transfer climate variables – such as peer support. Their explanation was that it is possible that the influence of transfer climate left little unique variance to be explained by supervisor support, which they relate to the cohesiveness of the work group in the study. In contrast to their study, however, results of this study showed no significant correlations between the components of supervisor support and motivation to transfer (for a similar result see Axtell et al., 1997). On the other hand, transfer climate and motivation to transfer correlate strongly. One possible explanation is that trainees in this study were believed to work in relatively autonomous work settings, possibly having rather little to do with their supervisors. In other words, the nature of the relationship between trainees and supervisors in a specific work setting might moderate the effect of supervisor support on trainees' motivation to transfer. It might be, for example, that the relationship between supervisor support and motivation to transfer will be stronger in a more directive and hierarchical work setting, in which work activities are to a large part determined by supervisors. Further research is needed to test the relationship between supervisor support and trainee motivation to transfer.

Another particular finding of this study is that the transfer climate has no direct effect on trainees' transfer outcomes. It was hypothesised that the transfer climate could enhance trainees' transfer outcomes directly by, for example, offering sufficient opportunities to use new knowledge and skills on the job. As the results indicated transfer climate to have a strong positive effect on trainees' motivation to transfer, however, it can be concluded that transfer climate does have a positive indirect effect on transfer outcomes. In this sense, the results indicate that a positive transfer climate is important with regard to transfer outcomes through affective aspects of trainees. The transfer climate does not affect post-training behaviour itself, but rather motivates trainees to use new knowledge and skills on the job. Tziner, Fisher, Senior, and Weisberg (2007) included trainee motivation to learn in their study, and similarly found the effect of transfer climate on transfer outcomes to be mediated by motivation to learn. They concluded that constructs such as trainee motivation have not been included frequently in research on the relationship between transfer climate and transfer of training, which might be a reason for finding a direct positive effect in other studies. Another point of view concerns the multidimensionality of the transfer climate. Whereas more or less "objective" aspects such as the opportunity to use knowledge and skills might directly affect transfer outcomes, more "subjective" measures such as experienced resistance against change might relate stronger to trainee motivation to transfer. It would therefore be useful to study the effects of separate dimensions/constructs of the transfer climate in relation to transfer outcomes, taking into account possible indirect effects by means of affective trainee characteristics. In a way, this suggests research on the transfer climate to distinguish between an affective, subjective and perceptional component, and a more objective component of the transfer climate.

Practical Implications

The study indicates trainees' motivation to transfer to have a strong effect on their transfer of training. In order to enhance transfer outcomes, organisations as well as trainers and others that are involved therefore best pay significant attention to trainees' motivational processes. On an organisational level, this refers to, for example, profiling itself as an organisation that values and stimulates employee learning and development. It also refers to matching organisational, job, and employee demands and wishes with regard to learning and development. Training that is adjusted to individual employee needs is likely to result in higher learning and transfer outcomes, and trainers and training departments subsequently have to be able to adapt training activities to these.

Results of the mean scores indicated trainees to perceive little support from their supervisors regarding training participation and transfer of training. In line with results of other studies (e.g. Nijman, Nijhof, & Wognum, 2003), supervisors thus hardly seem to promote trainees' use of new knowledge and skills on the job. Considering the direct and indirect effects supervisor support has on transfer outcomes, this study stresses the importance of supervisor attention for supporting transfer. Possible supportive behaviour could include the four distinguished components of social support, and should at least be directed at providing a positive transfer climate. Instrumental support can be provided by allowing trainees sufficient time to prepare for training, by creating opportunities to use new knowledge and skills on the job and by providing the right equipment to use these. Informational support consists of, for example, offering information about the relevance of the training programme and by offering information about when to use new knowledge and skills on the job. In appraisal, supervisors can provide support by offering rewards for taking part in the training programme and for applying new knowledge and skills after training, giving compliments when new knowledge and skills are used on the job, and by informing others about the successful use of new knowledge and skills. Emotional support can consist of creating a work climate that is open to change, showing confidence in successful training participation and transfer of training, and indicating understanding for possible difficulties in using new knowledge and skills on the job.

Limitations

It was stated earlier that the number of variables affecting transfer of training could be very large. This study incorporated supervisor support, transfer climate and trainees' motivation to transfer, selected on basis of their relationship with transfer outcomes or supervisor support in earlier research. The importance of examining transfer of training and factors affecting transfer from a more complete systemic point of views has been articulated before (e.g. Nijman, 2004), and it should be taken into account that other variables might have been overlooked in this study. For example, research has also indicated effects of, for example, relapse prevention modules and trainee self-efficacy (Cheng & Hampson, 2008). Future research therefore needs to work further towards an integrative systemic model of the transfer process, this study provided insight into a possible part of such a model.

References

Arbuckle, J. (2009). *Amos*™ *18 user's guide*. Chicago, IL: SPSS.

Axtell, C. M., Maitlis, S., & Yearta, S. K. (1997). Predicting immediate and longer-term transfer of training. *Personnel Review, 26*(3), 201–213.

Baarda, D. B., & De Goede, M. P. M. (1995). *Basisboek methoden en technieken: praktische handleiding voor het opzetten en uitvoeren van onderzoek* (2nd ed.). Houten: Stenfert Kroese.

Brinkerhoff, R. O., & Montesino, M. U. (1995). Partnerships for training transfer: Lessons from a corporate study. *Human Resource Development Quarterly, 6*(3), 263–274.

Browne, M. W., & Cudeck, R. (1993). Alternative ways of assessing model fit. In K. A. Bollen & J. S. Long (Eds.), *Testing structural equation models* (pp. 136–162). Newbury Park, CA: Sage.

Burke, L. A., & Baldwin, T. T. (1999). Workforce training transfer: A study of the effect of relapse prevention training and transfer climate. *Human Resource Management, 38*(3), 227–242.

Buunk, A. P. (1992). Affiliatie. In R. W. Meertens & J. Von Grumbkow (Eds.), *Sociale psychologie* (2nd ed., pp. 191–204). Groningen: Wolters-Noordhoff.

Cheng, E. W. L., & Hampson, I. (2008). Transfer of training: A review and new insights. *International Journal of Management Reviews, 10*(4), 327–341.

Chiaburu, D. S., & Lindsay, D. R. (2008). Can do or will do? The importance of self-efficacy and instrumentality for training transfer. *Human Resource Development International, 11*(2), 199–206.

Cohen, J., & Cohen, P. (1975). *Applied multiple regression/correlation analysis for the behavioral sciences*. Hillsdale, NJ: Lawrence Erlbaum.

Cohen, S., Underwood, L. G., & Gottlieb, B. H. (Eds.). (2000). *Social support measurement and intervention*. Oxford: Oxford University Press.

Colquitt, J. A., LePine, J. A., & Noe, R. A. (2000). Toward an integrative theory of training motivation: A meta-analytic path analysis of 20 years of research. *Journal of Applied Psychology, 85*(5), 678–707.

Den Ouden, M. D. (1992). *Transfer na bedrijfsopleidingen: Een veldonderzoek naar de rol van voornemens, sociale normen, beheersing en sociale steun bij opleidingstransfer. [Transfer of corporate training: A field study on the role of intentions, social norms, control and social support in transfer of training]* Doctoral dissertation. Amsterdam: Thesis Publishers.

Donovan, P., Hannigan, K., & Crowe, D. (2001). The learning transfer system approach to esti-mating the benefits of training: empirical evidence. *Journal of European Industrial Training, 25*(2/3/4), 221-228.

Facteau, J. D., Dobbins, G. H., Russell, J. E. A., Ladd, R. T., & Kudish, J. D. (1995). The influence of general perceptions of the training environment on pretraining motivation and perceived training transfer. *Journal of Management, 21*(1), 1–25.

Fitzgerald, C. G. (2002). *Transfer of training and transfer climate: the relationship to the use of transfer maintenance strategies in an autonomous job context.* Doctoral dissertation, University of Connecticut, Storrs, CT.

Fitzgerald, C. G., & Kehrhahn, M. T. (2003). *Transfer of training in an autonomous job context.* Unpublished Paper, University of Connecticut, Storrs, CT.

Ford, J. K., Quiñones, M. A., Sego, D. J., & Speer Sorra, J. (1992). Factors affecting the opportunity to perform trained tasks on the job. *Personnel Psychology, 45*(3), 511–527.

Foxon, M. (1997). The influence of motivation to transfer, action planning, and manager support on the transfer process. *Performance Improvement Quarterly, 10*(2), 42–63.

Gumuseli, A. I., & Ergin, B. (2002). The manager's role in enhancing the transfer of training: a Turkish case study. *International Journal of Training and Development, 6*(2), 80–97.

Hastings, S. L, Sheckley, B. G., & Nichols, A. B. (1995). Transfer of training: The impact of supervisory support, supervisory involvement, situational constraints, and self-efficacy on the application of technical skills training. In E. F. Holton, III (Ed.), *Academy of human resource development 1995 conference proceedings.* St. Louis, MO: AHRD.

Hoekstra, M. R. (1998). *Gedragsbeïnvloeding door cursussen: Een studie naar de effecten van persoons-, cursus- en omgevingskenmerken. [Influencing behaviour through training programmes: A study of the effects of personal, training programme and environmental characteristics]* Doctoral dissertation, Vrije Universiteit, Amsterdam, The Netherlands.

Holton, E. F., III. (1996). The flawed four-level evaluation model. *Human Resource Development Quarterly, 7*(1), 5–21.

Holton, E. F., III, Bates, R. A., & Ruona, W. E. A. (2000). Development of a generalized learning transfer system inventory. *Human Resource Development Quarterly, 11*(4), 333–360.

Holton, E. F., III, Bates, R. A., Seyler, D. L., & Carvalho, M. B. (1997). Toward construct validation of a transfer climate instrument. *Human Resource Development Quarterly, 8*(2), 95–113.

House, J. S. (1981). *Work stress and social support.* Reading, MA: Addison-Wesley.

Hu, L. T., & Bentler, P. M. (1999). Cutoff criteria for fit indexes in covariance structure analysis: Coventional criteria versus new alternatives. *Structural Equation Modeling, 6*(1), 1–55.

Kontoghiorghes, C. (1998). Training transfer as it relates to the instructional system and the broader work environment. In R. J. Torraco (Ed.), *Academy of human resource development 1998 conference proceedings* (pp. 466–473). Baton Rouge, LA: AHRD.

Kontoghiorghes, C. (2001). Factors affecting training effectiveness in the context of the introduc-tion of new technology – A US case study. *International Journal of Training and Development, 5*(4), 248–260.

Kontoghiorghes, C. (2004). Reconceptualizing the learning transfer conceptual framework: empir-ical validation of a new systemic model. *International Journal of Training and Development, 8*(3), 210–221.

Lim, D. H., & Johnson, S. D. (2002). Trainee perceptions of factors that influence learning transfer. *International Journal of Training and Development, 6*(1), 36–48.

Nijman, D. J. J. M. (2004). *Supporting transfer of training. Effects of the supervisor,* Doctoral dissertation, Twente University, Enschede.

Nijman, D.-J. J. M., Nijhof, W. J., & Wognum, A. A. M. (2003). Supervisory support and transfer of training: An explorative case study. In S. A. Lynham & T. M. Egan (Eds.), *Academy of human resource development 2003 conference proceedings* (Vol. 1, pp. 358–365). Bowling Green, OH: AHRD.

Noe, R. A. (1986). Trainees' attributes and attitudes: Neglected influences on training effectiveness. *Academy of Management Journal, 11*(4), 736–749.

Ouweneel, A. P. E., Taris, T. W., Van Zolingen, S. J., & Schreurs, P. J. G. (2009). How task characteristics and social support relate to managerial learning: Empirical evidence from Dutch home care. *The Journal of Psychology, 143*(1), 28–44.

Raykov, T., & Marcoulides, G. A. (2006). *A first course in structural equation modeling*. Mahwah, NJ: Lawrence Erlbaum.

Rouiller, J. Z., & Goldstein, I. L. (1993). The relationship between organizational transfer climate and positive transfer of training. *Human Resource Development Quarterly, 4*(4), 377–390.

Russ-Eft, D. (2002). A typology of training design and work environment factors affecting workplace learning and transfer. *Human Resource Development Review, 1*(1), 45–65.

Saks, A. M., & Belcourt, M. (2006). An investigation of training activities and transfer of training in organizations. *Human resource Management, 45*(4), 629–648.

Salas, E., & Cannon-Bowers, J. A. (2001). The science of training: A decade of progress. *Annual Review of Psychology, 52*, 471–499.

Scaduto, A., Lindsay, D., & Chiaburu, D. S. (2008). Leader influences on training effectiveness: motivation and outcome expectation processes. *International Journal of Training and Development, 12* (3), 158–170.

Seyler, D. L., Holton, E. F., III, Bates, R. A., Burnett, M. F., & Carvalho, M. A. (1998). Factors affecting motivation to transfer training. *International Journal of Training and Development, 2*(1), 2–16.

Smith-Jentsch, K. A., Salas, E., & Brannick, M. T. (2001). To transfer or not to transfer? Investigating the combined effects of trainee characteristics, team leader support, and team climate. *Journal of Applied Psychology, 86*(2), 279–292.

Stroebe, W. (2000). *Social psychology and health* (2nd ed.). Buckingham: Open University Press.

Tziner, A., Fisher, M., Senior, T., & Weisberg, J. (2007). Effects of trainee characteristics on training effectiveness. *International Journal of Selection and Assessment, 15*(2), 167–174.

Van der Klink, M. R., Gielen, E. W. M., & Nauta, C. (2001). Supervisory support as a major condition to enhance transfer. *International Journal of Training and Development, 5*(1), 52–63.

Velada, R., Caetano, A., Michel, J. W., Lyons, B. D., & Kavanagh, M. J. (2007). The effects of training design, individual characteristics and work environment on transfer of training. *International Journal of Training and Development, 11*(4), 282–294.

Viswesvaran, C., Sanchez, J. I., & Fisher, J. (1999). The role of social support in the process of work stress: A meta-analysis. *Journal of Vocational Behavior, 54*(2), 314–334.

Xiao, J. (1996). The relationship between organizational factors and the transfer of training in the electronics industry in Shenzhen, China. *Human Resource Development Quarterly, 7*(1), 55–73.

Chapter 7
Understanding the Relational Characteristics of Effective Mentoring and Developmental Relationships at Work

Andrew D. Rock and Thomas N. Garavan

Employees increasingly function in a world characterised by uncertainty, volatility, complexity, and ambiguity. This environment has resulted in changed career patterns, changing work and skill requirements, and a greater requirement to be self-directed in managing one's career. Particular sets of competencies are required to maintain employability and advance in the modern workforce. Singh, Ragins, and Tharenou (2009), for example, highlight the importance of career capital, which they define as *individual capital* and *relational capital*. Individual capital emphasises human and agentic capital, whereas relational capital highlights the importance of mentoring relationships and developmental networks. Individuals are expected to assume responsibility for their own career development and make decisions to continually develop both individual and relational capital.

Career theory traditionally assumed that individuals were independent, rational decision makers (see Parsons, 1909). Early theories highlighted autonomous approaches and the importance of person-career fit (Harmon, Hansen, Borgen, & Hammer, 1994; Holland, 1997). Career interventions traditionally focused on helping individuals assess and integrate information about themselves and the world of work utilising rational decision-making processes (see Davis, 1969). The emphasis on reasoning and objectivity failed to account for the subjective nature of career decision making, which involves ambiguity and uncertainty, and led to a focus on intuition, emotion, and interdependent processes (Hartung & Blustein, 2002).

A relational perspective views careers in the context of relationships (Blustein et al., 2001; Schultheiss, Kress, Manzi, & Glasscock, 2001). It views the use of others as a central resource in the career decision-making process. Interactions with others provide important opportunities for learning and insight (Greenhaus, Callanan, & DiRenzo, 2008). Individuals are confronted with complexity due to multiple life roles (Phillips, 1997), therefore, it makes sense to seek assistance and resources through mentoring and other developmental relationships. Scholars have

A.D. Rock (✉)
Department of Personnel & Employment Relations, Kemmy Business School, University of Limerick, Limerick, Ireland
e-mail: andrew.rock@ul.ie

R.F. Poell, M. van Woerkom (eds.), *Supporting Workplace Learning*, Professional and Practice-based Learning 5, DOI 10.1007/978-90-481-9109-3_7,
© Springer Science+Business Media B.V. 2011

emphasised that developmental relationships are important in helping individuals make career decisions (Ragins & Kram, 2007; Eby, Butts, & Lockwood, 2003). Hezlett and Gibson (2007) argued that it is useful to consider developmental relationships within the context of social relationships at work. Singh et al. (2009) found empirical support for this proposition in the context of "rising stars". Rising stars who exhibited help-seeking behaviours and utilised mentors enhanced their career competencies and career capital.

The overall aim of this chapter is to explore the relational characteristics of mentoring and other developmental relationships. It draws on a number of relational theories to understand the characteristics that make mentoring and other developmental relationships function effectively. These issues are discussed within the context of a relational perspective on careers.

Theoretical Context

Given that the focus of this chapter is on mentoring and developmental relationships within the frame of a relational perspective on careers, we first consider some of the definitional issues surrounding mentoring and developmental relationships.

Defining Mentoring and Other Developmental Relationships

Mentoring is frequently distinguished from other developmental relationships. However, Parker, Hall, and Kram (2008) suggest that traditional notions of what constitutes mentoring need to be challenged. Traditional, hierarchical mentoring is conceptualised as an intense meaningful dyadic relationship in which a more senior or more experienced mentor provides guidance and/or assistance to a less-experienced mentee or protégé. This has given way to conceptualisations that highlight the existence and importance of developmental relationship constellations (Higgins & Kram, 2001). Traditional mentoring as identified, in particular, by Kram (1983, 1985) has been conceptualised as a two-dimensional construct composed of career functions (coaching, sponsorship, exposure and visibility, protection, and providing challenging assignments) and psychosocial functions (counselling, role modelling, acceptance and confirmation, and friendship). As the relationship develops, more or different functions may be performed over time with the general assumption that the more that are served, the better the relationship (Kram, 1985). However, these functions occur in different ways in different relationships. All mentoring functions need not be present for a mentoring relationship to be effective (Ragins & Cotton, 1999). Subsequently, Scandura (1992) and Scandura and Ragins (1993) suggested role modelling as a third and distinct function. Therefore, a multiplicity of roles are possible for developers in developmental relationships including, for example, sponsor, career mentor, coach, role model, peer mentor/coach, or counsellor-friend. There are numerous possibilities beyond these examples.

Recent thinking emphasises multiple developmental relationships as a basis for developmental and career success. For example, Higgins and Kram (2001) conceptualised developmental relationships in terms of network diversity and relationship strength. They proposed a quadrant model incorporating weak-tie/strong-tie theory concepts (Granovetter, 1973) and elements of structural hole theory (Burt, 1992) where connections to otherwise unconnected entities provide non-redundant information and resources. Two of the relationship network types were based on weak ties: "receptive" networks (based on few weak ties from within the same social system); and "opportunistic" (based on several weak ties offering occasional assistance but from a diverse range). They labelled another relationship network type "traditional" and likely founded upon a primary, strong tie, classical mentoring relationship. In this case there may exist strong tie relationships with other developers, but these are likely from within the same context and network diversity potential is limited. They identified other relationships with developers from the network perspective through which there is enhanced potential for network diversity. Building upon what Burt (1992) identified as "entrepreneurial" developmental networks, Higgins and Kram illustrate how strong ties with developers that are otherwise unconnected can be useful for the acquisition of valuable, non-redundant information. The value of having various types of developmental relationships has been rapidly gaining credence among HRD practitioners, researchers, and in the workplace in general (e.g. Allen et al., 2004; Higgins, 2000; Higgins & Thomas, 2001; Ibarra, 2000; McManus & Russell, 2007). Understanding the processes or perhaps subtle differences in how these strong relationships function effectively will help both theoretical development and learning among individuals.

Bozionelos (2006) and Bozionelos and Wang (2006) have suggested that developmental relationships can be viewed as reciprocal learning relationships characterised by trust, respect, and commitment. Parker, Hall, and Kram (2008) suggested, in the context of a relational perspective on careers, that developmental relationships are characterised by: a focus on the personal and professional development of both parties, equal status of parties, the integration of reflection on practice, a focus on process as well as context issues, and accelerated career learning. They conceptualised career learning as a relational activity that consists of four key elements: (a) an ability to engage in self-reflection, (b) expanded self-awareness, (c) assessment of knowledge needs, and (d) a realignment of behaviour and attitudes to adapt to new learning. Ragins and Verbos (2007) highlighted that while the mentoring literature explains mentor behaviours and protégé outcomes, it does not address mutual relationship behaviours and relational outcomes (p. 95).

Table 7.1 synthesises the mentoring and developmental roles and functions and relates them to a number of theoretical perspectives on relationships. Our framework incorporates relationship characteristic elements that characterise a multiplicity of relationships types. However, this categorisation is not definitive and is not intended as a model.

Table 7.1 The spectrum of developmental relationships from a relational perspective

Focus of relationship	Developmental roles	Functions	Key relational theories and postulations relevant to all developmental relationships	Relationship characteristics emphasised by theories and relevant to all strong relationships
Career or job	Networking mentor	• Shares political knowledge and network experiences • Focus on enhancing social capital	*Social cognitive theory* • Cognitive schemas account for behavioural expectations, the construction of the relationship and perceptions of quality	*Trust* • Trust is essential to all developmental relationships. • Trust is multidimensional including resilient trust, competence trust, predictability trust, and goodwill trust.
	Coach	• Encourages learning, questioning and reflection on practice • Challenges the individual, provides feedback and supports new behaviours	*Social support theory* • Social support accounts for empathetic behaviours, how needs are fulfilled, and agentic capital enhancement behaviours	*Compatibility* • Compatibility of relationship members is essential to the on-going functionality of relationships.
Psycho-social or personal	Role Model	• Demonstrates appropriate behaviours, attitudes and values • Encourages imitation and mirroring of behaviours	*Social capital theory* • Explains relationship strength issues and mutual or reciprocal political learning and networking behaviours	• It is based on mutually satisfactory and harmonious thought processes, behaviours, and expectations.
	Counsellor–friend	• Provides friendly advice • Helps the individual to find answers • Focuses on coping strategies		

Table 7.1 (continued)

Focus of relationship	Developmental roles	Functions	Key relational theories and postulations relevant to all developmental relationships	Relationship characteristics emphasised by theories and relevant to all strong relationships
			Attachment theory • Explains feeling secure in close relationships through trust and dependability *Relatedness theory* • Explains relationship progression, mutual understanding, and shared experience *Self-in-relation theory* • Explains interdependence issues, relational competence, mutual validity, and esteem *Leader–member exchange theory* • Explains the establishment of connectivity between leaders and subordinates and how special developmental qualities emerge through reciprocal processes	*Authenticity* • Authenticity is essential in the free and determined pursuit of aspirations through relationships. • It is the means by which clarity is established to address goals effectively. *Dialogue, Reflection and Feedback* • These are the means through which deep learning occurs. • These drive both relationship interaction and have implications for relationship building *Relationship Proximity* • Relationship proximity is important in terms of beyond physical closeness. It also needs to be considered in terms of juxtapositions within or beyond organisational hierarchies. • Proximity has implications for how relationships are established and how they function. Proximity issues may account relationship intensity and how relationships are enabled or constrained

Source: Synthesis of selected commentators referenced throughout this chapter

Theoretical Perspectives on Relationships at Work

Various theoretical perspectives can be used to understand a relational perspective on careers and the characteristics of developmental relationships that are strong, meaningful, and "intense" as typically characteristic of mentoring relationships. We have selected the following theoretical perspectives: relational or social cognition theory, social support theory, social capital theory, attachment theory, Josselson's (1992) relatedness theory, self-in-relation theory (Surrey, 1991), and leader–member exchange theory (LMX) (Graen, Novak, & Sommerkamp, 1982) and discuss their implications for the characteristics of developmental relationships.

Relational or social cognitive theory explores how people mentally acquire and represent information about themselves and others through schematic mental knowledge structures that influence and shape behaviour. Ragins and Verbos (2007) argued that cognitive schemas represent "organised structures of tacit knowledge that serve to construct, construe and evaluate the behaviour of self, others and the relationship" (p. 100). This helps to explain behavioural expectations and how developmental relationships are understood by participants using cognitive maps. They envisage that these schemas will guide and frame how mentoring experiences and roles are constructed. Schemas adapt and evolve due to changing antecedents and behavioural feedback derived from the relationship and include various interpersonal scripts that will provide the "rules of the road" for developmental interactions. Furthermore, expectations, behaviours, and evaluation of those behaviours by both members of a developmental relationship are key factors in perceived quality of relationships (Ragins & Verbos, 2007). However, mentoring research has often measured relationship quality simply in terms of instrumental outcomes. The notion that developmental relationships evolve over time has long been emphasised (e.g. Kram, 1985). We assume that as the relationship and the functions it serves evolves, so too will the actual and perceived quality and effectiveness.

Quality and effectiveness is viewed in a relational sense rather than in attempt to measure instrumental or extrinsic outcomes. Social cognitive theory suggests that developmental relationships influence not only the reflexive construction of self but also the continual and reciprocal redefinition of the relationship over time. Therefore, a focus on the mutual and reciprocal, cognitive, and relational processes and structures is of substantial value to enhancing our understanding of how and why mentoring and other developmental relationships work.

Social support theory views relationships to be an important source of interpersonal support. This is defined as the fulfilment by others of ongoing social needs (Bowlby, 1983; Cutrona, 1996). Interpersonal support is conceptualised as a multidimensional construct based on interpersonal social functions considered to be vital for individual well-being. Cutrona and Russell (1990) suggest five core social functions: emotional support, social integration, esteem support, information support, and tangible assistance. Emotional support functions, in the context of mentoring and other developmental relationships, focus on concern, empathy, and the ability to turn to others for comfort and assistance. Social integration or network support relates to the feeling that the developmental relationship enables an individual to be a part of a network of individuals with similar interests and concerns. Esteem support functions as the boosting of self-confidence, belief in the other person's abilities, the validation of thoughts, feelings, and actions, and respect for what the other person has to offer. Information support functions are significant in that they may take the form of factual input, advice, guidance, appraisal of strengths and weaknesses, and developmental advice. Tangible assistance functions focus on the provision of resources or assistance with tasks. Supportive interactions can enhance self-esteem and self-efficacy beliefs. This could in turn lead to a reduction in interpersonal anxiety and an ability to participate in stronger, higher quality developmental relationships. They are also likely to contribute to what Singh et al. (2009) describe as agentic capital enhancement. This concerns an individual's proactive engagement in planned, motivated, and purposeful behaviours that enhance the achievement of career goals. Social support theory informs our understanding of mentoring and developmental relationships in terms of how a wide range of personal and career needs are fulfilled through such relationships. Social support theory particularly helps explain how needs are fulfilled through, mutual and reciprocal interactions that are based in learning and understanding more about others. Relationships built upon strong mutual understanding are likely to be deep and meaningful relationships that go beyond tangible assistance and instrumental engagement.

Social capital theories are increasingly used to explain the career benefits of mentoring and developmental relationships (Bozionelos, 2003, 2006; Bozionelos & Wang, 2006; Feeney & Boozeman, 2008; Hezlett & Gibson, 2007). However, our focus in this chapter is on the relational aspects rather than the outcomes of social capital. Nonetheless, it is difficult to completely isolate motivations for enhancing social capital and its career benefits from the relational and networking aspects. For example, political knowledge and skills can be a major component of developmental relationships (Blass, Brouer, Perrewé, & Ferris, 2007; Blickle et al. 2008). This is generally geared towards navigating networks and acquiring further social capital. While it is assumed that mentors possess more political knowledge and experience than their protégés, both members of the relationship can bring experiences with political behaviours of others into the dialogue. Hence, both members can reciprocally learn through an exchange of ideas and experiences about navigating networks and establishing contacts. Both members may have enhanced social capital as a goal. This reciprocal process and mutual learning will likely strengthen their own relationship, mutual appreciation, and the quality of the exchange.

Adler and Kwon (2002) offered multiple conceptualisations of social capital: First, social capital is the goodwill available to individuals or groups that is engendered by the fabric of social relations and that can be mobilised to facilitate action. Second, its source lies in the structure and content of the actors' social relations. Third, its effects flow from the information, influence, and solidarity it makes available to the actor. Or, more broadly, "social capital is the resource available to actors as a function of their location in the structure of their social relations" (Adler & Kwon, 2002, p. 18). Early research on social capital focused on the strength of the relationship as a basis for social capital formation (Granovetter, 1973). Later research extended this to mentoring and developmental networks with a focus on relationship strength as one key factor (of many) to distinguish different types of developmental relationships (Higgins & Kram, 2001). Social capital is embodied in information exchange, social trust, and norms of reciprocity that enhance cooperation for mutual advancement (Putnam, 1995; Woolcock, 1998). This accentuates the relational aspects of how social capital may operate through developmental relationships. Singh et al. (2009) suggested that career outcomes are influenced by an interplay between relational and individual career resources and that mentoring is just part of a portfolio or constellation of various resources that are weaved together to create the rich tapestry of career success.

Social capital theory is valuable to our understanding of mentoring and developmental relationships by helping to explain how and why developmental relationships emerge. De Janasz and Sullivan (2004) suggested that individuals in developmental relationships engage in the signalling of identity (knowing why), the signalling of performance (knowing how), and the signalling of social capital (knowing whom). Social capital operates through features of social organisation such as networks, norms, and social trust that facilitate coordination and cooperation for mutual benefit (Putnam, 1995, p. 67).

Attachment theory can be used to conceptualise and understand the importance of relationships in the context of development and career. In this theory attachment first emerged as a social cognitive, relational phenomenon in child–parent relationships (e.g. Ainsworth, Bleher, Waters, & Wall, 1978) and romantic partnerships (e.g. Hazan & Zeifman, 1994). This theory has been extended to include conceptualisations of attachment in supervisory relationships and leader–follower relations (Popper & Mayseless, 2003). Bowlby (1982) argued that individuals at any age are better adjusted when they have confidence in the accountability and responsiveness of a trusted other. Bowlby focused on the control role of attachments, which are defined as enduring emotional bonds of significant intensity that influence the development and ultimately participation in satisfying developmental relationships. Indeed, as Davidovitz, Mikulincer, Shaver, Izak, & Popper (2007) highlighted, "attachment theory can be applied to any adult relationship that fulfils three criteria: the maintenance of proximity (because people prefer to be near an attachment figure, especially in times of stress or need), the provision of a safe haven (an attachment figure often relieves an attached individual's distress and provides comfort, encouragement and support), and the provision of a secure base (an attachment figure increases an attached individual's sense of security, which in turn sustains exploration, risk taking, and self-development)" (p. 632).

According to attachment theory, human development occurs through active participation of the individual within significant relational contexts. Different patterns of attachment styles by both members in relationships significantly affect a wide range of behaviours, perceptions, cognitive conditions, and ultimately the functioning of relationships (Davidovitz et al., 2007). Furthermore, individuals who have a secure base established through attachment relationships are more resilient when they experience avoidance and lack of emotional availability from others (Davidovitz et al., 2007; Mikulincer & Shaver, 2007). Lopez (1995) found that continued participation in mutually satisfying relationships was important for many developmental activities across the life span. Attachment theory highlights the importance of trust, dependability, and mutuality in developmental relationships. It postulates that attachment styles by both members of the dyad in developmental relationships will have a strong impact on that relationship and it has implications for foundations in other meaningful relationships and other developmental activities. Attachment theory is valuable to our understanding of levels of trust, mutuality, levels and types of support functions, and the reciprocal nature of the connection between actors in mentoring and other developmental relationships.

Josselson (1992) proposed relatedness theory to explain the value of relationships arguing that interpersonal life is an ongoing effort to connect to others and overcome psychological and physical space between people. Relatedness is central to growth and development in the context of experience of self and becomes richer, more complex, broader and more differentiated over time. Josselson's theory identified eight stages of progression through which individuals connect with others and as development proceeds, they become more symbolic rather than physical or spatial: *holding* (feeling grounded), *attachment* (availability and predictability), *passionate experience* (intense affective experience), *eye-to-eye validation* (recognition that an individual has meaning to someone else), *idealisation and identification* (role modelling), *mutuality and resonance* (emotionally joining with another), *embeddedness* (the social context in which individuals define themselves), and *tending and caring* (the need to take care of others).

Aspects of relatedness theory have particular relevance to understanding mentoring and developmental relationships. Developers serve functions such as counselling and encouragement that can improve or maintain an individual's sense of groundedness. Members in developmental relationships will have some sense of attachment to their counterpart and the availability and predictability of this counterpart will impact on expectations and how the relationship functions. Members engaged in developmental relationships may not, of course, experience passion in its purest sense. However, affective experiences can be based in a passion for learning and success, motivation and commitment to learning, and engagement in meaningful relationships. Eye-to-eye validation, role modelling, mutuality and resonance, sensing embeddedness in context, and tending and caring are also states that can be readily experienced through developmental relationships. This has resonance in both developmental and network relationships. Especially, for instance, where dyad members have substantially mutual goals, shared responsibility, a history of similar experiences or where there is substantial reflective practice as part of the developmental relationship.

Self-in-relation theory (Surrey, 1991) was initially proposed as a theory of women's development. Surrey highlighted a paradigm shift from separation to relationship as the basis for development and self-experience. The basic goal of development is a deepening capacity for relationships and relational competence. Mutuality in relationships provides meaning to an individual's life and enhances self-esteem. Mentoring and other developmental relationships provide opportunities for self-other experiences in which the validity of both the individual's own experiences and those of the mentor or other party in the relationship may have value because they emphasise interdependence rather than independence and self-reliance. Self-in-relation theory postulates that mentoring and developmental relationships have significant interdependent qualities. Increased autonomous competence may be a goal in some situations. However, relational competence is increasingly important in the contemporary career. Relational competence will be important in explaining the operation of a developmental relationship. It is a competence that determines the successful functioning of developmental relationships as well as a competence that can be developed through developmental relationships.

Leader–member exchange theory (LMX) highlights the importance of dyadic relationships in the workplace. LMX is of value to a relational perspective of careers because it seeks to clarify perceptions about roles in relationships and how they are established (Graen, 1976). The quality of relationships between leaders and their subordinates varies. Early research suggested that because leaders had limited time available (Graen, 1976) leaders formed higher-quality relationships with an in-group and have lower-quality relationships with the out-group (Liden & Graen, 1980). Higher-quality LMX relationships are characterised by high levels of mutual trust, respect, liking, interaction, and obligation (Dienesch & Liden, 1986; Graen & Uhl-Bien, 1995). These factors are important in the establishment (role-making) phase of relationships and can grow or evolve as the relationship progresses (Graen & Uhl-Bien, 1995). Similarly, developmental relationship functions evolve as the relationship progresses over time (Kram, 1985). McManus and Russell (2007) suggested the integration of LMX with mentoring theory arguing that both are dyadic theories with significant developmental implications. They are also multi-dimensional and reciprocal constructs with a range of contextually based variables. Individuals provide assistance to others in expectation of receiving benefits of similar value in return in the future (Blau, 1964). These expectations will likely differ in content and timing depending on whether the leader or member or mentor or protégé is considered. LMX theory postulates that different subordinates can have drastically different perceptions of the same leader (Scandura & Schriesheim, 1994). Viewing high-quality LMX relationships from a relational perspective will provide insight to how mutual appreciation develops and how elements of friendship emerge in mentoring and other developmental relationships.

Characteristics of Effective Mentoring and Other Developmental Relationships

The theoretical perspectives discussed so far in this chapter highlight particular dimensions of mentoring or other developmental relationships that are important to the ability to enhance individual and relational career capital. We have decided to focus on specific dimensions here: trust; compatibility; authenticity; and dialogue, reflection, and feedback. Relationships will simply be less functional and effective without substantially positive levels of each of these dimensions. They are essential characteristics of high-quality relationships that foster personal and career development leading to the enhancement of individual and relational career capital. Relational/social cognitive theory, social support theory, social capital theory, attachment theory, relatedness theory, self-in-relation theory, and leader–member exchange theory provide various perspectives on how relationships operate. The absence of any of these quality characteristics will limit the relationship functionality that is illustrated through each of the theories. Furthermore, we highlight the important issue of relationship proximity as a relationship structure variable characteristic. We will discuss each of these characteristic dimensions and highlight some specific examples of their relevance to the theories identified.

Trust

Trust is highlighted as an important characteristics of an effective mentoring or other developmental relationships. Higgins and Kram (2001) summarise its salience in this way:

Although career functions such as protection and sponsorship may aid an individual's career advancement, an individual's clarity of identity and understanding of developmental needs and personal values are most likely to be realised through developmental relationships that are characterised by mutual trust, interdependence, and reciprocity (p. 278).

Trust resounds throughout the mentoring and developmental relationship literatures. It is also highlighted in a number of the theories we discussed earlier. For instance, trust is a key feature of social support theory (Cutrona, 1996), attachment theory (Bowlby, 1983), and leader–member exchange theory. Trust is a key source of social capital and it is realised through support (Adler & Kwon, 2002). Trust is a characteristic valued by protégés. Burke (1984) found that most protégés perceived in general that mentors had a reputation for being "trusted, respected, liked and admired" (p. 400). Trust is also mentioned by mentors as a key feature of a positive mentoring relationship. Young and Perrewé (2000) found that the met expectations of mentors and protégés were partially mediated by perceptions of relationship effectiveness and trust.

Parker, Hall, and Kram (2008) highlight that trust is a quality that develops over time. Trust based in interdependence and is built from sharing and mutuality (Rousseau, 1995). Sheppard and Sherman (1998) refer to predictability trust where trust is bolstered through series of reliable behaviours. Trust is important at the outset of the developmental relationship. Where trust is strong, it is more likely that the mentor or critical friend will be more comfortable asking difficult questions, offering feedback and criticism, and dealing with the difficult issues. Taking risks and receiving support can lead to more risk taking (Das & Bing-Sheng Teng, 1998). Trust is likely to be multidimensional in nature. Leana and van Buren (1999) make a distinction between fragile and resilient trust. The former exists when individuals in a developmental relationship make the decision to take a risk or demonstrate vulnerability in a transaction-by-transaction basis. Resilient trust is much more robust. It is derived from broader experiences of support with the other party. It can also deal more effectively with set-backs. A range of different types of trust issues can be identified (see Rousseau, Sitkin, Burt, & Camerer, 1998). In particular, it would be useful to consider competence trust, predictability trust, and goodwill trust and how they are established through reciprocity in mentoring and other developmental relationships.

Compatibility of Relationship Members

Compatibility among individuals is of paramount importance. We define relationship compatibility as effective relationship functioning through mutually satisfactory and harmonious thought processes, behaviours, and expectations. This does not require absolute similarity; differences of opinion will compliment the learning process and add value. However, strong dissonance will be disruptive. There will be perceptions of compatibility in naturally occurring developmental relationships. Relationships are constructed and evaluated through cognitive maps (social cognitive theory). Armstrong, Allinson, and Hayes (2002) suggested that naturally occurring developmental relationships will occur where both parties have complimentary or similar cognitive styles or quality would be negatively affected and the relationship would become dysfunctional and cease. Effective compatibility is also essential to interpersonal social support (social support theory) and the enduring emotional bonds established through attachment (attachment theory). The establishment of compatible relationships is manifest through the stages of progression of attachment identified by Josselson (1992). Self-in-relation theory highlights interdependence that is present in all relationships to varying degrees and the relational competence that is integral to this interdependence. For this to occur, compatibility is essential. High-quality relationships are based in mutual liking, trust, and respect (Thomas & Lankau, 2009). Therefore, compatibility is an important feature for all developmental relationships.

The issue of compatibility of the pair is particularly important in formally established mentoring and other developmental relationships. Viator (1999) suggested that input into the matching (pairing) process is associated with perceptions of a more positive relationship. Eby, Butts, Lockwood, and Simon (2004) found that effective matching was as a key feature of an effective formal mentoring programme. The consequences of mismatches or poor compatibility are highlighted in the literature (Eby & Lockwood, 2005; Eby & McManus, 2004). Perceived similarity may be a key feature of compatibility between both parties in the relationship and has been associated with more positive perceptions of relationship quality (Allen & Eby, 2003). Effective developmental relationships are more likely to be based on mutual attraction and respect and develop because mentors and protégés readily identify with each other. Clutterbuck (2004) highlighted the importance of an organisation seeking a balance between the formal and informal, and this will help avoid the risk of flawed compatibility and dysfunctionality often associated with mismatches.

"Our thinking increasingly is that the mentoring 'package' that will give organisations the greatest value is one that integrates both formal and informal mentoring, so that they become mutually supportive. Furthermore, there has been some consensus that an environment where successful mentoring can flourish would contain some elements of structure in the form of support available, but require no third party intervention in pairings. Rather it would allow market forces to drive both the matching process and the quality control of the mentoring provided" (p. 17).

Authenticity

Authenticity is associated with issues of trust, esteem, and efficacy. Authentic exchanges are enabled by trust, esteem, and efficacy, which in turn can bolster trust, esteem, and efficacy. Trust has already been established as a crucial element of relationships. However, the interplay of this with esteem and efficacy is important. There must be a sufficient level of both esteem and efficacy to engage authentically; and authentic exchanges can build perceptions of esteem and efficacy. The interdependence of these issues is complex and has implications for relationships as conceptualised by relational theories. For example, the emotional bond formed through attachment (Bowlby, 1983) and progressive relatedness (Josselson, 1992) will be significantly limited in the absence of authentic exchanges. Mutual esteem and self-efficacy are somewhat important at the foundation of the relationship and can grow as the relationship progresses. Authenticity and the building of interdependence associated with self-in-relation theory may be mutually reinforcing. Relational competence is a crucial element of this theory and this is associated with efficacy. Furthermore, mutual esteem and the boosting of self-esteem are particularly important elements highlighted by self-in-relation theory. These examples highlight relevant aspects of authentic relationships.

Authenticity received substantial attention through George (2003) who emphasised the importance of authentic leadership. While valuable for informing what it takes to be a truly great leader, a number of issues that George highlighted have pertinence to developmental relationships. He suggested the following as essential components of authenticity: learning from your life story, knowing your authentic self, practising your values and principles, balancing you intrinsic and extrinsic motivations, building your support team, and integrating your life by staying grounded (George, Sims, McLean, & Mayer, 2007). Leaders and followers or peers and colleagues that approach developmental relationships in the same manner will be able to maximise the true potential of the relationship. Therefore, authenticity has emerged as an important issue in mentoring and developmental relationships. It suggests that there is limited value in simply emulating someone else's behaviours no matter how positive they may be. Maniero and Sullivan (2006) suggested that authenticity is "striving to be genuine to one's true self" (p. 159). Kernis (2003) made this subtle distinction: "Authenticity is not reflected in a compulsion to be one's true self, but rather in the free and natural expression of core feelings, motives, and inclinations" (p. 14). Individuals who are authentic have a strong understanding of their values, priorities, and preferences, and this may manifest itself in a number of ways. It may represent a longing for purpose or it may involve striving for growth. It may also represent a need to follow one's own path or a desire for unrealised aspirations. Parker, Hall, and Kram (2008) suggested that authenticity is an important characteristic of a peer coaching relationship. They highlight the need for both parties to be honest and open with themselves and each other. Herriott (2001) pointed out that effective social relationships enable the reformation of self to acquire characteristics of authenticity including expressions of empathy, warmth, and generousness. Where individuals bring authenticity to the process, it enables more effective management of tensions. Schlegal et al. (2009) found that self-reported authenticity was positively related to important outcomes such as self-actualisation, self-concept clarity, self-esteem, and career clarity. Authenticity is also related to general subjective well-being, hope, and positive affect. These issues indicate that higher levels of mutual authenticity would likely augment the perceived and actual effectiveness of a developmental relationship for personal and career growth.

Dialogue, Reflection, and Feedback

Dialogue, reflection, and feedback are key features of developmental activities (Parker, Hall, & Kram, 2008). Dialogue is an important element of meaning-making that occurs between parties in a developmental relationship as highlighted by social cognitive theory. Dialogue in developmental conversations is the vehicle or means of expression that carries learning, understanding, and growth forward through deep and meaningful interaction. These are fundamental elements of developmental activities that should pervade more or less throughout any relationship. The absence of at least sufficient levels of dialogue, reflection, and feedback would severely limit the establishment of mutuality and the reciprocal nature of high-quality relationships as identified by each of the relational theories presented.

Parker et al. (2008) suggest that dialogue is different from conversations in that the former facilitates a greater degree of shared thinking and that the role of the mentor, developer or peer is to listen, question, and ensure that there is an appropriate emotional and cognitive space. There is some debate about whether dialogue and conversation are the same or different. Parker and colleagues prefer to "promote the concept of dialogue as posited by Issacs (1999, p. 22) as it 'raises the level of shared thinking, it impacts how people act, and in particular, how they all act together'" (p. 498). While Baker, Jenson, and Kolb (2005) settle for using the terms interchangeably, they bring attention to distinctions that are important to relational concepts. Dialogue and/or conversation should not be considered simply in terms of reciprocally talking, discussing, or debating. They highlight that root definitions indicate that dialogue is actually more associated with the spoken word and that it can be traced back to Latin definitions of debate with pejorative connotations such as conflict and strife; but that conversation in its historically literal sense is more associated with broader social activity, sharing space, intimacy, and collaboration (Baker et al., 2005, p. 414). We, like Baker and colleagues, do not wish to descend into a debate where one term is chosen as more positive and comprehensive. Nonetheless, it is important to emphasise that the notion that reciprocating through the spoken word is not sufficient to capture the depth and complexity of the interaction. We have chosen "dialogue" for its contemporary connotations of being deeper and more complex than "conversing". The issue of dialogue is important to many of the relational perspectives previously discussed. In order to achieve deep meaning and mutual understanding, the participants engaged in dialogue in developmental conversations need to be highly receptive and empathetic, dynamic and adaptive, inquisitive and sincere.

Reflection and feedback are emphasised as important elements that contribute to increased self-awareness. Raelin (2002) is a particularly strong proponent of reflection and argues that developmental relationships are ideal opportunities for this to occur. Most commentators advocate deep reflection, which is facilitated through pointed and powerful questions, challenging and follow-through, and the development of alternatives. Boud, Keogh, and Walker (1985) argue that attending to feelings is an important component of reflection. This involves utilising positive feelings and removing obstructive feelings. They use the term "revaluating experience" as an important outcome of reflection. Reynolds (1998) makes a distinction between "reflection" and "critical reflection". Critical reflection focuses on asking questions of purpose and confronting the taken-for-granted that influences individuals' thoughts and actions. Van Woerkom (2004) argues that reflection performs five important functions. It enables individuals to learn from mistakes, to engage in vision sharing, to share knowledge, to challenge groupthink, and to ask for feedback. Feedback is a constant in much of the literature on mentoring and developmental relationships.

Feedback enables individuals to become more reflective, to develop deeper levels of consciousness, and to change behaviours where appropriate. Feedback processes, in general, range from formal to informal. However, their effectiveness will be enhanced or limited by the openness of the individual to be receptive to the feedback and by their willingness to act on the feedback (Gilbert & Trudel, 2005). Feedback can be intricately incorporated into processes of dialogue and reflection. Mentoring relationships frequently involve protégés using mentors as sounding boards to test ideas and clarify perceptions about career options (Lankau & Scandura, 2002). Furthermore, feedback is part of the process of helping people resolve issues for themselves rather than simply providing prescriptions (Kram, 1985). This occurs through a reciprocal and perhaps cyclical process of generating dialogue and reflecting on past career experiences. Feedback is an important part of the process and can be considered figuratively as the punctuation in the process where progress is assessed, decisions are made, or values established. From a relational perspective, dialogue, reflection, and feedback are integral to cognitive construction. They are also the processual instruments for career decision making through relational support.

Relationship Proximity

A key consideration for effective mentoring and other developmental relationships concerns the structural proximity of the network of members. It is implied through all of the relational theories presented that there must be the opportunity for closeness in order for optimal relationship characteristics to be established. In other words, there must be significant proximity in order for a strong tie developmental relationship to be established and to be effective through significantly mutual and/or reciprocal processes. Proximity is considered a particularly important aspect of attachment theory (Davidovitz et al., 2007). We consider proximity in organisations in terms of how individuals are connected or related structurally within or beyond an organisation as well as their perceptions of "closeness". Considering a strong developmental relationship in organisations, the opportunity for "closeness" or proximity is an important consideration. Is the relationship intradepartmental or interdepartmental? Or is it intra- or inter-organisational? Is it a direct reporting relationship or not? Ragins, Cotton, and Miller (2000) found that having an interdepartmental mentor led to stronger commitment to and satisfaction with the mentoring process. However, Allen, Eby, and Lentz (2006) found little evidence for the significance of having a mentor from a different department. They did, however, acknowledge the argument that having a mentor from a different department may provide opportunities for more diverse learning, greater exposure, and it may avoid role clash that may occur with a intradepartmental mentor; however, contrastingly, they suggested having a mentor from the same department might provide greater opportunity for career mentoring based on more immediate knowledge and increased scope for interaction. Protégés reported receiving greater career mentoring from mentors within the same department, and mentors reported providing more psychosocial mentoring to protégés from the same department (Allen, Eby, & Lentz, 2006, p. 575). Even so, it would be counterintuitive to suggest that an interdepartmental or inter-organisational mentor would not be able to provide objective advice about career trajectory or the counselling that is often gained through psychosocial mentoring. It is important to continue to consider relationship proximity, degrees of formality, and the nature of hierarchical relationships in the theoretical development of a relational perspective on mentoring and other developmental relationships.

Conclusions and Implications for Research

A relational perspective on mentoring and other developmental relationships helps us to more fully understand their contribution to personal learning, support, and career development. There is a broad and deep body of theory supporting the view that self is more fully developed through effective relationships with others. It is likely that mentoring and other developmental relationships will play a significant role in individuals' professional and career development into the future. Research suggests that relationships with others provide a critical resource that can inform decision making in a variety of areas related to self and career. We know that mentoring and other developmental relationships have the potential to be very fruitful experiences. Various developmental relationships can occur naturally in an organisation. However, mentoring and other developmental relationships are also viewed as interventions that facilitate a process of helping, development, exploration, and shared understanding. They are increasingly structured or formalised (Allen, Eby, Poteet, Lentz, & Lima, 2004; Burke & McKeen, 1989; Douglas & McCauley, 1999; Ragins & Cotton, 1999). Whether they are naturally occurring or formally arranged, relational helping may take many forms, such as mentoring, coaching, peer coaching, counselling, and role modelling. There is significant overlap and common elements or functions throughout this conventional nomenclature. While these relationship titles have often been inconsistently differentiated, we continue to struggle to understand the developmental relationship construction and process, let alone concrete definitional aspects. However, Clutterbuck and Lane (2004) argued, "To some extent, definitions do not matter greatly if those in the role (...) have a clear and mutual understanding of what is expected of them and what they in turn should expect" (p. xvi). Delving more deeply into the relational qualities and processes of mentoring and other developmental relationships will help clarify how these expectations are formed, how they operate, how they change, and how they are satisfied.

The spectrum of relational theories discussed in this chapter highlight particular characteristics that are important for mentoring and other developmental relationships to flourish. These are trusting relationships that facilitate risk taking and exploration for learning and support; compatible relationships that allow the positive operation of interdependence, attachment, and the formation of shared meaning; authentic relationships that foster openness and reduce inhibition. Finally, relationships characterised by high levels of dialogue, reflection, and feedback as catalysts to learning will be more dynamic and productive.

The selected relationship theories highlighted in this chapter signal an opportunity for researchers to incorporate a range of perspectives for the exploration of mentoring and other developmental relationships. In particular, they provide useful alternatives to incorporate a range of variables in the investigation of how and why highly effective developmental relationships work. Reciprocal and mutual processes are not sufficiently understood or explained empirically. Ragins and Verbos (2007) suggest exploring social cognitive theory to better understand the relational implications. Furthermore, there are opportunities to build the theoretical basis of mentoring and developmental relationship constructs and phenomena through further incorporation of social support theory, social capital theory, attachment theory, relatedness theory, self-in-relation theory, and leader–member exchange theory. However, this list is not exhaustive. There is scope for a comprehensive integration that includes a range of other leadership, relationship, social, and psychological perspectives. This could focus, for instance, on the relational process that enables individuals to achieve an effective balance between interdependence and independence. This would also contribute greatly to our discovery of the optimal conditions and processes through which personal and career learning flourishes reciprocally and mutually through developmental relationships.

References

Adler, P. S., & Kwon, S. W. (2002). Social capital: Prospects for a new concept. *Academy of Management Review, 27*(1), 17–40.

Ainsworth, M. D. S., Blehar, M. C., Waters, E., & Wall, S. (1978). *Patterns of attachment: Assessed in the strange situation and at home.* Hillsdale, NJ: Erlbaum.

Allen, T. D., & Eby, L. T. (2003). Relationship effectiveness for mentors: Factors associated with learning and quality. *Journal of Management, 29,* 469–486.

Allen, T. D., Eby, L. T., & Lentz, E. (2006). Mentorship behaviors and mentorship quality associated with formal mentoring programs: Closing the gap between research and practice. *Journal of Applied Psychology, 91*(3), 567–578.

Allen, T. D., Poteet, M. L., Eby, L. T., Lentz, E., & Lima, L. (2004). Career benefits associated with mentoring for protégés: A meta-analysis. *Journal of Applied Psychology, 89*(1), 127–136.

Armstrong, S. J., Allinson, C. W., & Hayes, J. (2002). Formal mentoring systems: An examination of the effects of mentor/protégé cognitive styles on the mentoring process. *Journal of Management Studies, 39*(8), 1111–1137.

Baker, A. C., Jensen, P. J., & Kolb, D. A. (2005). Conversations as experiential learning. *Management Learning, 36*(4), 411–427.

Blass, F. R., Brouer, R. L., Perrewé, P. L., & Ferris, G. R. (2007). Politics understanding and networking ability as a function of mentoring: The roles of race and gender. *Journal of Leadership & Organizational Studies, 4*(2), 93–105.

Blau P. M. (1964). *Exchange and power in social life.* New York: Wiley.

Blickle, G., Meurs, J. A., Zettler, I., Solga, J., Noethen, D., Kramer, J., et al. (2008). Personality, political skill, and job performance. *Journal of Vocational Behavior, 72*(3), 377–387.

Blustein, D. L., Fama, L. D., White, S. F., Ketterson, T. U., Schaefer, B. M., Schwam, M. F., et al. (2001). A qualitative analysis of counseling case material: Listening to our clients. *The Counseling Psychologist, 29*(2), 242–260.

Boud, D., Keogh, R., & Walker, D. (1985). Promoting reflection in learning: A model. In D. Boud, R. Keogh, & D. Walker (Eds.), *Reflection: Turning experience into learning* (pp. 18–40). London: Kogan Page.

Bowlby, J. (1982). *Attachment and loss. Volume 1: Attachment* (2nd ed.). New York: Basic Books.

Bozionelos, N. (2006). Mentoring and expressive network resources: Their relationship with career success and emotional exhaustion among Hellenes employees involved in emotion work. *International Journal of Human Resource Management, 17*(2), 362–378.

Bozionelos, N., & Wang, L. (2006). The relationship of mentoring and network resources with career success in the Chinese organizational environment. *International Journal of Human Resource Management, 17*(9), 1531–1546.

Burke, R. (1984). Mentors in organisations. *Group and Organisation Studies, 9*(3), 353–372.

Burke, R. J., & McKeen, C. A. (1989). Developing formal mentoring programs in organizations. *Business Quarterly, 53*(3), 76–99.

Burt, R. S. (1992). *Structural Holes: The social structure of competition.* Cambridge, MA: Harvard University Press.

Feeney M. K., & Bozeman, B. (2008). Mentoring and network ties. *Human Relations, 61*(12), 1651–1676.

Clutterbuck, D. (2004). Making the most of informal mentoring: A positive climate is key. *Development & Learning in Organizations, 18*(4), 16–17.

Clutterbuck, D., & Lane, G. (Eds.). (2004). *The situational mentor: An international review of competencies and capabilities in mentoring.* Burlington, VT: Gower.

Cutrona, C. E. (1996). *Social support in couples: Marriage as a resource in times of stress.* Thousand Oaks, CA: Sage.

Cutrona, C. E., & Russell, D. W. (1990). Type of social support and specific stress: Toward a theory of optimal matching. In: B. R. Sarason, I. G. Sarason, & G. R. Pierce (Eds.), *Social support: An interactional view* (pp. 319–366). New York: Wiley.

Das, T. K., & Bing-Sheng Teng, (1998). Between trust and control: Developing confidence in partner cooperation alliances. *Academy of Management Review, 23*(3), 491–512.

Davidovitz, R., Mikulincer, M., Shaver, P. R., Izak, R., & Popper, M. (2007). Leaders as attachment figures: Leaders' attachment orientations predict leadership-related mental representations and followers' performance and mental health. *Journal of Personality and Social Psychology, 93*(4), 632–650.

Davis, H. V. (1969). *Frank Parsons: Prophet, innovator, counselor.* Carbondale, IL: Southern Illinois University Press.

de Janasz, S. C., & Sullivan, S. E. (2004). Multiple mentoring in academe: Developing the professional network. *Journal of Vocational Behaviour, 64*(2), 263–283.

Dienesch, R. M., & Liden, R. C. (1986). Leader–member exchange model of leadership: A critique and further development. *Academy of Management Review, 11*(3), 618–634.

Douglas, C. A., & McCauley, C. D. (1999). Formal developmental relationships: A survey of organizational practices. *Human Resource Development Quarterly, 10*(3), 203–220.

Eby, L. T., Butts, M., & Lockwood, A. (2003). Predictors of success in the era of the boundaryless career. *Journal of Organizational Behavior, 24*(6), 689–708.

Eby, L., Butts, M., Lockwood, A., & Simon, S. (2004). Protégé's negative mentoring experiences. *Personnel Psychology, 57*(2), 411–447.

Eby, L. T., & Lockwood, A. (2005). Protégé's and mentors reactions to participating in formal mentoring programs: A qualitative investigation. *Journal of Vocational Behavior, 67*(3), 441–458.

Eby, L. T., & McManus, S. (2004). The protégé's role in negative mentoring experiences. *Journal of Vocational Behavior, 65*(2), 255–275.

George, B. (2003). *Authentic leadership: Rediscovering the secrets to creating lasting value.* San Francisco: Jossey-Bass.

George, B., Sims, P., McLean, A. N., & Mayer, D. (2007). Discovering your authentic leadership. *Harvard Business Review, 85*(2), 129–138.

Gilbert, W., & Trudel, P. (2005). Learning to coach through experience: Conditions that influence reflection. *Physical Educator, 62*(1), 32–43.

Graen, G. (1976). Role-making processes within complex organizations. In M. D. Dunnette (Ed.), *Handbook of industrial and organizational psychology* (pp. 1201–1245). Chicago: Rand McNally.

Graen, G., Novak, M., & Sommerkamp, P. (1982). The effects of leader-member exchange and job design on productivity and satisfaction: Testing a dual attachment model. *Organizational Behavior and Human Performance, 30*(1), 09–131.

Graen, G. B., & Uhl-Bien, M. (1995). Relationship-based approach to leadership: Development of leader–member exchange (LMX) theory of leadership over 25 years: Applying a multi-level multi-domain perspective. *Leadership Quarterly, 6*(2), 219–247.

Granovetter, M. S. (1973). The strength of weak ties. *American Journal of Sociology, 78*(6), 1360–1380.

Greenhaus, J. H., Callanan, G. A., & DiRenzo, M. (2008). A boundaryless perspective on careers. In C. Cooper & J. Barling (Eds.), *The sage handbook of organizational behavior* (pp. 277–299). Thousand Oaks, CA: Sage.

Harmon, L. W., Hansen, J. C., Borgen, F. H., & Hammer, A. L. (1994). *Strong interest inventory: Applications and technical guide.* Stanford, CA: Stanford University Press.

Hartung, P. J., Blustein, D. L. (2002). Reason, intuition, and social justice: Elaborating on parson's career decision-making model. *Journal of Counseling & Development, 80*(1), 41–47.

Hazan, C., & Zeifman, D. (1994). Sex and the psychological tether. In K. Bartholomew & D. Perlman (Eds.), *Advances in personal relationships: Attachment processes in adulthood* (Vol. 5, pp. 151–177). London: Jessica Kingsley.

Herriott, P. (2001). Future work and its emotional implications. In R. L. Payne & C. L. Cooper (Eds.), *Emotions at work: Theory, research and applications in management.* (pp. 307–325). Chichester: Wiley.

Hezlett, S. A., & Gibson, S. K. (2007). Linking mentoring and social capital: Implications for career and organization development. *Advances in Developing Human Resources, 9*(3), 384–412.

Higgins, M. C. (2000). The more the merrier? Multiple developmental relationships and work satisfaction. *Journal of Management Development, 19*(4), 277–296.

Higgins, M. C., & Kram, K. E. (2001). Reconceptualizing mentoring at work: A developmental network perspective. *Academy of Management Review, 26*(2), 264–288.

Higgins, M. C., & Thomas, D. A. (2001). Constellations and careers: Toward understanding the effects of multiple developmental relationships. *Journal of Organizational Behaviour, 22*(3), 223–247.

Holland, J. L. (1997). *Making vocational choices: A theory of vocational personalities and work environments*. Lutz, FL: Psychological Assessment Resources.

Ibarra, H. (2000, March/April). Making partner: A mentor's guide to the psychological journey. *Harvard Business Review, 78*(2), 146–155.

Issacs, W. (1999). *Dialogue and the art of thinking*. New York: Currency.

Josselson, R. (1992). *The space between us: Exploring the dimensions of human relationships*. San Francisco: Jossey-Bass.

Kernis, M. H. (2003). Toward a conceptualization of optimal self-esteem'. *Psychological Inquiry, 14*(1), 1–26.

Kram, K. E. (1983). Phases of the mentoring relationship. *Academy of Management Journal, 26*(4), 608–625.

Kram, K. E. (1985). *Mentoring at work: Developmental relationships in organisational life* Glenview, IL: Scott Foresman.

Lankau, M. J., & Scandura, T. A. (2002). An investigation of personal learning in mentoring relationships: Content, antecedents, and consequences. *Academy of Management Journal, 45*(4), 779–790.

Liden, R. C., & Graen, G. (1980). Generalizability of the vertical dyad linkage model of leadership. *Academy of Management Journal, 23*(3), 451–465.

Leana, C., & van Buren, H. (1999). Organizational social capital and employment practices. *Academy of Management Review, 24*(3), 538–555.

Lopez, F. G. (1995). Contemporary attachment theory: An introduction with implications for counseling psychology. *The Counseling Psychologist, 23*(3), 395–415.

Mainero, L., & Sullivan, S. (2006). *The Kaleidoscope career*. Mountain View, CA: Davies-Black.

McManus, S. E., & Russell, J. E. A. (2007). Peer mentoring relationships. In B. R. Ragins & Kram, K. E. (Eds.), *The handbook of mentoring at work: Research, theory and practice* (pp. 273–297). Los Angeles, CA: Sage.

McManus, S. E., & Russell, J. E. A. (1997). New directions for mentoring research: An examination of related constructs. *Journal of Vocational Behavior, 51*(1), 145–161.

Mikulincer, M., & Shaver, P. R. (2007). *Attachment in adulthood: Structure, dynamics, and change*. New York: Guilford Press.

Noe, R. A. (1988). An investigation of the determinants of successful assigned mentoring relationships. *Personnel Psychology, 41*, 457–479.

Parker, P., Hall, D. T., & Kram, K. E. (2008). Peer coaching: A relational process for accelerating career learning. *Academy of Management Learning & Education, 7*(4), 487–503.

Parsons, F. (1909). *Choosing a vocation*. Boston, MA: Houghton-Mifflin.

Phillips, S. D. (1997). Toward an expanded definition of adaptive decision making. *Career Development Quarterly, 45*(3), 275–287.

Popper, M., & Mayseless, O. (2003). Back to basics: Applying a parenting perspective to transformational leadership. *Leadership Quarterly, 14*(1), 41–65.

Putnam, R. D. (1995). Bowling alone: America's declining social capital. *Journal of Democracy, 6*(1), 65–78.

Raelin, J. A. (2002). "I don't have time to think!" versus the art of reflective practice. *Reflections, 4*(1). 66–79.

Ragins, B. R., & Cotton, J. L. (1999). Mentor functions and outcomes: A comparison of men and women in formal and informal mentoring relationships. *Journal of Applied Psychology, 84*, 529–550.

Ragins, B. R., Cotton, J. L., & Miller, J. S. (2000). Marginal mentoring: The effects of type of mentor, quality of relationship, and program design on work and career attitudes. *Academy of Management Journal, 43*(6), 1117–1194.

Ragins, B. R., & Kram, K. E. (2007). *The Handbook of mentoring at work: Research, theory and practice*. Los Angeles, CA: Sage.

Ragins, B. R., & Verbos, A. K. (2007). Positive relationships in action: Relational mentoring and mentoring schemas in the workplace. In J. E. Dutton & B. R. Ragins (Eds.), *Exploring positive relationships at work* (pp. 91–116). Mahwah, NJ: Lawrence Erlbaum.

Reynolds, M. (1998). Reflection and critical reflection in management learning. *Management Learning, 29*(2), 183–200.

Rousseau, D. M. (1995). *Psychological contracts in organizations: Understanding written and unwritten agreements*. Thousand Oaks, CA: Sage.

Rousseau, D., M., Sitkin, S. B., Burt, R. S., & Camerer, C. (1998). Not so different after all: A cross discipline view of trust. *Academy of Management Review, 23*(3), 393–404.

Scandura, T. A. (1992). Mentorship and career mobility: An empirical investigation. *Journal of Organizational Behavior, 13*(2), 169–174.

Scandura, T. A., & Ragins, B. R. (1993). The effects of sex and gender role orientation on mentorship in male-dominated occupations. *Journal of Vocational Behavior, 43*(3), 251–265.

Scandura, T. A., & Schriesheim, C. A. (1994). Leader-member exchange and supervisory career mentoring as complementary constructs in leadership research. *Academy of Management Journal, 37*(6), 1588–1602.

Schultheiss, D. E. P., Kress, H. M., Manzi, A. J., & Glasscock, J. M. J. (2001). Relational influences in career development: A qualitative inquiry. *The Counseling Psychologist, 29*(2), 216–241.

Sheppard, B., & Sherman, D. (1998). The grammars of trust: A model and general implications. *Academy of Management Review, 23*(3), 433–437.

Singh, R., Ragins, B. R., & Tharenou, P. (2009). What matters most? The relative role of mentoring and career capital in career success. *Journal of Vocational Behavior, 75*(1), 56–67.

Surrey, J. L. (1991). The "self-in-relation": A theory of women's development. In J. V. Jordan, A. G. Kaplan, J. B. Miller, I. P. Stiver, & J. L. Surrey (Eds.), *Women's growth in connection: Writings form the Stone Center* (pp. 51–66). New York: Guilford Press.

Thomas, C. H., & Lankau, M. J. (2009). Preventing burnout: The effects of LMX and mentoring on socialization, role stress, and burnout. *Human Resource Management, 48*(3), 417–432.

Van Woerkom, M. (2004). The Concept of critical reflection and its implications for human resource development. *Advances in Developing Human Resources, 6*(2), 178–192.

Viator, R. E. (1999). An analysis of formal mentoring programs and perceived barriers to obtaining a mentor at large public accounting firms. *Accounting Horizons, 13*, 37–53.

Woolcock, M. (1998). Social capital and economic development: Toward a theoretical synthesis and policy framework. *Theory and Society, 27*(2), 151–208.

Young, A. M., & Perrewé, P. L. (2000). The exchange relationship between mentors and protégés: The development of a framework. *Human Resource Management Review, 10*(2), 177–209.

Chapter 8
Learning How Things Work Here: The Socialization of Newcomers in Organizations

Russell Korte

"I wish someone had taught me how to play the political game here." This wish typifies a common complaint from several newcomers interviewed about their experiences starting a new job. Mostly, they referred to learning about the unwritten rules governing work and social behavior—also known as the social norms of the organization. Preliminary investigations of the experiences of newcomers indicated that the most troublesome experiences in starting a job were learning how to work within the informal social systems of the organization.

Aim of This Chapter

Much of the organizational socialization (henceforth called socialization) literature and practice perceives the socialization of new employees as a learning process. Although the organization's practices surely influence newcomer learning, it is generally believed that it is the responsibility of the newcomer to learn to fit into the organization (Ashforth, Sluss, & Saks, 2007; Ashforth & Saks, 1996; Chao, O'Leary-Kelly, Wolf, Klein, & Gardner, 1994; Cooper-Thomas & Anderson, 2006; Holton, 1996, 2001; Ostroff & Kozlowski, 1992; Van Maanen & Schein, 1979; Wanous, 1992). This "sink or swim" perspective tends to take a narrow, individualistic view of learning in the context of the organization (Moreland, Levine, & McMinn, 2001) and underestimates the influences of other people and practices in the organization that affect the socialization of newcomers.

Interviews with newly hired employees (newcomers) in a study of organizational socialization indicated the presence of strong influences on their learning that were outside the control (and responsibility) of the newcomers. Examining the nature of newcomers' experiences when beginning a new job will enhance our current understanding of how they learn to work and develop their expertise in the workplace. Furthermore, increasing the understanding of the socialization process becomes

R. Korte (✉)

Assistant Professor, Human Resource Development, Fellow, Illinois Foundry for Innovation in Engineering Education, University of Illinois at Urbana-Champaign, 1310 South 6th Street, Champaign, IL 61820, 217-333-0807
e-mail: korte@illinois.edu

R.F. Poell, M. van Woerkom (eds.), *Supporting Workplace Learning*, Professional and Practice-based Learning 5, DOI 10.1007/978-90-481-9109-3_8,
© Springer Science+Business Media B.V. 2011

important to individuals and organizations. Most individuals spend considerable time and effort in the workplace and achieving success (however defined) is an important goal of working life. Organizations spend considerable time and effort hoping to improve employee performance, along with satisfaction, engagement, commitment, and retention.

This chapter describes the findings of a study of newly hired engineers in a large, global manufacturing organization. First, this chapter briefly reviews the literature on organizational socialization along with a theoretical framework offering insights for examining the learning processes in organizational settings. The second section is a brief description of the study of the socialization process of newcomers as they began their employment. The third section presents the findings of the study followed by conclusions and implications for practice.

Literature Review and Theoretical Context

Many researchers of organizational socialization based their work on individual learning (Bauer, Bodner, Erdogan, Truxillo, & Tucker 2007; Cooper-Thomas & Anderson, 2006; Saks & Ashforth, 1997; Saks, Uggerslev, & Fassina, 2007). Yet, an important factor in newcomer learning is the interaction between the newcomer and others in the organization (Billett, 2002; Koopmans, Doornbos, & van Eekelen, 2006). Effective developmental interactions, such as newcomer learning, include personal, relational, and communication factors (Eddy, D'Abate, Tannenbaum, Givens-Seaton, & Robinson, 2006), as well as cultural and social factors (Lemke, 1997). The interactions among these factors for the purpose of learning a new job can be conceptualized as a form of social exchange in which the newcomer seeks information on various aspects of the workplace from more experienced members of the organization in the hope of becoming a more productive member. Interactions between workers have been characterized as social exchanges by various organizational behaviorists, as described in the next section. Furthermore, the literature on learning often describes the importance of the interactions between instructors and learners as a give-and-take relationship. Instructors provide access to knowledge and expertise or help learners construct new knowledge and acquire expertise in return for learners making efforts to learn. In addition to information and knowledge, there are myriad interpersonal, psychological, and environmental factors that influence the learning process, such as respect, empathy, safety, norms, readiness, relevance. It is commonly believed that learning must be mutually constituted between the instructor and the learner, to be effective. From this perspective, the research on social exchange is informative.

Social Exchange Theory

Social exchange theory (SET) describes a type of ongoing, dynamic relationship between people (actors) as a series of interactions in which actors exchange resources guided by rules of exchange, such as social norms (Cropanzano &

Mitchell, 2005). However, scholars differ on the inclusiveness of their definitions of social exchange. Some, like Blau (1986), excluded economic or negotiated exchange and stated that social exchange involved the more ambiguous and relationally oriented exchange based on reciprocity. Cohen and Bradford (1989) posited that the basis of many organizational interactions was reciprocity and that most people expected exchanges in organizations to gradually become balanced—either through the reciprocal return of favors from others or if not reciprocated, the reduction of exchange efforts.

More recent theorizing began to move social exchange theory beyond its behavioral and economic roots to include cognitive and affective constructs (Lawler, 2001; Molm, 2003). Lawler proposed an affective theory of social exchange that directly links emotions and sentiments to an individual's perception of fairness, satisfaction, solidarity, trust, leniency, and commitment to exchange relationships. This link to affective characteristics provides a rich explanation of the judgments that actors make related to the exchange relationship.

A particular type of social exchange related to socialization is role-making theory. An important premise of the theory is that organizational roles are ill-defined; therefore, newcomers must negotiate and clarify roles through interactions (exchanges) between members (Graen, 1986). Thus, newcomers acquire information about the behavioral constraints and demands of the job, negotiate alternatives, accept patterns of behavior, and gradually modify these patterns of behavior (Miner, 2002) based on exchanges with others in the organization.

Leader–member exchange is another type of social exchange theory that states that work roles are developed and established over time through a process of exchanges, or "interacts" between a leader and member. The leader offers increased responsibility and membership benefits to the subordinate, and in return the subordinate offers increased commitment and contribution to the work group (Graen & Uhl-Bien, 1995). The quality of leader–member exchanges are unique to each individual dyad and may develop into high-quality relationships based on trust and respect, or degenerate into low-quality relationships merely fulfilling the employment contract (Bauer & Green, 1996). According to Graen and Uhl-Bien's (1995) model of leader–member exchange, high-quality relationships are characterized by higher levels of trust, respect, and mutual obligations between the leader and member.

Once the newcomer joins the group, initial relationships form quickly and the characteristics of these initial relationships tend to endure (Miner, 2002). Although relationships continue to develop over time, the strength of initial judgments or "first impressions" continues to influence the quality of the relationship. This makes the initial interactions between the newcomer and manager extremely important, consequently affecting attitudes, satisfaction, and performance into the future. This is especially important for the socialization process.

Another important research finding on leader–member exchange theory is that perceptions of a relationship often differ significantly between the leader and member. Studies have shown a low correlation between subordinates' and leaders' perceptions of their relationships (Gerstner & Day, 1997). This difference in perceptions may confound attempts to socialize newcomers by fostering misperceptions, misunderstandings, and misinterpretations of events, exchanges, and expectations during the socialization process.

Critics of the current state of the literature on socialization point to the fragmented nature of the work and the lack of a holistic view of the process (Bauer, Morrison, & Callister, 1998; Saks & Ashforth, 1997). While most of these views tend to regard socialization as an individual learning process, they pay less attention to the interactions (exchanges) between the newcomer and the environment. Broader views of learning account for the social interaction processes that influence how and what individuals learn.

Learning in Social Settings

Many models of socialization describe stages through which newcomers pass as they become organizational members (Wanous, 1992). Learning is a common thread throughout these models as newcomers learn specific job tasks and responsibilities, work-group procedures, management's expectations, and the values and mission of the organization (Bauer et al., 1998; Ostroff & Kozlowski, 1992). Yet, many of these models focus on the newcomer and underestimate or ignore strong interdependence between internal psychological processes and external interactional processes in learning (Illeris, 2005).

Recent developments in learning theories tend to emphasize the relational factors between the learner and the environment as an important influence on learning outcomes. More holistic views of learning integrate cognitive, emotional, and social factors into an interdependent system (Illeris, 2003; Yang, 2004). For example, Illeris proposed a tripartite model of learning based on interdependencies among cognitive, affective, and social dimensions. The interactions between the internal psychological processes (cognitive and affective) with external environment (social) take multiple forms—from passive perceptions to active participation.

Similarly, Yang (2004) proposed a theory of learning by explaining the interdependencies among domains of technical, practical, and affectual knowledge. There is a useful correspondence between these broader views of learning and the requirements of learning in the socialization process—learning what to do (technical knowledge), how to do it (practical knowledge), and why it is done this way (Van Maanen & Schein, 1979).

Others take a stronger social view of learning as social constructivism in which the unit of analysis is the practices and processes of the social system in which individuals interact (Lave & Wenger, 1991; Lemke, 1997). These perspectives on learning ground individual action in relationships and communal interchange (Gergen, 1999) emphasizing the subjective and situational idiosyncrasies of the learning process, as well as the interaction between the individual and the social system, which describes learning as a process embedded in a participatory system (Illeris, 2002). In this interactive or participatory system, Wildemeersch (cited in Illeris, 2002) emphasized the concept of social responsibility coupled with social obligation as the responsibility of a society to help socialize the individual—rather than focusing solely on the individual's responsibility to learn. Thus, individual learning in social settings (e.g., socialization) is both socially and individually determined.

While these views of learning differ subtly in the descriptions of the learning process, they agree that a significant amount of learning in work settings occurs informally and relies on learning from others and from doing the work. Of course, organizations and industries vary in the amount of learning required of individuals. Some industries are naturally more learning intensive. Skule (2004) identified characteristics of work that composed a more learning-intensive workplace. These characteristics include exposure to high demands and responsibilities coupled with high levels of interaction and communication among workers, managers, customers, and suppliers. In addition, Skule stated that demanding situations without support and guidance (interaction and communication) from others reduce the amount of learning and increase the stress related to the work. It seems plausible that the demands and responsibilities facing workers vary as well at different times in a job. The pressures on newcomers to become proficient and excel make the socialization process an intensive learning situation that can be facilitated with higher levels of support and guidance from others. The practices of organizations to "throw them [newcomers] into the fire" or expect a "sink or swim" process to produce the best employee jeopardizes the socialization process and causes undue stress and failure for newcomers and organizations alike.

Thus, the conceptualization of socialization as a learning process requires a broader view. If relationships and interactions influence learning in the social realm—especially about relatively intangible concepts (such as norms) embedded in social structures—it seems that the current perspectives on socialization as an individualistic learning process must be broadened to emphasize the importance of the social interactions between the newcomer and members of the work group. The following study of socialization in an organization focused on *how newcomers learned the social norms of the organization* as they began their employment. Preliminary investigations into the phenomenon of socialization through the literature and from pilot interviews with practicing engineers and managers indicated that the socialization process was problematic—especially regarding what and how newcomers learned to work in the organization. One of the key findings was that the quality of relationships that formed between newcomers and others in work groups strongly affected the quality of learning experienced by newcomers. The following section describes this study in more detail.

Method

This study was a qualitative case study that enabled the author to explore the learning of newcomers in a large global manufacturing organization. Several authors described a qualitative methodology as not only appropriate, but also more likely to provide insights into complex social phenomena (Eisenhardt & Graebner, 2007; Patton, 2002; Silverman, 2005). Yin (2003) described case study designs as relevant strategies for research questions of *how* and *why*, as well as relevant strategies for research focused on contemporary events within a real-life context and in which the researcher had little to no control over events. Thus, the characteristics of this study (examining a complex social phenomenon in context) seemed most appropriate to a qualitative case study research design.

This study investigated the socialization process in one of the world's largest manufacturers, employing more than 250,000 people around the world. The company, headquartered in the United States, has been a global engineering and sales leader for decades. During the 2 years preceding this study the company hired nearly 200 new engineers—of which 30 participated in this study. The newcomers came from 26 different work groups. In addition, the author interviewed six managers and several human resource executives for the purpose of triangulating the data analyzed. Specific questions guiding this study were as follows:

- How do newcomers learn the social norms of the organization?
- What factors enable and constrain this learning process in the organization?
- What factors determine how well newcomers learn and integrate into the workplace?

Sample

All newcomers participating in this study had been with the company at least 6 months and none had been employed within the company longer than 18 months. Participants represented a mix of men and women, as well as a mix of those who had previous job experience and those for whom this was their first job after graduating from school. Three groups comprised the sample:

- New grads: 17 newly hired engineers starting their first job out of school (recent graduates from higher education).
- Experienced hires: 13 newly hired engineers with previous job experience.
- Managers: 6 managers of work groups with newly hired engineers.

Data Collection and Analysis

Participant data came from semistructured interviews conducted and recorded by the author following the critical incidents technique (Ellinger & Watkins, 1998; Flanagan, 1954; Gremler, 2004). Questions prompted participants to recall a specific event or incident in which they learned something about the "way things work here." Subsequent questions probed for specifics such as what was the incident, what happened, who was involved, and what did the participant learn from this. In some cases, participants said there was no specific incident and recounted a relatively continual series of small experiences that accumulated over time giving them an increasing understanding of their work in the organization.

The analysis of the interview transcripts followed qualitative analysis procedures recommended by Miles and Huberman (1994) and Strauss and Corbin (1998).

Specifically, the researcher (a) carefully read the transcripts and attached predetermined codes to specific statements that described learning and norms; (b) retrieved all statements coded as learning and norms, carefully reread the retrieved statements, and proceeded to open-code (Strauss & Corbin, 1998) the statements at a finer level of detail, staying close to the participants' language; (c) sorted the open codes into categories and identified the categorical themes emerging from these data.

Findings

The data indicated that the quality of relationship building between the newcomers and members of their work groups mediated the quality of learning by newcomers. Overall, newcomers reported the necessity of building high-quality relationships with coworkers and their managers as a means for learning *what to do, how to do it well,* and *why it was done this way.* Two major themes emerged from the analysis of the data gathered from newcomers:

1. *Relationship building was the primary driver* of the socialization process—not individual capability for learning.
2. The *work group was the primary context* for socialization—not the organization.

Based on a frequency count of learning incidents reported and attributed to different sources, coworkers were the primary source of learning the social norms of the job (65% of learning incidents reported). Newcomers also reported learning from managers (15%). Most of the remaining learning incidents reported were personal reflection based on past experiences (18%). Further analysis of these three sources of learning (coworkers, managers, and self) revealed several subthemes that provided more detail about the learning processes during the socialization of these newcomers. The following sections describe these subthemes in more detail.

Learning from Coworkers

Within the category of learning from coworkers, two subthemes emerged: (a) developing a specific *mentoring relationship* with an experienced coworker in the group and (b) becoming accepted by others as a *member of the work group.* The most satisfying learning experiences reported by newcomers resulted from developing high-quality mentoring relationships with an experienced coworker and being accepted by others as a member of the group. In a few work groups, the manager formally assigned a coworker to serve as a mentor to the newcomer; however, in most work groups the newcomer sought or accepted the help of a willing coworker informally. These informal mentoring relationships subsequently helped newcomers learn what to do on the job, how to do it, and oftentimes why it was done that way. While much of the content of this learning focused on the tasks of the job, newcomers also reported learning important insights about the way things worked in the group and the organization, including the formal and informal rules (social norms) guiding behavior in the work group. For example, one newcomer reported,

> Some of the senior guys know how to do that [*work around the rules*] and they've got the years that they can do that. But when you're new, you're really frowned on if you try to go around the system.

Although the company had a formal mentoring program, the program was not very useful for newcomers. The formal program paired junior employees with senior mentors, usually in different departments, for guidance about advancing one's career in the company. However, newcomers needed someone locally (in their work group) that knew the details of the work and could guide them through the initial process of learning their jobs and how to get things done. One newcomer commented,

> Questions came up a lot because the instructions didn't really go into any detail about that. And so, I was asking my coworkers a lot of those type of questions. Like, why are we doing this? What exactly is this doing? You know, just like getting more explanation on why we were doing that stuff.

From the perspective of the newcomer, a major factor influencing the success of these mentoring relationships was the quality of the relationship, which seemed to mediate the quality of learning experienced by the newcomer. Newcomers recounted a wide range of experiences—from good to bad—with developing a mentoring relationship. For example,

> And he's been extremely helpful and I have to remind myself, how much time out of the day he's taking, leaving what he's working on and helping me out. It was a lifesaver. There's no way I would have been able to finish those projects in half the time if he hadn't been there to help out.
>
> [*My coworkers are*] approachable, but you kind of get the feeling like—don't bother me. You can go ask them questions and stuff like that, but then their cell phone rings or something comes up and then it's kind of like—I have to take this call or I have to do something else. So you kind of, there's this feeling of—ask questions but don't take too much of my time.
>
> There are some [*mentors*] that are like very quiet and then there was that one that loves you because you get to do all the work and he just gets to supervise you. And then there's the one that wants to teach you that everything you learned in school is wrong and this is the real world.

There comes a time when the newcomers must become more self-reliant and make decisions based on what they have learned. Developing the confidence to make decisions is helped by supportive relationships with others in the work groups. The following statement describes a newcomer's realization that he has learned enough about some things to make decisions without validating his decisions with his mentor. This point also indicates a change in status, as the newcomer becomes a functional member of the work group.

> I would go to him and ask him questions a lot, but at one point I realized that he was okay with however I did it for the most part. He said, 'I trust your judgment.' So I stopped going to him. I just realized that I kind of answered my own question or he would tell me what I already thought.

Obtaining membership in the group was the second subtheme that emerged from the category of learning from coworkers. Newcomers learned by observing and listening to how others interacted in the group. Much of the content of this learning domain focused on the social interactions and the norms governing these social interactions. Learning how to interact with others helped newcomers build relationships and facilitate their integration into the group. However, this was not always the outcome. Coworkers, as well as the newcomer, had to contribute to the relationship-building process. Some newcomers reported disappointment with the poor quality of the response and help they received from coworkers and the seemingly one-sided relationships they experienced in their work groups. Again, newcomers reported a range of experiences regarding efforts to integrate into the work group.

> We all go on this trip together. And being with the same people for that long, like 24 hours a day, you're going out to dinner and stuff and being in a social atmosphere with those people, it was the most remarkable thing. After that trip, I am part of this group. I'm not an outsider anymore. And we just got to know each other and I got to know more about how things work.
>
> I've been here a year and I don't feel completely comfortable with everybody I work with, because I think you have a lot of engineers that are very into their work and they kind of shut the world off around them. I get the impression my group doesn't know what to do with these new people that they're getting.

Learning from the Manager

Another source of learning the norms of the work group for newcomers was their manager. However, with few exceptions, newcomers in this organization had little contact with their managers. Two subthemes emerged from the manager category. The first subtheme described the need for newcomers to *learn the expectations of the manager*. Newcomers perceived these expectations as important norms they must learn to help them integrate into the group and be successful on the job. A primary method for newcomers to learn about their managers' expectations was by trying to get to know their managers better personally and professionally. Despite a general low frequency of interaction with their managers, the few newcomers who were able to build high-quality relationships with their managers reported learning valuable insights about the way things worked in their work group, in other work groups, and in the organization. Some also reported gaining insights about how to make sense of the way things worked in the organization. For example,

> And my boss I have now is really good. He's like, the process is there to help people who don't know what they're doing. If you don't know how to do something, you look it up. But when you find a better way—do it. It's about getting the work done and getting it done right and making the customer happy. If you find someone that won't do it, find someone who will.

The second subtheme to emerge described the efforts of newcomers to build relationships with their manager as a means to enhance their position in the group and the organization. Many newcomers believed that higher-quality relationships with their manager enhanced their membership in the group and afforded greater opportunities for development and advancement in the organization. For example, one newcomer remarked,

> People say it's who you know. I said—well, it's not really who you know. The question is—who knows you?

Another reported,

> Then he just kind of got into his expectations for where he saw my career [*going*] for the next couple of years.

And in another case, a newcomer believed,

> The projects I get is a big indication to me that, you know, my boss trusts me with some very highly visible things where I'm meeting with people very high up in our company.

Because most newcomers had little contact with managers, there were few examples of very high-quality relationships between newcomers and managers. Most newcomers reported neutral relationships—neither good nor bad (medium quality). They accepted the fact that managers generally were not available or responsible for day-to-day guidance.

> I mean, I didn't have a lot of contact with my official boss. You know, the way I saw it, his job was more to organize a group.

Learning from Self-Knowledge and Past Experiences

Newcomers also reported learning to understand and adapt to the social norms of the organization by reflecting on their personal knowledge and past experiences. Understandably, new grads did not report a wealth of experiences in organizations compared to experienced hires. However, they had previous experience with social norms from group projects, extracurricular programs, internships, and cooperative learning experiences in school. Experienced hires often interpreted their current perceptions of the social norms of the work group based on previous employment experiences. For example, one individual expressed frustration at the obstacles he faced getting work done in this company compared to his previous experience.

> I'm like, I need this now, I'm trying to get stuff done. It's just the way it's done in the rest of the industry. It's just not part of the culture [*here*]

Individually, some newcomers appeared to have a richer set of these past experiences and stronger propensities toward social interactions.

Newcomers often reflected on their past experiences to help them interpret the social information they perceived in their present jobs.

> Like in a previous company we'd do this. This is the type of behavior, the goals, the expectations.

Also, through the process of self-reflection, some indicated undertaking a process of internalizing the social norms of the work group and conformed their personal knowledge about the way things work in organizations to the current norms they encountered.

> Well, at first, I felt discouraged because I'm a person who always likes to do my best ... So, I was kind of discouraged like—okay, what am I doing wrong? And I felt bad. But as I got used to it, it got fine.

Differences Between New Grads and Experienced Hires

During the interviews and analysis of the transcripts, the researcher perceived apparent differences between the socialization experiences of new grads and experienced hires. Thematic analysis of the interviews indicated that experienced hires reported more difficulty integrating into the work group than new grads. Using the Mann–Whitney test (for non-parametric data) to compare means between independent groups (experienced hires and new grads), evidence of a significant difference was found, indicating that experienced hires experienced lower-quality relationship building during socialization ($p = 0.03$). This finding corroborated the qualitative analysis, which indicated noticeably higher levels of conflict and frustration, as well as lower levels of satisfaction reported by experienced hires.

It seemed that much of the source of this conflict and frustration stemmed from the expectations held by experienced hires that clashed with the expectations and norms of others in the work group. In extreme cases, members of the work group seemed threatened by the experienced newcomer—especially if the newcomer had more experience or expertise than others in the group. A few of the newcomers in this situation reported great difficulty getting access to information and integrating with the group. One newcomer described this situation as a matter of trust.

> Here I would say, of the companies I've worked at, [this company] is really not very quick to accept new people in that there is the lifer mentality, that if you didn't come here [out of] of college and [were] raised in [the company] perspective and way of life, then why should we trust you? How do we know what you're doing and all you know is reasonably sound?

The difficulties reported by experienced hires had a negative effect on their ability to learn on the job and integrate into their work groups. It was easier for new grads to form relationships with coworkers because they were more open to instruction and relatively inexperienced (less threatening to the group). Thus, new grads received more guidance (learning interactions) and were accepted into the group more quickly.

Managers' Views of the Socialization Process

To capture another perspective on the socialization process, this study analyzed data gathered from interviews with six work-group managers who recently hired new engineers. The conversations provided additional insights into the contextual factors influencing the characteristics of the work groups, as well as the managers' perceptions and beliefs about the socialization and learning processes for newcomers.

These managers reported knowing from experience that newcomers were more successful at learning the norms of the group when they had the opportunity to learn from coworkers in strong mentoring relationships. Corroborating the successful experiences reported by newcomers, successful managers perceived that building high-quality relationships with one or more coworkers was a precursor to learning the social and technical aspects of the job. One manager reported,

> Well, as much as possible I like to assign them someone to work with, someone that they're going to take over part of their job, someone that they can get technical direction from and answer questions and give them [*guidance*].

Most of these managers recognized the importance of helping newcomers integrate into the work group and the organization. They fostered a collaborative environment and mentoring relationships, and ensured that newcomers met key people in the organization and attended important meetings. They believed relationship building was as much a responsibility of coworkers and managers as it was of the newcomer.

Conclusions and Discussion

The questions guiding this study arose from several exploratory discussions with engineers and managers about their experiences with newcomers "learning the ropes" in the workplace and the consequences of their learning on job performance, satisfaction, and retention. These discussions indicated that learning to work at a new job was problematic regarding how well newcomers learned the social norms in organizations.

This study found that, for newcomers, it was the quality of the relationships within the work group that appeared to mediate how newcomers learned the norms, tasks, and procedures of their jobs. For example, several newcomers at the organization reported frustration at the lack of direction, instruction, and support they received from their coworkers and manager. In these situations, newcomers often attributed these difficulties as a lack of interest, respect, or attention from others. At the other extreme, several newcomers reported receiving valuable direction and support, along with highly satisfying experiences while learning the particulars of their jobs.

The primacy of relationships for learning as found in this study support what Ashforth and Sluss (2006) described as the "fundamental embeddedness of individuals in dense networks of interpersonal relationships" (p. 8). Obviously, newcomers are not embedded at the early stages of their employment, and achieving a high quality of embeddedness is an important objective of socialization. In this organization, newcomers relied on their relationships with others for information and help in learning what to do on the job, how to do it, and why it was done this way.

The exchange of information and knowledge between newcomers and coworkers is a critical means for newcomer learning in organizations. Theories of social exchange state that the relationship between actors will become stronger if both parties reciprocate efforts to enhance the relationship. Otherwise, the development of the exchange relationship will stall or decline (Blau, 1986; Molm, 2003). Graen and Uhl-Bien (1995) defined the quality of a relationship as a range from high to low based on the levels of trust, respect, and mutual obligation developed between actors. Tierney (1999) added the dimensions of frequency of interaction and degree of interpersonal support as factors contributing to the quality of exchange relationships. In addition, the quality of the exchange relationship influences the perceptions of the actors toward each other, as well as their perceptions toward the work group and organization (Bauer & Green, 1996; Lawler, 2001).

Newcomers offered their contributions and commitment to the organization in exchange for information and membership in the organization. The quality of these exchanges influenced the perceptions newcomers formed of the organization as "the way things are done here." For example, some newcomers received little help or direction and consequently perceived the organization as a place where people rarely collaborated and interaction was minimal. The opposite was also true for newcomers that received meaningful direction from their coworkers.

Lawler's (2001) affect theory of social exchange explained how joint activities among actors generate positive or negative emotions that individuals consequently attribute to the social group, thereby producing stronger or weaker ties between the actors and the group. Relationship building between newcomers and other members of the work group is just such a joint activity, and the data in this study indicated the emotional consequences of relationship building on newcomers' perceptions of their job and the organization. Lawler went on to state that these positive or negative emotions attributed to the group affected the quality of future relationships among individuals and the group. The emotional assessment of the group's relationship structure by the newcomer and others in the work group likely affects future interactions in a self-fulfilling manner. Many newcomers implied that their impressions and expectations of future support and attention from others in the company formed out of their initial experiences with coworkers. They learned which individuals they could ask for help, who was not helpful, who had important information, and how to manage these relationships to accomplish their work.

Rather than view newcomer socialization as an individual responsibility of the newcomer to learn to fit in, work groups are responsible as well by enabling or constraining their learning and integration as new members. Much of the tacit knowledge required to do the work of an organization is constructed among workers mediated by the relationship structure of the group (Ashforth & Sluss, 2006; Gergen, 1999; Schwandt, Ayvaz, & Gorman, 2006). The reports by newcomers in this study continually referred to the strong influence of relationships on the quality of their learning and working. What newcomers perceived and experienced at the beginning of their jobs became their perceptions of "the way things are done here."

The experiences of newcomers during socialization have important consequences for their careers and for the organization. The socialization process itself is a social norm of the workplace from which newcomers infer how the organization values employees. The social system or relational structure of an organization mediates the entry of newcomers by affecting what and how they learn to do their work. It also affects the quality of the work and experiences of newcomers and incumbents alike.

Even in work that is considered highly technical, such as engineering, there was a remarkable level of social and political influence affecting what newcomers learned and how the work was done.

Newcomers in this study often seemed surprised at the preeminence of the social and political influences they encountered. The new grads especially seemed surprised that learning to do their jobs was not more of an objective instructional process similar to what they experienced in school. They quickly learned that the quality of their relationships were critical factors affecting their learning and membership in the group.

Compared to the new grads, many experienced hires reported greater frustration learning how to integrate in the organization. They brought with them expectations and work habits formed from previous experiences. Some explicitly described how this company's capabilities compared to their previous workplace. For example, one participant reported, "I just realized that there wasn't the same maturity level and software process that I'm used to." These expectations and work habits often clashed with the established habits of the new work group. In addition, many experienced hires were hired because of their expertise and without first carefully building relationships with the work group; these newcomers encountered resistance and rejection from the incumbents in the group. A couple of the experienced hires attributed this resistance as a result of the members of the work group feeling threatened. Another difficulty reported by some experienced newcomers related to their career development. They were more eager for promotion and advancement than the new grads and expressed more frustration at the delays they perceived in their career track. This frustration was often focused on their managers' perceived lack of interest in promoting them or assigning them to high-profile projects.

Viewing the workplace as a complex, socially constructed system makes the transfer of information and learning a mutually constitutive process based on the relationships among individuals. Learning to function in the relational structure becomes as important as learning the procedures and tasks of the work. Several newcomers in this study reported that their perceptions of engineering had changed from a primarily objective view of solving technical problems to a more subjective view of a collaborative, interpersonal process. The importance of the relational qualities of newcomers' experiences and the salience of the work group as the context for these experiences suggest a shift is needed in the emphasis of organizational socialization from a focus on the newcomer's capability and responsibility for learning to a focus on the mutual constitution of relationships within the work group as a mediator of newcomer socialization.

Implications for Human Resource Development and Socialization Practices

Increasing interest in the socialization of individuals into organizations has produced more studies over the past few years, yet the prevailing focus of these studies has continued to emphasize the responsibility of the newcomer to learn to fit in. The evidence provided by this study indicates that building relationships in the contexts of small work groups is a primary driver of socialization for newcomers—especially in knowledge-intensive work.

Traditional views of socialization tend to underestimate the influence of the dynamic relational processes among members of the work group. Schwandt, Ayvaz, and Gorman (2006) argued that the creation of knowledge (i.e., learning) and its utilization depended on the specific structure of relationships and values found in the group. The collective nature of organizational work suggests that HRD scholars and practitioners attend to the social dynamics (especially the relational dynamics) among members of the work group—not just the competencies or skill sets of individual members entering and working in organizations.

Enhancing the socialization of newcomers into an organization is an important strategy for developing personal careers and improving organizational performance. For individuals entering organizations, focusing on the process of building high-quality relationships along with the technical tasks of the job will increase the potential for a successful transition into the organization. For example, the advice offered by newcomers for enhancing the socialization process included making an extra effort to get to know others personally, socialize outside of work, and seek opportunities to interact and collaborate with others on the job. Organizations looking to increase the capacity of their workforce, improve their competitive advantage, and develop future capabilities might improve the outcomes of newcomer job satisfaction, performance, commitment, and ultimately retention by facilitating the development of high-quality relationships between newcomers and others in the organization. Managers corroborated many of the findings in this study stressing the importance of getting newcomers connected to others in the work group. They assigned mentors, organized the work to be collaborative, provided meaningful assignments to newcomers early, and frequently provided advice and opportunities for newcomers to interact with others in the organization.

As a result of this study, the participating organization changed their "onboarding" program (orientation and socialization processes) to include informing managers of the importance of social experiences for newcomers to build relationships, assigning a local mentor to newcomers, and fostering greater interaction among newcomers, coworkers, and managers. Recognizing that what newcomers learn develops within the constraints of the relationship structures within work groups suggests that organizations might foster and enhance the relationship-building processes in work groups through which newcomers become productive members of the organization. In addition, future research in learning, development, and performance in organizations might include or focus on the complex social interactions, exchanges, and relationships among members within and across work groups in organizations. These complex interrelationships seem to be strong mediators of the learning and work performed in organizational settings.

Acknowledgements The author wishes to express his deepest gratitude to members of the research team that supported this research, including Sheri Sheppard, Steve Barley, Karl Smith, Andrew Van de Ven, Baiyin Yang, and the members of the organization who participated in the study. Additional support came from the Center for the Advancement of Engineering Education, funded by NSF grant # ESI-0227558, and the Department of Management Science and Engineering at Stanford University.

References

Ashforth, B. E., & Saks, A. M. (1996). Socialization tactics: Longitudinal effects on newcomer adjustment. *Academy of Management Journal, 39*(1), 149–178.

Ashforth, B. E., & Sluss, D. M. (2006). Relational identities in organizations: Healthy vs. unhealthy. In O. Kyriakidou & M. F. Ozbilgin (Eds.), *Relational perspectives in organizational studies: A research companion* (pp. 8–27). Cheltenham: Edward Elgar.

Ashforth, B. E., Sluss, D. M., & Saks, A. M. (2007). Socialization tactics, proactive behavior, and newcomer learning: Integrating socialization models. *Journal of Vocational Behavior, 70*, 447–462.

Bauer, T. N., Bodner, T., Erdogan, B., Truxillo, D. M., & Tucker, J. S. (2007). Newcomer adjustment during organizational socialization: A meta-analytic review of antecedents, outcomes, and methods. *Journal of Applied Psychology, 92*(3), 707–721.

Bauer, T. N., & Green, S. G. (1996). Development of leader-member exchange: A longitudinal test. *Academy of Management Journal, 39*(6), 1538–1567.

Bauer, T. N., Morrison, E. W., & Callister, R. R. (1998). Organizational socialization: A review and directions for future research. In G. R. Ferris (Ed.) *Research in personnel and human resources management* (Vol. 16, pp. 149–214). Stamford, CT: JAI Press.

Billett, S. (2002). Toward a workplace pedagogy: Guidance, participation, and engagement. *Adult Education Quarterly, 53*(1), 27–43.

Blau, P. M. (1986). *Exchange and power in social life* (2nd ed.). New Brunswick, NJ: Transaction Books.

Chao, G. T., O'Leary-Kelly, A. M., Wolf, S., Klein, H. J., & Gardner, P. D. (1994). Organizational socialization: Its content and consequences. *Journal of Applied Psychology, 79*(5), 730–743.

Cohen, A. R., & Bradford, D. L. (1989). Influence without authority: The use of alliances, reciprocity, and exchange to accomplish work. *Organizational Dynamics, 17*(3), 5–17.

Cooper-Thomas, H. D., & Anderson, N. (2006). Organizational socialization: A new theoretical model and recommendations for future research and HRM practices on organizations. *Journal of Management Psychology, 21*(5), 492–516.

Cropanzano, R., & Mitchell, M. S. (2005). Social exchange theory: An interdisciplinary review. *Journal of Management, 31*(6), 874–900.

Eddy, E. R., D'Abate, C. P., Tannenbaum, S. I., Givens-Skeaton, S., & Robinson, G. (2006). Key characteristics of effective and ineffective developmental interactions. *Human Resource Development Quarterly, 17*(1), 59–84.

Eisenhardt, K. M., & Graebner, M. E. (2007). Theory building from cases: Opportunities and challenges. *Academy of Management Journal, 50*(1), 25–32.

Ellinger, A. D., & Watkins, K. E. (1998). Updating the critical incident technique after forty-four years. In R. J. Torraco (Ed.), *1998 Academy of human resource development conference proceedings*. Baton Rouge, LA: Academy of Human Resource Development.

Flanagan, J. C. (1954). The critical incident technique. *Psychological Bulletin, 51*(4), 327–358.

Gergen, K. R. (1999). *An invitation to social construction*. London: Sage.

Gerstner, C. R., & Day, D. V. (1997). Meta-analytic review of leader-member exchange theory: Correlates and construct issues. *Journal of Applied Psychology, 82*, 827–844.

Graen, G. B. (1986). Role-making processes within complex organizations. In M. D. Dunnette (Ed.), *Handbook of industrial and organizational psychology* (pp. 1201–1245). New York: Wiley.

Graen, G. B., & Uhl-Bien, M. (1995). Relationship-based approach to leadership: Development of leader-member exchange (LMX) theory of leadership over 25 years: Applying a multi-level multi-domain perspective. *Leadership Quarterly, 6*(2), 219–247.

Gremler, D. D. (2004). The critical incident technique in service research. *Journal of Service Research, 7*(1), 65–89.

Holton, E. F., III. (1996). New employee development: A review and reconceptualization. *Human Resource Development Quarterly, 7*(3), 233–252.

Holton, E. F., III. (2001). New employee development tactics: Perceived availability, helpfulness, and relationship with job attitudes. *Journal of Business and Psychology, 16*(1), 73–85.

Illeris, K. (2002). *The three dimensions of learning*. Malabar, FL: Krieger.

Illeris, K. (2003). Towards a contemporary and comprehensive theory of learning. *International Journal of Lifelong Education, 22*(4), 396–406.

Illeris, K. (2005). A Comprehensive understanding of human learning. In P. Jarvis & S. Parker (Eds.), *Human learning: An holistic approach* (pp. 87–100). New York: Taylor and Francis.

Koopmans, H., Doornbos, A. J., & van Eekelen, I. M. (2006). Learning in interactive work situations: It takes two to tango; Why not invite both partners to dance? *Human Resource Development Quarterly, 17*(2), 135–158.

Lave, J., & Wenger, E. (1991). *Situated learning: Legitimate peripheral participation*. Cambridge: Cambridge University Press.

Lawler, E. J. (2001) An affect theory of social exchange. *American Journal of Sociology, 107*(2), 321–352.

Miles, M. B., & Huberman, A. M. (1994). *Qualitative data analysis* (2nd ed.). Thousand Oaks, CA: Sage.

Miner, J. B. (2002). *Organizational behavior: Foundations, theories, and analyses*. Oxford: Oxford University Press.

Molm, L. D. (2003). Theoretical comparisons of forms of exchange. *Sociological Theory, 21*(1), 1–17.

Moreland, R. L., Levine, J. M., & McMinn, J. G. (2001). Self-categorization and work group socialization. In M. A. Hogg & D. J. Terry (Eds.), *Social identity processes in organizational contexts* (pp. 87–100). Philadelphia, PA: Psychology Press.

Ostroff, C., & Kozlowski, S. W. J. (1992). Organization socialization as a learning process: The role of information acquisition. *Personnel Psychology, 45*, 849–874.

Patton, M. Q. (2002). *Qualitative research and evaluation methods* (3rd ed.). Thousand Oaks, CA: Sage.

Saks, A. M., & Ashforth, B. E. (1997). Organizational socialization: Making sense of the past and present as a prologue for the future. *Journal of Vocational Behavior, 51*, 234–279.

Saks, A. M., Uggerslev, K. L., & Fassina, N. E. (2007). Socialization tactics and newcomer adjustment: A meta-analytic review and test of a model. *Journal of Vocational Behavior, 70*, 413–446.

Schwandt, D. R., Ayvaz, M. T., & Gorman, M. D. (2006). Relational perspectives on collective learning and knowledge creation. In O. Kyriakidou & M. F. Ozbilgin (Eds.), *Relational perspectives in organizational studies: A research companion* (pp. 56–73). Cheltenham, UK: Edward Elgar.

Silverman, D. (2005). *Doing qualitative research: A practical handbook* (2nd ed.). London: Sage.

Skule, S. (2004). Learning conditions at work: A framework to understand and assess informal learning in the workplace. *International Journal of Training and Development, 8*(1), 8–20.

Strauss, A., & Corbin, J. (1998). *Basics of qualitative research: Techniques and procedures for developing grounded theory* (2nd ed.). Thousand Oaks, CA: Sage.

Tierney, P. (1999). Work relations as a precursor to a psychological climate for change: The role of work group supervisors and peers. *Journal of Organizational Change Management, 12*(2), 120–133.

Van Maanen, J., & Schein, E. H. (1979). Toward a theory of organizational socialization. *Research in Organizational Behavior, 1*, 209–264.

Wanous, J. P. (1992). *Organizational entry: Recruitment, selection, orientation and socialization of newcomers* (2nd ed.). Reading, MA: Addison-Wesley.

Yang, B. (2004). Holistic learning theory and implications for human resource development. *Advances in Developing Human Resources, 6*(2), 241–262.

Yin, R. K. (2003). *Case study research: Design and methods* (3rd ed.). Thousand Oaks, CA: Sage.

Chapter 9
Learning Vocational Practice in Relative Social Isolation: The Epistemological and Pedagogic Practices of Small-Business Operators

Stephen Billett

The knowledge required for effective vocational practice arises from historical and cultural sources, with the actual requirements for performance at work being manifested in particular ways in specific workplace settings. In order to construct this knowledge (i.e. learn it), individuals need to engage with social partners, artefacts, and practices that provide access to the procedural, conceptual, and dispositional forms of the knowledge. Much is understood about how this learning progresses in situations that provide direct access to this knowledge through more experienced social partners (e.g. teachers in schools and colleges, experts in workplaces). However, many individuals (e.g. shift workers, home workers) are working and learning in relative social isolation and often in the absence of such expert partners. Moreover, perhaps most learning occurs through experiences in working life in the absence of expert guidance. Consequently, there must be ways of learning socially derived knowledge in the absence of more experienced partners. This chapter discusses learning in relative social isolation to advance a conception of the process of learning in these kinds of situations. It does this by re-engaging with learning theorists whose ideas are informative and by elaborating these processes through explanations of small-business operators' epistemological and pedagogic practices as they learnt new work tasks. In combination, both localised contributions and these workers' agency are held to be central to their learning in these circumstances. This account informs the means by which other kinds of socially isolated workers might come to know and learn through their working life. Such considerations are important for those concerned with developing the capacities of workforces, particularly for the many, perhaps the majority, of those individuals who work and learn in relative social isolation.

Learning Vocational Practice in Relative Social Isolation

There has been great interest for a long time in understanding how individuals learn in circumstances where more experienced or expert partners are available to

S. Billett (✉)
Faculty of Education, Griffith University, Australia
e-mail: s.billett@griffith.edu.au

R.F. Poell, M. van Woerkom (eds.), *Supporting Workplace Learning*, Professional and Practice-based Learning 5, DOI 10.1007/978-90-481-9109-3_9,
© Springer Science+Business Media B.V. 2011

assist. These circumstances are seen as almost the standard way in which learning of socially derived knowledge occurs. The strongest association is perhaps that between learners and the people teaching them the knowledge that they are required to learn. Studies of learning through schools, colleges, and workplaces that afford direct support by more knowledgeable partners have dominated the field of inquiry into learning and have, understandably, emphasised the interpersonal process of learning. Yet, we also need models of the much more common learning processes in which workers engage, for instance, when undertaking relatively independent forms of work. In addition, there are salient procedural and conceptual purposes. Procedurally these kinds of circumstances represent those through which most of learning throughout working life likely often progresses. Many, if not most, workers (e.g. shift workers, home workers, workers who are the sole experts in their workplace) work and learn in relative social isolation. In many countries, workers employed in small businesses far outnumber those who work in large enterprises (Coopers & Lybrand, 1995) and who have greater access to more experienced and expert coworkers. Yet, even those working in large organisations often practise and, therefore, learn in situations of low social guidance. For some, the private practice of the classroom, office, surgery, or car or the kinds of engagement with work tasks are beyond the gaze and hearing of more expert others. Given that learning is ongoing through everyday work activities, whenever and wherever workers are engaged in these activities they are learning (Rogoff & Lave, 1984), albeit often without access to more expert social partners who can interpersonally provide direct guidance. Of course, in most of these situations there will be, by different degree, accessible social forms and practice to observe, listen to, and imitate. Indeed, these forms of indirect social guidance are often reported as assisting learning more frequently than expert guidance (Billett, 2001a). Yet, knowledgeable partners can provide access to the kinds of conceptual and procedural knowledge individuals are unlikely to learn through discovery alone. Therefore, there is need to understand how those working in the absence of more expert partners can learn the knowledge required for their work that is usually provided through direct engagement with more expert social partners.

The conceptual salience of understanding how learning proceeds in these circumstances is to advance contemporary accounts of learning. Over the past two decades, much inquiry into and theorising about learning has emphasised the importance of close interpersonal interactions between more and less experienced partners and joint problem solving that occurs between them as a premise for optimum socially guided development. In particular, many of these accounts have emphasised interpsychological interactions (i.e. those between individuals and social sources, principally other individuals). Drawing on Vygotskian-inspired precepts, this chapter proposes that these interactions, and in particular, the interpersonal ones, lead to intrapsychological socially derived legacies (i.e. learning). This learning process comprises the knowledge of the more expert partner (e.g. teacher, skilled worker) being made accessible by joint activities and being appropriated by the less experienced partners (e.g. students, novice workers). There are good reasons to emphasise these kinds of interactions in regard to learning to perform occupational tasks. The knowledge required for occupational practice arises from cultural sources, is transformed through history, and is manifested in particular ways in specific workplace situations, because of localised performance requirements. To construct (i.e. learn) this knowledge, individuals need to engage with social partners, artefacts, and practices that provide access to this knowledge. Within Vygotskian-derived traditions, this knowledge is seen to be sourced in phylogenesis (the development of the species), shaped into sociocultural practices (e.g. occupations), and engaged with and appropriated through microgenesis (i.e. moment-by-moment learning) that contributes to individuals' ontogeny (i.e. development across a life course) (Scribner, 1985). Yet, the moment-by-moment learning that constitutes individuals' ontogenetic development most commonly occurs in circumstances where expert guidance is not present. Workers are required to secure novel learning outcomes in the absence of expert guidance and often manage to do so (Billett, 2006). Moreover, it has also been shown that much of children's learning before going to school is indirect and independent, premised on active learning and imitation (Bransford, Sherwood, & Hassellbring, 1985, cited in Pea, 1987), not a product of teaching by others, such as parents. Indeed, across their lives individuals engage constantly in processes of learning in the absence of experts as they participate in and develop the capacities to perform a range of roles (e.g. parenting) in and outside of work. Similarly, the kinds of active engagement with the social world that Vygotsky identified in children's play (Valsiner & van der Veer, 2000) suggest the potential scope for their learning resided not only in more experienced social partners but in the child's agency.

Consequently, current accounts of interpsychological processes that are premised on the access to more experienced partners may not be wholly explanatory of much of the learning processes in which individuals engage throughout their lives. Here, it is proposed that in the absence of direct social guidance individuals exercise their personal epistemology more agentically in their engagement with the world beyond them, when engaging in everyday activities in work and other social settings. That is, they not so much as compensate for the absence of experts, but are quite used to and adept at engaging with the social world from which they learn socially derived practices. Perhaps, most strongly when they are interested, individuals exercise their active and strategic capacities for actively extracting meaning from the available social forms and partners, to paraphrase Gibson and Levin (1975). It follows that for workers employed in circumstances of relative social, geographic, or physical isolation, and working in circumstances where more experienced social partners are unlikely to be encountered, there may well be the case for developing workers' capacity and encouraging the workers to exercise a higher level of strategy and intentionality in their construction of knowledge. The findings of an investigation into how small-business operators learnt novel conceptual and procedural capacities (Billett, Ehrich, & Hernon-Tinning, 2003) are used to illustrate this point. The study identified the small-business operators' interpsychological processes as being largely premised on learner agency and engagement, including a considered engagement with and critical scrutiny of locally available sources of knowledge. Differences in the purposes, scope, and intentionality of learning-related interactions

and activities and their outcomes were largely premised on small-business operators' agency. Although this investigation identified contributions of social partners
and artefacts, the qualities of engagement and critical appraisal characterising these
interactions were largely premised on learner agency.

In advancing its case, this chapter first discusses the conceptual bases for considering the active role of learners in constructing knowledge by reviewing some
accounts that refer to the agency that individuals employ in learning from the world
beyond them. These ideas are then used to illuminate the epistemological and pedagogic practices of small-business operators in their learning of new work tasks:
those associated with the introduction of a goods and service tax. It was found in
this study that, in combination, localised support and the agentic actions of workers are central to their learning in these circumstances. This suggests the means
by which other kinds of socially isolated workers might come to know and learn
through their working life. Hence, the central role of personal epistemology within
interpsychological processes (i.e. those between the worker and the social world) are
emphasised here. In conclusion, some considerations for promoting learning in these
circumstances are advanced, with a focus on the active processes of observing and
listening, the organisation of learning experiences, and the assisting of individuals
to develop criticality in their thinking and acting.

Learning and Engagements with the Social and Physical Environment

The processes shaping individuals' learning through engagement with the world
beyond them has long been considered within psychological accounts of human
development. Many of these accounts emphasise the agentic way in which individuals engage with and construe and construct meaning from what they encounter in
the physical and social world beyond them. That is, they are not merely learning
what is suggested by sources external to them. Instead, a consistent line of theorising holds that individuals construct knowledge premised on their interpretations
and renderings of what they experience. Indeed, some of the earliest psychological
accounts emphasise individuals' active role in these processes. Baldwin, Claparède,
and Janet in different ways all emphasise the active and person-dependent interpre-
tative role of the individual. Baldwin (1894) proposed that children, from an early
age, begin to understand through their dealings with the social world that it can
be inconsistent or unpredictable. He claimed this inconsistency in what is afforded
them leads to the *projective* stage in the growth of personal consciousness, which
shapes individuals' responses to what they subsequently experience. These variations in responses to experiences from the world beyond them lead to the learning
of principles of interpretation. Here arises the prospect for the potential of imitation:
the copying of social partners' behaviours through observation. Imitation provides
an early example of interpsychological processes, although Baldwin does not use
that term. In all, as part of the development of personality, the child learns principles of interpretation. Later, Baldwin (1898, p. 6) proposes these processes were

underpinned by selective thinking by referring to a broadly accepted view within psychology that "the growth of the mind depends upon the constant reception of new materials-materials which do not repeat from experiences simply, but constitute in some sense 'variations' upon them". Hence, the relations between the person and the social are construed and constructed by the individuals, and are mediated by what arises through the individuals' personal histories. Janet, according to Piaget (1968), proposed that a distinction must be drawn between "primary action" or the relation between subject and object (intelligence, etc.) and "secondary action" or subjects' response to their own actions. Moreover, this reaction, which constitutes elementary feelings, regulates primary actions and moderates the release of energy and intentionality available within the organism. Besides these regulations that shape "the energetics or inner economy of behaviour" (Piaget, 1968, p. 5), Janet proposes that we must consider those factors that "govern its [i.e. behaviour's] ends and values, and such values that characterise an energetic or economic interaction with the external environment" (p. 5). So, here the locus of engaging with and learning through what is experienced is premised on how individuals direct their intentionality. Similarly, Claparede (cited in Piaget, 1968) proposes that feelings appoint a goal for behaviour, with intelligence providing only the means for that goal to be realised. Hence, Claparede suggests that individuals continually modify their goals for actions and, in doing so, shape (i.e. negotiate) meaning with the world that is external to them. He is held by Piaget (1968) to have concluded that individuals' feelings directs behaviour by attributing a value to its ends, and therefore directs the energy necessary for action premised on its value to the individual. In this way, Claparede is held to refer to readapting what the person experiences, on the basis of their needs and conceptions.

Importantly, these early accounts were advanced before the rise and domination of behaviourism, which as a movement tended to downplay the active role of learners in construing what they experienced independently of what was suggested by the social world beyond the individual. Instead, behaviour was proposed as being a learnt response to a particular stimulus. Indeed, rather than a consideration of mind, observable behaviour became the key emphasis within this school of psychological thought. It was perhaps only with the rise of the cognitive revolution that the dominant psychological view came to reemphasise the importance of accounting for the human processing of what is experienced. Indeed, cognitive psychology made a virtue out of the human capacity to remember and manipulate what was experienced, rather than viewing behaviour as a learnt and therefore predictable response to a specific experience. However, others were exploring these kinds of relationships far earlier than those within cognitive psychology. Piaget (1968), for instance, offered accounts that emphasised the particular kinds of negotiations that occurred when individuals encountered novel experiences.

Indeed, to explain these active processes of meaning making, Piaget (1968) had advanced the concept of equilibrium: the individual actively seeking to overcome disequilibrium. Within this account of active meaning making, assimilation was used as a term to describe individuals' process of aligning what they experienced with what they already knew or had learnt. That is, this sense making was shaped by previous engagements with the same or similar objects. Accommodation, however, was the individual making sense of a new experience through developing new categories of knowledge and ways of knowing, often through elaborating or extending what they already know. Piaget (1968, p. 7) proposed, "every relation between a living being and the environment has its particular characteristic; instead of submitting passively – modification by imposing on it a structure of its own." It is noteworthy that Piaget's work is described as genetic epistemology, not psychology, thereby emphasising an active engagement with sources of knowledge. Importantly, Piaget's central concept of equilibrium was framed by concerns about how persons negotiated contributions from both the physical and social world beyond them. Consequently, it has a strong emphasis on the presence and activities of a personal epistemology. In these ways, rather than emphasise either the personal or the social contribution, the focus of human development was based upon negotiations between subject and object, but included the social world and the world of nature. In this way, both brute and institutional factors (Searle, 1995) were accounted for in these negotiations. It is important to be reminded of these contributions to the process of equilibrium, because Piaget's work is often characterised as being too focused on nature and biological development in particular, and excluding social contributions to that development. Yet, clearly, his accounts included the consideration of social contributions to human development, and individuals' negotiation of them with social partners. Indeed, Piaget's original consideration of these ideas dates back to the 1940s, when he discussed successive processes of equilibrium as being "organised along two dimensions–intrapersonal and social (interpersonal)" (1968, p. 50). Therefore, prior to the rise of the behaviourism, the cognitive revolution, and more recent accounts of sociocultural theories, a range of accounts had emphasised active processes of negotiation between persons and the social and physical environments beyond them. These accounts emphasised the active human role of construing, negotiating, and constructing meaning from what was experienced. Moreover, the kinds of activities described above are analogous to what in contemporary terms is described as reflexivity: a capacity to consider one's own responses to particular experiences.

As noted, in Vygotskian-inspired traditions, relations between the social world and the individual are referred to as interpsychological processes (i.e. between the person and the social world) that lead to intrapsychological outcomes (i.e. changes called "learning" in the individual). Within this tradition, human development (i.e. learning) is seen as arising from individuals engaging with social partners, cultural forms, and norms. A key concept attributed to Vygotsky is the zone of proximal development (ZPD). This concept proposes that individuals' capacity to learn richly is premised by engagement with a more knowledgeable partner who can extend the scope of the individuals' learning through joint problem solving. That is, because they know more than the novice, more experienced partners can open possibilities, options, and understandings for learners. In this way, dyads such as those between parent and child, teacher and student, and tradesperson and apprentice are seen to epitomise models of human development based upon access to proximal guidance, and in particular models for learning what Vygotsky (1978) referred to as scientific knowledge. These premises are emphasised in views of learning through apprenticeship-like arrangements (Brown & Palinscar, 1989; Collins, Brown, & Newman, 1989; Lave & Wenger, 1991). Within the Vygotskian tradition, and possibly directly from, is also an acceptance of the importance of engagement with the brute world. Indeed, Vygotsky deliberately adopted biological concepts and applied them to the social and cultural genesis of knowledge and human development, because he wanted to emphasise the social contributions to knowledge. For instance, terms such as proximal (i.e. close) and distal (i.e. distant) and also phylogeny (i.e. the development of the species) and ontogeny (i.e. personal development across a life course) were appropriated from their biological origins to inform processes that are inherently cultural and social.

However, these accounts' emphasis on the social and collective contributions to human development have been advanced in the past two decades possibly at a cost of considerations of humans' active thinking and responding to what they experience. Much of this emphasis on the immediate social contribution to cognition was directed as a correction for the dominance of cognitive theory, which emphasises the importance of humans' manipulation of knowledge, as in conception of expertise (Ericsson & Lehmann, 1996; Glaser, 1989), and a downplaying of the social and physical world's contributions. However, beyond sociocultural theory other perspectives that have a strong cultural and social orientation propose a more central and negotiated role for individuals. For instance, the cultural psychologist Valsiner (1998, p. 393) proposes, "most of human development takes place through active ignoring and neutralisation of most of social suggestions to which the person is subjected to in everyday life". According to this view, the negotiation with the social world is essential to buffer individuals' personalities against the constant demands of social suggestions. He continues, "Hence, what is usually viewed as socialisation efforts (by social institutions or parents) is necessarily counteracted by the active recipients of such efforts who can neutralise or ignore a large number of such episodes, aside from single particularly dramatic ones" (p. 393).

Here, Valsiner suggests that there are real limits to potency of the social suggestion and the degree to which it can shape the core human cognition. Such considerations are important given the role that personal constructions of events play in thinking and acting and how these constructions are also shaped through individuals' earlier experiences (Gergen, 1994). In this way, not only is personal history important, but also the agency of the individual in utilising and exercising the legacy of that personal history or ontogeny in their ongoing microgenetic development. Given the social and cultural emphases in Vygotskian-inspired accounts of human development, perhaps surprisingly, it seems that Vygotsky concluded that social guidance was secondary to individual agency in the development of psychological functions. In referring to children's play, he noted, "In play, the child is always higher than his average age, higher than his usual everyday behaviour; he is in play as if a head above himself. The play contains, in a condensed way, as if in the focus of a magnifying glass, all tendencies of development; it is as if the child in play tries to accomplish a jump above the level of his ordinary behaviour. ... Play is the resource of development and it creates the zone of nearest development. Action in the imaginary field, in the imagined situation, construction of voluntary intention, the formulation of life plan, will motivate – this all emerges in play" (Vygotsky, 1966, pp. 74–75, translated and cited in Valsiner, 2000, p. 43).

What is suggested here is that not only are individuals' interest and volition central to their development, but also that the scope of that development is shaped as much by the agency of the learner as by other partners. These propositions might seem quite distinct from the widely accepted accounts of Vygotsky-derived theorising. Yet, the founder of cultural historical activity theory, Cole (2002), also claims that in learning and remaking cultural practices individuals' agency is paramount. He reports that he is unable to assist his education students learn how to manage classrooms in turbulent American high schools. Instead, he suggested that these students need to determine what works in that particular school by themselves. In doing so, he suggests that the historically developed cultural practices of classroom management that have been developed and refined over time will not be helpful for these novice teachers. Moreover, the kind of guidance which he might provide as their teacher would also be insufficient. Instead, they had to largely work it out for themselves in uncertain and often difficult circumstances. Beyond individuals' learning, these propositions also suggest that individuals play a central role in remaking cultural practices such as classroom management. It is the application of personal agency when enacting culturally, and socially derived practices to particular situations that is generative of the kinds of practices that are undertaken and are being remade through the application and potentially transformed through their enactment.

In all, these accounts suggest that the intentional, active, and focussed engagement that constitutes the process of learning and remaking of practice is shaped by individuals' interests and capacities that comprise their personal epistemologies. Adopting such a concept provides a base to understand learning through and for work as a more active and person-centred process than many recent accounts propose. It also assists understanding of how new learning is developed by those engaged in relatively isolated social circumstances.

Small-Business Operators' Personal Epistemologies

To elaborate the character of these epistemologies, and how they shape learning through working life in different ways, it is helpful to draw on investigations of learning through work. The particular instance discussed here is from businesses whose workforces are small and may also lack the kinds of direct social guidance by experts often found in workplaces with larger workforces. So, unlike workplaces where there are more experienced or expert coworkers to observe, and with whom to engage to discuss and evaluate work tasks, small businesses often lack such accessible sources of knowledge and guidance. Consequently, there arises a question about what kind of interpsychological processes workers in small businesses engage when seeking to learn new tasks. Given the lack of direct social guidance, to what degree do these workers have to be more personally agentic and directed in their thinking, acting, and learning? That is, do these workers have to compensate for the absence of easily accessible socially derived knowledge from experts and have to develop a more agentic personal epistemology?

The accounts here are derived from a study of how small-business operators learnt to implement the goods and service tax during its introduction in Australia (Billett et al., 2003). Unlike in Europe, in Australia, small businesses are those with ten or fewer employees and include sole operated businesses. Given the well-reported reluctance of small-business operators to participate in vocational education programmes (Coopers & Lybrandt, 2005), this study aimed to understand how these operators acquire new knowledge and respond to innovations. The procedural outcomes of this study aimed to be helpful in suggesting the kinds of models of learning support that might be most appropriate for such workers. One form of learning support would be assisting workers to find ways to secure access to forms of localised support that are appropriate for and informed about their particular circumstances and understood the particular learning that these small-business operators require. However, the study also drew attention to conceptual considerations for learning in situations that lacked direct access to more informed social partners (i.e. proximal guidance). The procedural concerns come together with conceptual development. As noted, current understanding about learning through work situations is largely premised on richly social affordances, including the availability of more informed social partners. Less is known about learning through work in the absence of these kinds of dyads and other forms of social partnerships.

The study referred to here used interviews and case studies of 25 small businesses to identify the processes through which small-business operators learnt how to implement the goods and service tax in their businesses. The small-business operators were guided through a series of questions about (i) their business; (ii) the preparations they undertook before the implementation of the goods and service tax; (iii) the scope of learning that was required by the informant; (iv) how that learning occurred; (v) the relative contributions of a range of learning supports; and (vi) perceptions of the ideal way that this task could have been learnt. Undertaking the task of implementing the goods and service tax comprised, for many businesses, a significant body of new learning. It required understanding the conceptual premises of administering the tax, which were not always straightforward, and the procedural means for calculating, gathering, and forwarding the tax to the Australian Taxation Office; for many small businesses this requirement meant they had to address for the first time electronically organised business management procedures. Despite being a nationally uniform process, the implementation of the goods and service tax meant quite different things for each of the businesses interviewed. This was because of the breadth and complexity of the taxation requirements within and across business activities. Some small businesses had access to different kinds of assistance outside of their business. These included business consultants and accountants who were employed to manage the acquisition of this new knowledge or to do it for the business operators. Others used their bookkeepers to learn about and implement this new requirement, thereby avoiding having to learn about and implement it themselves. For others still, however, the learning process was essential. For some, developing these capacities was necessary to be free themselves from the burden of employing accountants, consultants, and others to do this work. Because it was a national initiative, there was also a range of more distant forms of support provided by the government, and industry groups and local chambers of commerce, etc. to help small-business operators understand the principles, processes, and obligations associated with their administration of this tax. Importantly, this process had to be implemented by all Australian businesses, except the very smallest, by the beginning of the new financial year. Consequently, learning about this tax and the processes supporting it were being widely discussed in many forums and by business operators who had to learn its principles and practices to meet their legislated obligations and maintain the viability of their businesses. Therefore, it is a topic for discussion and evaluation across many forums with which these workers engage, particularly outside of the small businesses.

The interviews were conducted 2 years after the implementation of the goods and service tax and, as such, allowed the operators to reflect, retrospectively, upon their experiences. The interviews provided data that permitted identification of available forms of support outside of operators' workplaces, and the degree and ways by which these were reported as being helpful to these small businesses. In general, support was most helpful when the source of that support understood the nature of the specific business and could identify the particular implications of the goods and service tax upon that business. Support was least valued when it offered principles without being able to advise how the tax would impact on the particular business. Significantly, in terms of outside support, trust was identified as being an essential quality in judging the support as being helpful. Thus, there was an active consideration by these learners (i.e. business operators) of the bases on which information was being provided. Importantly, judgements about the worth of the forms of support with which individuals engaged arose from their engagement with and critical considerations of these forms of support. Yet, this trust and view of the worth of informants were developed through active consideration of and appraisal by the small-business operators. These operators claimed to be engaged in seeking and accessing advice, and also making decisions about the veracity of that advice. They reported actively listening to speakers talk about the goods and service tax when attending meetings sponsored by local commerce groups, in order to assess the worth of what was being stated, and to asses and test their own knowledge of these schemes. Hence, these operators were not passive recipients of such information; rather, they tested out its applicability, standing, and value, in ways analogous to what is referred to as critical appraisals of knowledge. Thus, even when engaging with other sources of information, these workers reported being agentic, critical, and comparative. That is, they were engaged in a highly active and strategically focused learning process characterised by the exercise of an agentic personal epistemology.

Beyond engaging with others, the small-business operators also reported being pragmatic and selective in their efforts at conscious learning. They reported trying to identify what they needed to know and then direct their energies in very selective, but active, ways to learn what they needed to know, and for the specific requirements of the small business. For instance, one proactive learner was an entrepreneur who owned a number of businesses of different kinds. Business profitability, not the kind of business or professional practice, was his key motivation. In contrast, two of the small businesses comprised professional practices (i.e. a veterinary surgeon and an optometrist). Both of these professionals reported finding as quite uninteresting the processes of business administration and, in particular, the accounting components and requirements of the business. They were more interested in their professional practice and hired bookkeepers to do their administrative and accountancy work. Hence, their approach to goals for learning and efforts were commensurate with their interests. In short, they delegated the majority of the responsibility to their paid bookkeepers. They only wanted to know what they had to understand about the principles under which the goods and service tax operated. So, their focus on, approach to, and engagement in learning this task were relative to and quite distinct from those of the entrepreneur, for instance. However, what was common was that these individuals directed their interests and focuses towards their particular ends. Important here is the selective nature of these workers' epistemological actions.

Then, as noted, there were small-business operators who were keen to learn how to administer the goods and service tax in order to avoid the expense of accountants and bookkeepers that had arisen during the implementation phase. These individuals, like the entrepreneur, were often highly proactive, engaged, and eager to learn the processes of administering this tax. For them, the intention for learning was about reducing the cost of running their business and assisting in its financial viability. Consequently, they were pragmatic, engaged, and interested in what they needed to learn in order to effectively adopt this innovation and thus remove the financial burden of paying accountants and bookkeepers. Then, there was one business owner, a bookshop owner, who had few local sources of advice (i.e. proximal guidance). He actively and selectively sought advice from and engaged in reciprocal learning with another bookshop owner in another state, communicating electronically in sharing information about what the goods and service tax meant to their businesses and how best they could implement it with little or no impact on their businesses. In some ways, this process builds upon existing practice by bookshop owners who often use their own networks to swap stock in order to fulfil customer requests. In all, these examples demonstrate the ways in which personal agency, which extended to the identification of credible sources of information, was enacted by workers who had to acquire new knowledge in the absence of immediate expertise and guidance (Billett et al., 2003).

However, the exercise of personal epistemologies was not always effective. One small-business owner, who was quite socially and geographically isolated, relied upon his own resources and expertise. These comprised quite rudimentary, albeit effective, business aids including a manual entry system to note sales and manage stock. However, the advent of the goods and service tax required all small-business operators to use a software package to administer their businesses and fulfil their taxation administration obligations. This particular business operator had never used a computer, had no experience with business management software, and did not know how to translate his current business management strategy into one based upon the use of computer. However, his individual and self-directed approach to learning concepts and procedures (epistemological adventures, if you like) led to a range of difficulties, embarrassment, and, ultimately, high levels of anxiety. In all, his capacities and approach (i.e. personal epistemology) were inadequate for the task to be learnt, as was the degree and means by which he engaged with others who could assist and help him implement his business management systems. Essentially, the gaps in his knowledge were too great to be closed by discovery learning alone. He required the assistance of particular kinds of experts to assist him to secure the very specific kinds of knowledge needed to operate the technology effectively. Yet, it seems also that his beliefs and values, and perhaps social competence, rendered him reluctant to engage with others to secure sources of advice and assistance with learning new concepts and procedures. Consequently, the inadequacy of his personal epistemology, including not working to overcome his socialisation, was limiting the process and scope of what was, for him, necessary learning.

Hence, while providing illustrative instances of agentic learning for particular purposes, this chapter needs to state the consequences of an inappropriate reliance upon personal epistemologies. These epistemologies and their exercise are not of unqualified effectiveness. Instead, they need to be seen as being used selectively, and in ways that depend upon the particular qualities of the learner and the scope of the learning to be undertaken. At their best, these personal epistemologies were both driving and guiding the process of trying to make sense of this new business requirement in ways consonant with Piagetian accounts of securing equilibrium and viability, and also with the kinds of critical and reflexive processes that have been identified as being necessary in recent accounts of lifelong learning, for instance (Dyke, 1997; Edwards, Ranson, & Strain, 2002). These workers were trying in an active way to understand what was required of them and were guided by desires to be clear about the process and its requirements and were deploying their way of seeing and engaging with the world, making sense, and responding to the social world in a highly active way. Yet, there can be no guarantee that the learning can be negotiated by individual efforts alone, particularly if the gap between what the individual knows and what they need to learn is great. There is a point at which the limits of personal agency are understood and guidance by more expert others becomes essential, as the example above demonstrates. In these ways, personal epistemologies were exercised to understand the knowledge required for these work tasks and the boundaries (e.g. scope, limitations, strengths, and weaknesses) of what the individuals know. However, within this mix is the need for individuals to know at what point it is necessary to engage with others to secure kinds of knowledge that they need to learn.

It follows, therefore, that personal epistemologies are seen as being a premise to understand the intentional, agentic, and selective learning in which these small-business operators needed to engage. Perhaps most noticeable in their accounts is how they had to engage proactively and critically, not accepting the worth of advice received from others, but appraising that advice in terms of its application to the particular issues they had to address and the circumstances in which those responses had to occur. Yet, in all of this, there is the sense of these workers reaching out to secure new knowledge, identify viable sources of information, and actively appraise that information in the absence of the kinds of close guidance that is available elsewhere. As discussed earlier, these processes are distinct from individuals' manipulation of their existing knowledge, which would never been sufficient in these circumstances, because the knowledge to be learnt had to be secured from elsewhere. Yet, more than perhaps what is proposed in contemporary sociocultural accounts, there is also evidence here of an engagement which seems to be quite distinct from that proposed to occur between experts and novices. The learners here were not looking directly to experts to provide the knowledge they needed. Instead, they engaged with them in a way that was testing and pressing the expertise that was available to them. All of this suggests that accounts of intrapsychological processes require further elaboration in order to explain kinds of learning processes that can be found in these accounts. The zone of nearest or proximal development was that being created often by the learner in seeking to establish the problem space to which they needed to respond and also actively identifying and locating interlocutors from whom to secure the kinds of understandings and procedures that they needed to learn. Indeed, it seems as though these learners delineated the scope of the learning that they desired and the degree by which others could assist them secure the knowledge that they needed to learn.

It follows that the kinds of models of human resource development that might be afforded to such workers would likely have a design and be enacted in ways different from those proposed in many current accounts of learning new knowledge through work. That is, models of learning through work in social isolation ought to emphasise the active engagement of the learner rather than the guidance of an expert.

Supporting Learning in Situations of Limited Social Guidance

This book has as its rationale advancing key considerations for advising and guiding human resource development practitioners in assisting workers learn the knowledge they need to secure for effective work practice. Here, it is proposed that in the absence of more expert coworkers, particular approaches to learning are required. These are premised on the agentic epistemological activities of learners. What needs to be stated upfront is that social guidance is provided not only through the close guidance of a more expert coworker but also in a range of ways as organised and selected by the learners. Indeed, in a series of studies across a range of industries and workplaces, people were found to learn through everyday work activities typically and largely in the absence of direct guidance (Billet, 2001a). Perhaps the most commonly cited forms of support by workers across these studies were engaging in work activities (e.g. "just doing it"), observing and listening to others, and the contributions of the physical workplace setting. In essence, these workers reported what has been found in anthropological studies of the learning of culturally derived practices, which is that the majority of that learning occurs through processes that do not involve the close guidance of more expert partners (Lave, 1990). Consistent with findings of the anthropological studies were the workers' reports that the active engagement in tasks and with the physical and social environment of the work-places in which those tasks were undertaken provided the goals for, procedures of, and premises for undertaking that work (Billett, 2001a). In short, the media-tion of individuals' cognitive capacities fuelled by their interests and values largely shaped the goals for and processes of learning in these physical and social environ-ments. Yet, having said this, there is also recognition in both the anthropological and workplace studies that there are limits to this self-directed and personally mediated form of learning. For instance, anthropological studies identify instances of teach-ing knowledge that would not be secured through discovery alone. One example was the need of Micronesian fishermen to learn star patterns by which to navigate at night (Pelissier, 1991). Here, jetsam and pebbles on the beach were used to illustrate the position of stars and help the fishermen identify them. Also, in the workplace learning studies, it was found necessary to use a range of pedagogic strategies to overcome concerns about the development of specific procedures and conceptual understanding that were not going to be learnt effectively through practise alone.

Consequently, there are both strengths and limitations to the exercise of personal epistemologies in learning through and for work. Both strengths and limitations are likely found in the extent of the individuals' domain-specific knowledge, that is, their knowledge of a particular domain of activities, such as their occupation or business, and the extent of the gap between their personal domain of knowledge and the knowledge that needs to be learnt to effectively undertake the new tasks. Hence, in considering approaches to assisting workers learn in this way, a starting point is the understanding of the gap between what workers already know and what they need to know in order to effectively complete the new task. So, the scope or the zone of the new learning becomes an essential consideration. However, the scope of the learning, rather than being somehow fixed, is shaped by the extent and depth of individuals' knowledge and the gap between that and what has to be learnt. Thus, as so many have suggested before (Ausubel & Novak, 1978), an important starting place is understanding learners' knowledge and readiness to engage in what needs to be learnt. For some, such as the accountants and bookkeepers, in this study, the new tasks represented something which was easily negotiable using their personal epistemologies and domain-specific knowledge. However, for the individual lacking the financial, taxation, and information technology knowledge required to operate a business management system, the scope of the task to learn that new knowledge might be quite large and impossible to negotiate without the assistance of more knowledgeable others. Consequently, the first task is to decide whether the scope of the learning required is something that can be negotiated by the individual agenti-cally, or requires the assistance of others, and the degrees by which such support is required. However, not only is this task likely to be person dependent, but it is also likely to be situationally specific. Earlier studies have indicated that the particu-lar performance requirements for workplaces differ quite markedly (Billett, 2001b). So, it is important to appraise the individuals' competence and readiness against the requirements of the domains of activities that they will be required to learn, not some uniform standard.

Second, there is a need to understand the kinds of knowledge that are required to be learnt (i.e. conceptual, procedural, and dispositional) and the best means by which these can be developed more generally. Hence, individualised considerations of the kinds of knowledge that are required to be learnt, and what kind of support is most likely to be helpful, are required. For instance, particular emphases on conceptual, procedural, or dispositional dimensions of the knowledge required for effective performance may well require particular kinds of interventions. The development of conceptual capacity might require making accessible to these learners knowledge which otherwise remains hidden from them. The development of procedural capacity likely will require expert engagement and opportunities to practise, refine, and hone, so that the learner can progressively realise more mature approximations of the procedures needed to effectively enact those tasks. In addition, dispositional development might well arise from opportunities to observe effective models. While all of this might sound demanding, for many workers the need for this kind of learning support will be the exception, rather than frequently required. This is because much of that learning can progress without the need for such interventions because it arises through observation, imitation, and practise that assist that imitation to become increasingly mature approximations of the tasks to be learnt. All of this is directed by individuals' personal epistemologies.

In concluding, the key point made here is that much of our learning arises without the need for direct guidance. The quality about learning appears to be premised upon the degree by which learners engage actively, intentionally, and with criticality. The agency of the learner can do much to access the kinds of knowledge that are available in the social world and need to be constructed by the learner and, in doing so, close the gap between their personal domain of knowledge and that required for effective performance in their workplace. Consequently, there is no need for constant access to expert guidance; rather, this access is needed only when expert guidance is required. Therefore, at the same time it is important that individuals' personal epistemologies be opened to and aware of their limits in securing knowledge that is outside of the zone that constitutes the scope of learning that they can realise agentically. It is in the areas beyond that zone that they will need to access guidance by more expert partners.

References

Ausubel, D. P., & Novak, J. D. (1978). Meaningful reception learning and retention. In D. P. Ausubel, J. D. Novak, & H. Hanesian (Eds.), *Educational psychology: A cognitive review* (pp. 114–160). New York: Holt Reinhardt and Winston.

Baldwin, J. M. (1894). Personality-suggestion. *Psychological Review, 1*, 274–279.

Baldwin, J. M. (1898). On selective thinking. *The Psychological Review, 5*(1), 1–24.

Billett, S. (2001a). *Learning in the workplace: Strategies for effective practice*. Sydney: Allen and Unwin.

Billett, S. (2001b). Knowing in practice: Re-conceptualising vocational expertise. *Learning and Instruction, 11*(6), 431–452.

Billett, S. (2006). *Work, change and workers*. Dordrecht: Springer.

Billett, S., Ehrich, L., & Hernon-Tinning, B. (2003). Small business pedagogic practices. *Journal of Vocational Education and Training, 55*(2), 149–167.

Brown, A. L., & Palinscar, A. M. (1989). Guided, cooperative learning and individual knowledge acquisition. In L. B. Resnick (Ed.), *Knowing, learning and instruction: Essays in honour of Robert Glaser* (pp. 393–451). Hillsdale, NJ: Erlbaum & Associates.

Cole, M. (2002, April). *Building centers of strength in cultural historical research.* Paper presented at the annual meeting of the American Educational Research Association, New Orleans, LA.

Collins, A., Brown, J. S., & Newman, S. E. (1989). Cognitive apprenticeship: Teaching the crafts of reading, writing and mathematics. In L. B. Resnick (Ed.), *Knowing, learning and instruction: Essays in honour of Robert Glaser* (pp. 453–494). Hillsdale, NJ: Erlbaum & Associates.

Coopers & Lybrand. (1995). Small business: A review of training evaluation and effectiveness. In *Enterprising nation* (Research Report Volume 2. Document no. TD/TNC 49.73). Canberra: Industry Task Force on Leadership and Management Skills, Australian Government Publishing Service.

Dyke, M. (1997). Reflective learning as reflexive education in a risk society: Empowerment and control? *International Journal of Lifelong Education, 16*(1), 2–17.

Edwards, R., Ranson, S., & Strain, M. (2002). Reflexivity: Towards a theory of lifelong learning. *International Journal of Lifelong Education, 21*(6), 525–536.

Ericsson, K. A., & Lehmann, A. C. (1996). Expert and exceptional performance: Evidence of maximal adaptation to task constraints. *Annual Review of Psychology, 47*, 273–305.

Gergen, K. J. (1994). *Realities and relationships: Soundings in social construction.* Cambridge, MA: Harvard University Press.

Gibson, E. J., & Levin, H. (1975). *Psychology of reading.* Cambridge, MA: MIT Press.

Glaser, R. (1989). Expertise and learning: How do we think about instructional processes now that we have discovered knowledge structures? In D. Klahr & K. Kotovsky (Eds.), *Complex information processing: The impact of Herbert A. Simon* (pp. 269–282.). Hillsdale, NJ: Erlbaum & Associates.

Janet, P. (1930). In C. Murchison (Ed.), *Pierre Janet A history of psychology in autobiography* (pp. 123–133). Worcester, MA: Clark University.

Lave, J. (1990). The culture of acquisition and the practice of understanding. In J. W. Stigler, R. A. Shweder, & G. Herdt (Eds), *Cultural psychology* (pp. 259–86). Cambridge: Cambridge University Press.

Lave, J., & Wenger, E. (1991). *Situated learning: Legitimate peripheral participation.* Cambridge: Cambridge University Press.

Pea, R. D. (1987). Socializing the knowledge transfer problem. *International Journal of Educational Research, 11*(6), 639–663.

Pelissier, C. (1991). The anthropology of teaching and learning. *Annual Review of Anthropology, 20*, 75–95.

Piaget, J. (1968). *Six psychological studies.* New York: Vintage.

Rogoff, B., & Lave, J. (Eds.). (1984). *Everyday cognition: Its development in social context.* Cambridge, MA: Harvard University Press.

Scribner, S. (1985). Vygostky's use of history. In J. V. Wertsch (Ed.), *Culture, communication and cognition: Vygotskian perspectives* (pp. 119–145). Cambridge: Cambridge University Press.

Searle, J. R. (1995). *The construction of social reality.* London: Penguin.

Valsiner, J. (1998). *The guided mind: A sociogenetic approach to personality.* Cambridge, MA: Harvard University Press.

Valsiner, J., & van der Veer, R. (2000). *The social mind: The construction of an idea.* Cambridge: Cambridge University Press.

Vygotsky, L. S. (1978). *Mind in society: The development of higher psychological processes.* Cambridge, MA: Harvard University Press.

Part III
Encouraging Collective Learning

Chapter 10
Team Coaching in Teacher Teams

Marianne van Woerkom

Higher education is a sector that has to deal with many changes. Where in the past teachers were mainly expected to transfer information to students, they are now supposed to coach students in self-directed learning (Vermunt & Verloop, 1999). More and more, students are supposed to work together on projects and curricula are increasingly being integrated (Isaacson & Bamburg, 1992). All these new expectations presuppose new skills and knowledge of teachers (Van Eekelen, Boshuizen, & Vermunt, 2005). One way to facilitate the development of these new competencies is to combine the different sets of knowledge, skills, experiences, and perspectives of several teachers (Castka, Bamber, Sharp, & Belohoubek, 2001) by working together in teacher teams and by stimulating the process of team learning. Several studies (Borko, 2004; Garet, Porter, Desimone, Birman, & Yoon, 2001) have shown that the alignment of the professional development activities of teachers and the encouragement of communication among them are crucial factors in the success of educational innovation.

Teamwork is a way to stimulate collective learning (Critchley & Casey, 1996; Conley, Fauske, & Pounder, 2004; Kluijtmans, Becker, Crijns, & Sewandono, 2005) and to take individual teachers out of their isolated and individual roles (Conley et al., 2004; Muncey & Conley, 1999). A team can be defined as a group of people within a larger organization, who have a clearly defined team membership and who have a shared responsibility for a team product or service (Edmondson, 1999). Real teams have (1) all team members held responsible for the performance of the overall task, (2) clear boundaries to distinguish members from non-members, and (3) at least moderate stability of team membership (Wageman et al., 2005).

Research shows that teachers in colleges for higher professional education indicate to learn most of meetings with other teachers, followed by having more informal conversations with them (Van Eekelen et al., 2005). Teachers working in teams are responsible for a broad range of work-related issues and therefore have the opportunity to develop themselves more broadly (Pounder, 1999). Also, teachers

M. van Woerkom (✉)
Department of Human Resource Studies, Tilburg University, Tilburg, The Netherlands
e-mail: m.vanwoerkom@uvt.nl

R.F. Poell, M. van Woerkom (eds.), *Supporting Workplace Learning*, Professional and Practice-based Learning 5, DOI 10.1007/978-90-481-9109-3_10, © Springer Science+Business Media B.V. 2011 who work in a team have been found to be more committed to their job, to communicate more with their colleagues, and to have a broader knowledge of the curriculum and their students, in comparison to teachers who do not work in a team (Pounder, 1999).

The cohesion of a teacher team may be an important predictor of the collective learning that takes place in this team (Montes, Moreno, & Morales, 2005; Williams & Duray, 2006). Team cohesion refers to the extent to which team members feel attracted to one another and want to remain part of the team (Dobbins & Zaccaro, 1986; Williams & Duray, 2006). Cohesive teacher teams have been found to communicate more (Prien, 2000) and to develop a better cooperation among the individual teachers (Kidwell, Mossholder, & Bennet, 1997), which may lead to more team learning (Van Woerkom & Sanders, 2010).

It can also be expected that the coaching behavior of a team leader will influence the collective learning in a teacher team. Coaching leaders see mistakes as learning experiences (Yukl, 1998), discuss problems openly in the team (Ellinger & Bostrom, 1999), and give feedback to the team (Ellinger, Ellinger, & Keller, 2005), thereby giving an impetus to the learning activities in the team (Knight, Tait, & Yorke, 2006; Edmondson, 1999). Especially, in a team of highly educated teachers, coaching leadership might be important since, especially in Western cultures, these professionals will not easily tolerate a more autocratic leader. It can also be expected that coaching leaders will positively influence the team cohesion since they build a collective commitment to the task (Wageman et al., 2005) and stimulate the development of high-quality interpersonal relationships in the team (Wageman, 2001). The few studies that are available on managerial coaching behaviors are mostly related to performance (Ellinger, Ellinger, & Keller, 2003; Ellinger et al., 2005).

This chapter reports the results of a study of the relationships between team coaching, team cohesion, and team learning. As far as we are aware, the relationship between team coaching and team learning has not been studied before. We expect that team cohesion partly mediates the relationship between coaching leadership and team learning. When a team leader acts as a coaching leader, this can be expected to lead to a stronger attraction among the team members (Wageman et al., 2005), which in turn may lead to a greater willingness to share and discuss information (Montes et al., 2005; Williams & Duray, 2006) and thereby to team learning. Although teamwork is becoming increasingly popular in organizations (Gittleman, Horrigan, & Joyce, 1998; Osterman, 2000) and also in educational institutions, there is scant research into coaching leadership in the context of work teams (Hackman & Wageman, 2005; Ellinger et al., 2003; Ellinger, 2003).

Theoretical Framework and Hypotheses

Coaching Leadership

In spite of the increasing popularity of coaching leadership in the context of work teams, there is only little empirical research about this concept and its influence on employee perceptions and performance (Popper & Lipshitz, 1992; Yukl, 1994; Hackman & Wageman, 2005). Coaching team leaders do not determine what team members should do and how they should go about this (Wageman et al., 2005; Senge, 1990). They feel responsible for the team members to constantly develop their capabilities in order to deal with the complexity around them and in order to build shared mental models. By entrusting task autonomy to the team, the team leader indicates to trust the team. Team members may react to this by an increased commitment to the task (Goleman, 2000). A coaching leader might, for instance, try to make the team feel responsible for the team performance, provide feedback and information, help the team in developing problem solving strategies to improve the way that team members carry out their tasks (Wageman, 1997), strengthen interpersonal relationships, solve conflicts, and motivate the team for a common purpose (Wageman et al., 2005). The short-term goal of team coaching is to improve the team processes and team performance, the long-term goal is, however, to develop the team's capability to deal with changing circumstances (Egberts, Verheul, Fisscher, & Vinke, 1993).

Team Cohesion

One can distinguish between two forms of team cohesion, namely, social cohesion and task cohesion (Van Vianen & De Dreu, 2001). Social cohesion refers to the attraction of an individual to the group as a consequence of the positive relationships among the other group members and the wish to remain part of the team (Michalisin, Karau, & Tangpong, 2004; Dobbins & Zaccaro, 1986; Williams & Duray, 2006; Shaw, 1981; Yukl, 1998). Task cohesion refers to the extent to which individuals are attracted to the group as a result of a shared commitment to the group task (Zaccaro, 1991). In this study we focus on social cohesion since we expect that team learning will especially benefit from social cohesion (Montes et al., 2005; Williams & Duray, 2006). In a cohesive group team members feel close to each other, resulting in an increased consensus about the group goals (Houldsworth & Mathews, 2000), more cooperative behavior (Kidwell, Mossholder, & Bennett, 1997; Sanders & Van Emmerik, 2004), openness (Berman, West, & Richter, 2002), and knowledge-sharing among team members (Van Woerkom & Sanders, 2010). Since team learning can be seen of as a form of cooperative behavior and knowledge-sharing behavior of team members, we expect that team learning will be affected by social cohesion.

The Relationship Between Team Coaching and Team Cohesion

Team leaders are likely to influence the internal group processes. Burke, Stagl, Klein, Goodwin, Salas, and Halpin (2006) show that coaching leadership can be characterized by 'consideration' for developing social relationships in the group (one of the elements of transformational leadership) and developing group cohesion. This has been confirmed by the study of Thornhill and Saunders (1998) who found that subordinates with a coaching leader feel more committed to the team. Although the relationship between team coaching and team cohesion has not been studied before, we can therefore expect that there is a positive relationship between team coaching and team cohesion. Therefore we expect that:

H1: There is a positive relationship between team coaching and team cohesion.

Team Learning

There is no universal definition of the concept of team learning (Wilson, Goodman, & Cronin, 2007). Some researchers see team learning as an outcome (Ellis, Hollenbeck, Porter, Ilgen, West, & Moon, 2003), a permanent change in the team's collective level of knowledge and skills that is developed by the shared experiences of team members (Ellis et al., 2007). Other researchers see team learning as a process which may, but not necessarily will, lead to an improved performance (Edmondson, 1999; Van Offenbeek, 2001). In this study we choose to define team learning as the process of information acquisition, information distribution, information interpretation and information storage and retrieval, by which teams may create knowledge for themselves or others (Huber, 1991; Kasl, Marsick, & Dechant, 1997; Van Offenbeek, 2001). By information acquisition team members obtain information by scanning or inquiring into the environment. By information distribution and interpretation they distribute information to each other and give shared interpretations to this information. By information storage and retrieval, they store the information that has been shared in their collective memory (Van Woerkom & Van Engen, 2009) or by putting it on paper, entering it into meeting minutes or adding it to a database and use it again in the future (Van Offenbeek, 2001).

The Relationship Between Team Cohesion and Team Learning

It can be expected that team cohesion raises the knowledge exchange between team members (Williams & Duray, 2006; Prien, 2000) as has also been shown by Van Woerkom and Sanders (2010). Cohesive teams have a high collective group identification and shared norms and values (Yukl, 1998). The common interest of the group is more important than in low cohesive teams (Shaw, 1981) as a result of which team members will not withhold important information from each other. Because the team members of cohesive teams feel attracted to each other, they are more inclined to collaborate and communicate with each other (Prien, 2000; Kidwell et al., 1997). Because team members in cohesive teams are more sensitive toward each other, they tend to give help and assistance to each other (Schachter, Ellertson, McBride & Gregory, in Kidwell et al., 1997). For these reasons, it can be expected that both the quality and the quantity of the interaction in the team will be influenced by the team's cohesiveness (Shaw, 1981). Cohesive teams will have more positive social contacts (Kidwell et al., 1997; Shaw, 1981) and will develop an atmosphere of trust and cooperation which will positively affect the team-learning process (Williams & Duray, 2006). Cohesiveness will diminish the interpersonal conflicts in the group so that team members can pay more attention to the task (Dobbins & Zaccaro, 1986). Cohesive teams can also be expected to have lower levels of employee turn-over (Forsyth, 1983) which may have a positive effect on the storage and retrieval of information.

Several studies show a positive relationship between team cohesion and team learning (Montes et al., 2005; Williams & Duray, 2006). Van Woerkom and Sanders (2010) show that a high level of group cohesion is positively related to team members asking and giving advice to each other and to an openness for different opinions and perspectives which can be seen as essential aspects of team learning (Wilson et al., 2007). Therefore we hypothesize that:

H2: There is a positive relationship between team cohesion and team learning.

The Relationship Between Team Coaching and Team Learning

Edmondson (1999) showed that coaching leadership by the team leader is positively related to team learning. Team coaches may create a safe climate in which team members feel free to be open about mistakes and discuss these with other team members (Edmondson, 1999). Coaching leaders tend to see mistakes made by team members as learning experiences instead of as personal failure (Yukl, 1998) and therefore they may enhance the learning process in the long run (Goleman, 2000). Ellinger et al. (2005) indicate that coaching leadership may result in employees interpreting team activities and experiences as an input for learning. Furthermore, coaching managers stimulate learning processes in teams by openly discussing problems and working toward a solution for these problems (Ellinger & Bostrom, 1999). By the feedback that the coaching leaders give, effective performance will be stimulated while ineffective performance will be noticed (Ellinger et al., 2005). It can be expected that team members will feel free to experiment when they know they will receive constructive feedback (Goleman, 2000). This may lead to team members learning on an individual basis, but when they share the outcomes of their experiments with other team members, also to team learning. A coaching leader is also likely to stimulate reflection in the team by stimulating individuals to analyze their behavior and talk about this with others, which will lead to learning experiences (Engelen, 2002). Ellinger (2003) showed that managers define the term 'coach' as 'facilitator of learning.'

Other studies showed a positive relationship between coaching leadership and team performance (Ellinger et al., 2003, 2005). Although the underlying process leading to an improved performance has not been included in these studies, it seems plausible that team learning will play a mediating role in the relationship between team coaching and team performance, since several studies have shown that team learning is a powerful predictor of team performance (Chan, Lim, & Keasberry, 2003; Edmonson, 1999; Savelsbergh, 2010; Van Woerkom & Croon, 2009; Van

Woerkom & Van Engen, 2009; Zellmer-Bruhn & Gibson, 2006). Therefore we expect that:

H3: There is a positive relationship between team coaching and team learning.

The Mediating Effect of Team Cohesion

It seems likely that team cohesion is a partial mediator in the relationship between team coaching and team learning. When a team leader displays coaching leadership behaviors, this will result in a stronger attraction among team members (Wageman et al., 2005) which will in turn result in increased levels of team learning (Montes et al., 2005; Williams & Duray, 2006). Since we also expect a direct effect of team coaching on team learning (see above), we therefore expect that

H4: The relationship between coaching leadership and team learning is partially mediated by team cohesion.

The conceptual model that summarizes our hypotheses is represented in Fig. 10.1.

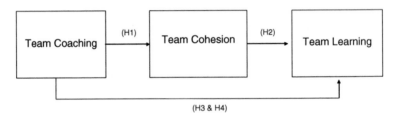

Fig. 10.1 Conceptual model of the study

Method

We conducted cross-sectional survey research, collecting data by means of a written questionnaire among 90 teacher teams within 13 of all 52 institutions for higher professional education in the Netherlands (CBS, 2007). These institutions were contacted by email or telephone, after which an appointment was made with a contact person (usually a managing director or a manager of an educational program). In the following step, questionnaires were distributed to the teacher teams by two MSc students who participated in this research project. The following teams participated in our study: teams of teachers with a similar expertise (for instance, all language teachers), teams that were formed around a program year (for instance, all teachers involved in the first year of an educational program) or teams that were formed around a specialization in the program.

We distributed 891 questionnaires of which 399 were returned, resulting in a response rate of 45%. After teams with response rates below 20% were deleted from the data set, the final data set consisted of 72 teams with an average of 10 team members. Of the 371 respondents that were included in the data set 47.3% were women, which is almost the same as in the population of teachers working in higher professional education (in the year 2005 43.5% of this population was female) (CBS, 2007). The average age in our sample was 44.9 years, which also equals the age in the population (45 years old) (CBS, 2007). Thirty-three percent of the respondents had an educational background in higher professional education, while 63% of the respondents had an academic background. This is slightly different from the population, in which 50% of the teachers have an academic background, while 40% have a higher professional education background, and 10% have an uncompleted academic education. Team members in our sample had an average team tenure of five and a half years.

Instruments

Team members were asked to indicate their perceptions of team coaching, team cohesion, and team learning. Unless otherwise stated, we assessed all variables by questionnaire items with a response scale ranging from 1, 'strongly disagree' to 7, 'strongly agree.'

Team Coaching. The variable team coaching was measured by using the scales task-focused coaching and interpersonal coaching developed by Wageman and Hackman (2005). Together, these scales consisted of eight items. Example items are 'the team leader helps the team identify and use well each member's unique talents' and 'the team leader helps members to resolve any conflicts that may develop among them.' A Principal Components Analysis (PCA) and Catell's scree test showed that all items loaded on one component, team coaching. The alpha of this scale was 0.95.

Team Cohesion. To measure team cohesion we used a scale developed by Dobbins and Zaccaro (1986) consisting of eight items, for example: 'the members of my team get along well' and 'if I had the chance, I would leave my team and join another team.' After deletion of one item this scale had an alpha of 0.87.

Team Learning. We measured team learning with a scale from Van Offenbeek (2001) consisting of 26 items. In previous research (Van Woerkom & Van Engen, 2009) this scale showed a reliability (Cronbach's alpha) of 0.97. Example items of this scale are 'in my team we search for professional information and knowledge outside the organization' 'in my team we challenge each other to take new perspectives concerning our work,' and 'my team refers to documents made previously.' A Catell scree test showed that a one-factor solution was the most appropriate and that all items loaded sufficiently on this component. Cronbach's alpha in this study was 0.94.

As can be seen in Table 10.1, all ICC1 values (referring to the proportion of the total amount of variance in the data that is between the teams) and all ICC2 values (representing the reliability of the group means) of the scales described above were acceptable, allowing for aggregation to the team level.

Control Variables. We controlled for the extent to which teams in our sample were 'real' teams (Wageman et al., 2005) in terms of having some degree of

Table 10.1 ICC1 and ICC2
Scores of team learning, team
cohesion, and team coaching

Variable	ICC1	ICC2
Team learning	0.27	0.62
Team cohesion	0.12	0.63
Team coaching	0.23	0.57

stability of team membership, having clear boundaries and the extent to which team members were independent in their task execution. For this purpose we used nine items developed by Wageman and Hackman (2005). An example item of stability of membership was 'this team is quite stable, with few changes in membership.' An example items for boundedness was 'team membership is quite clear – everybody knows exactly who is and who isn't on this team.' An example item (negative) for task interdependency was 'Members of this team have their own individual jobs to do, with little need for them to work together.' A PCA on the nine items showed a simple structure with items referring to boundedness, stability, and interdependency loading on separate factors. Stability had an alpha of 0.76 (3 items), boundedness had an alpha of 0.68 (3 items), and interdependency had an alpha of 0.64 (3 items).

Analysis

Since our theoretical concepts were all on the team level, we aggregated our data to the team level by taking the mean value of the team members' scores. We tested our hypotheses in hierarchical multiple regression models.

Results

Table 10.2 reports the descriptive statistics and the correlations among the aggregated variables. As can be seen, team coaching is positively related to team learning ($r = 0.43$, $p < 0.01$), to team cohesion ($r = 0.54$, $p < 0.01$), and to boundedness ($r = 0.28$, $p < 0.05$). Moreover, team cohesion is positively related to team learning ($r = 0.67$, $p < 0.01$), to task interdependency ($r = 0.38$, $p < 0.01$), and to boundedness ($r = 0.31$, $p < 0.01$). Also, team learning is positively related to interdependency ($r = 0.48$, $p < 0.01$) and to boundedness ($r = 0.45$, $p < 0.01$). Although stability was not related to any of the other variables, we decided to include all three features of a real team in our subsequent regression analyses. Since gender ratio, average age, average level of education, average team tenure, and team size were not related to our main variables, we decided not to include these variables in the regression analyses.

Regression Analyses

We tested our hypotheses in a hierarchical multiple regression model (see Table 10.3). In step 1 we predicted team cohesion from team coaching while in

Table 10.2 Descriptive statistics and correlations

	Mean	SD	1.	2.	3.	4.	5.	6.	7.	8.	9.	10.
1. Team learning	4.74	0.59										
2. Team cohesion	5.04	0.70	0.67***									
3. Team coaching	4.77	0.84	0.43***	0.54***								
4. Gender ratio (0 = male, 1 = female)	0.47	0.30	0.11	0.05	0.15							
5. Average age	44.9	6.03	−0.13	−0.06	−0.01	0.24**						
6. Educational background	1.66	0.27	−0.04	−0.09	−0.05	−0.10	0.09					
7. Average team tenure	4.70	4.48	0.01	0.05	−0.09	−0.23***	0.24**	−0.09				
8. Team size	9.93	5.74	−0.13	−0.06	−0.19	−0.02	−0.13	0.07	0.24**			
9. Interdependency	4.84	0.66	0.48***	0.38***	−0.03	−0.06	0.21*	0.06	0.08	−0.16		
10. Stability	4.66	1.12	0.04	0.18	0.17	−0.13	0.21*	−0.22*	−0.03	−0.21*	−0.06	
11. Boundedness	5.54	0.84	0.45***	0.31***	0.28**	−0.04	0.20*	−0.22*	0.14	−0.21*	0.35***	0.31***

***$p < 0.01$ **$p < 0.05$, *$p < 0.10$

Table 10.3 Results of the regression analyses predicting team cohesion from team coaching

	Team cohesion	
Independent variables	β	β
Team coaching	0.54***	0.54***
Control variables		
Interdependency		0.41***
Stability of membership		0.13
Team boundedness		−0.02
R^2	0.29	0.46
Delta R^2		0.17
F	0.27.64***	13.70***

$N = 72;\ ***p < 0.01$

Table 10.4 Results of regression analyses predicting team learning from team coaching, mediated by team cohesion

	Team learning					
Independent variables	β	β	β	β	β	β
Team coaching	0.43***	0.40***			0.10	0.15
Team cohesion			0.67	0.54***	0.61***	0.45***
Control variables						
Interdependency		0.41***		0.18*		0.23**
Stability of membership		−0.06		−0.12		−0.18
Team boundedness		0.22*		0.26***		0.23**
R2	0.19	0.46	0.45	0.56	0.46	0.57
Delta R2	0.19	0.28	0.45	0.11	0.46	0.12
F	15.44***	13.79***	55.84***	20.95***	27.53***	16.96***
Sobel test						3.27***

$***\ p < 0.01,\ **\ p < 0.05,\ *p < 0.10$

step 2 we controlled for stability, boundedness, and interdependency. As we can see in Table 10.3, both model 1 ($F = 27.64, p < 0.01$) and model 2 ($F = 13.70, p < 0.01$) are significant and team coaching is positively related to team cohesion ($\beta = 0.54$, $p < 0.01$) (hypothesis 1 corroborated).

Table 10.4 shows the results of the regression analyses of team coaching and team cohesion on team learning. To test for the hypothesized mediation effect we applied the procedure suggested by MacKinnon, Fairchild, and Fritz (2007) who argue that a mediation exists if (1) the independent variable (team coaching) has a significant effect on the mediating variable (team cohesion), and (2) the mediating variable (team cohesion) has a significant effect on the dependent variable (team learning) in a regression analysis of the independent and mediating variable on the dependent variable. If, in this analysis, team coaching has no significant effect on team learning, we have a case of pure mediation. If team coaching (in addition to team cohesion) does have a significant effect on team learning, we have a case of partial mediation.

The analyses show that there is a significant positive relationship between team coaching and team learning, which remains significant after the control variables have been added ($\beta = 0.40$, $p < 0.01$). Team cohesion is also positively related to team learning, also when we control for the real-team characteristics ($\beta = 0.54$, $p < 0.01$) (hypothesis 2 corroborated). When we add both team coaching and team cohesion to the equation, the significant effect of team coaching disappears ($\beta = 0.15$, n.s.), while the effect of team cohesion remains significant ($\beta = 0.45$, $p < 0.01$), indicating that team cohesion is a full mediator in the relationship between team coaching and team learning, also evidenced by the Sobel test for mediation. This means that hypothesis 3 (there is a positive relationship between team coaching and team learning) cannot be confirmed. The control variables interdependency ($\beta = 0.23$, $p < 0.05$) and boundedness both appear to be positively related to team learning equally strongly ($\beta = 0.23$, $p < 0.05$).

All findings are summarized in Fig. 10.2.

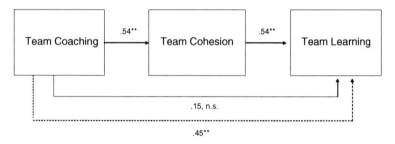

Fig. 10.2   Summary of the study findings (dotted line represents the mediated relationship)

Discussion

This study shows that team-learning processes may be stimulated by creating team cohesion. This is in line with earlier studies (Montes et al., 2005; Williams & Duray, 2006). Cohesion is likely to lead to more and better communication (Prien, 2000) and a better collaboration (Kidwell et al., 1997; Prien, 2000) resulting in higher levels of team learning. Van Woerkom and Sanders (2010) conclude that cohesion is a precondition for knowledge-sharing. Furthermore, team coaching seems to be a good way to develop team cohesion by stimulating a collective commitment to the task. Other studies showed that minimizing hierarchy (Pettigrew & Whipp, 1991), encouraging transformational leadership (Pillai & Williams, 2004), and implementing self-directed teams (Moravec, 1997) can be antecedents of team cohesion. As far as we are aware, the present study is the first to show that cohesion can also be stimulated by team coaching.

Furthermore, our results show that team coaching does not lead directly to team learning but is able to create conditions for team learning by helping the team members to build a collective commitment and to improve their interpersonal relationships. Also teams with clear boundaries and high interdependency among members experience more team learning than other teams. It seems likely that in these teams there is a greater need and commitment to use the collective knowledge and skills of all team members to get the work done.

Also, team cohesion proves to be higher in teams with a high interdependency and clear boundaries. This means that another way to stimulate team cohesion, and thereby also team learning is to create a team structure in which team members really need to communicate and coordinate among each other to get the work done, and to be very clear about the membership of the team, for instance, by labeling the team and by organizing team activities that emphasize the team identity.

Institutions for higher professional education need to deal with many changes (Vermunt &Verloop, 1999; Isaacson & Bamburg, 1992) which imply new demands on the knowledge and skills for teachers (Van Eekelen et al., 2005). By working in teams, collective learning can be stimulated (Critchley & Casey, 1996; Conley et al., 2004) which may take individual teachers out of their isolated roles (Conley et al., 2004; Muncey & Conley, 1999) and which may make it easier for them to develop the required competencies. Moreover, whereas teachers used to have a relatively autonomous position within their classrooms and their institutions, pedagogical changes ask for more collaboration between teachers (Lieberman, 2000; Seezink & Van der Sanden, 2005; Van Woerkom, 2010). Increasingly, the learning process of students is not just seen as the responsibility of one teacher but as a collective responsibility of all teachers (Van Veen, Sleegers, Bergen, & Klaassen, 1999). In many countries collaborative structures inside schools are being built to reverse the isolation felt by many teachers (Lieberman, 2000). Therefore, teachers will need a greater readiness to work and learn collaboratively in the school community (Niemi, 2002).

Practical Implications

For institutions for higher professional education that want to stimulate their teachers teams to be innovative and to remain up to date in terms of knowledge and skills and that want to stimulate collaboration and collective responsibility among teachers, it is wise to pay attention to team cohesion. According to a manager who participated in this study, teachers who work on the same team do not have to like each other, but need to be professional and be able to share knowledge with their colleagues even if they do not like each other too much. However, since this study shows that the chance of team learning taking place increases when team members do feel attracted to each other, it seems important to stimulate the interpersonal relations in a team and to make this an explicit goal for team leaders. Team leaders might be selected on the basis of their coaching skills and assessed in their appraisal interviews on the energy that they put into strengthening team cohesion. Furthermore, it is important to keep investing in the coaching skills of team leaders by training and development or by creating a team of team leaders, which may serve as a platform to exchange ideas and perspectives on their jobs.

The concept of team coaching as a form of leadership is relatively new compared to more established leadership theories (such as the theory about transactional, transformational, and laissez-faire leadership; Bass, 1990). However, this concept does seem to have a high validity in the context of teacher teams in higher education. In these teams, team leaders need to manage relatively small teams of teachers, are often also participating in the team as one of the team members, but are taking on an extra role as team leader. It is likely that the highly educated teachers, who are experts in their area of teaching, will demand a large degree of autonomy and are not likely to accept a transactional leader. On the other hand, the concept of charismatic leadership or transformational leadership seems to be too 'strong' for a leader who is also participating as one of the team members in a small team. Creating positions for coaching leaders, who facilitate positive team processes such as team learning and knowledge-sharing and who help the team in coordinating and monitoring its own work, may be a solution for the sometimes disappointing results of self-directed teams, which are nevertheless becoming increasingly popular in educational institutions (Van der Linden, Teurlings & Vermeulen, 2003).

Implications for Further Research

In this study, we have focused on the role that team leaders can play in stimulating team-learning processes. A next interesting step for research might be to investigate to what extent coaching leaders can also enhance the development of individual team members. Further research might also focus on the difficulties that team leaders may face in their role of learning facilitator. Team leaders may feel that they are not recognized or rewarded for this role, see their developmental role as a distraction from their managing role, or more as a responsibility of the training and development department (Ellinger & Bostrom, 1999). Also, it may be difficult to unite the role of team leader and the role of coach (Ellinger & Bostrom, 2002). While the management role implies being in charge, telling, judging, and controlling, the coach role means helping and empowering people to succeed. Further research might therefore investigate the dilemmas of team leader coaching, addressing how team leaders balance between direct control versus process consultation, the interest of individual team members versus the collective interest of the team, and sustaining long-term results versus responding to short-term performance demands.

Acknowledgements The author would like to thank Renée van Schaik, MSc, and Tessa de Nijst, MSc, for their work on this research project.

References

Akgün, A. E., & Lynn, G. S. (2002). Antecedents and consequences of team stability on new product development performance. *Journal of Engineering and Technology Management, 19*, 263–286.

Argote, L. (1999). *Organizational learning: creating, retaining and transferring knowledge.* Boston, MA: Kluwer.

Bass, B. M. (1990). From transactional to transformational leadership: Learning to share the vision. *Organizational Dynamics, 18*, 19–31.

Bliese, P. (2000). Within-group agreement, non-independence, and reliability. In K. Klein & S. Kozlowski (Eds.), *Multi-level theory, research, and methods in organizations* (pp. 349–381). San Francisco: Jossey-Bass.

Bolhuis, P., Hoffius, R. G. H., & Grijpstra, D. H. (2007). Zwaar weer op komst. Arbeidsmarktmonitor voor personeel in het hbo 2007 [Severe weather to come: Labor market statistics personnel in Higher Education]. Retrieved May 19, 2008, from http://www.arbeidsmarktvisie.nl/media/pdf/B3268.pdf

Borko, H. (2004). Professional development and teacher learning: Mapping the terrain. *Educational Researcher, 33*(8), 3–15.

Burke, C. S., Stagl, K. C., Klein, C., Goodwin, G. F., Salas, E., & Halpin, S. M. (2006). What type of leadership behaviours are functional in teams? A meta-analysis. *The Leadership Quarterly, 17*, 288–307.

Castka, P., Bamber, C. J., Sharp, J. M., & Belohoubek, P. (2001). Factors affecting successful implementation of high performance teams. *Team Performance Management, 7*, 123–134.

CBS (2007). Jaarboek onderwijs in cijfers 2007. [Year book education in numbers 2007] Voorburg: Centraal bureau voor de statistiek. Retrieved May 19, 2008, from http://www.cbs.nl/NR/rdonlyres/7776AD12-1045-4177-9423-1201982C8247/0/2007f162pub.pdf

Chan, C. A., Lim, L., & Keasberry, S. K. (2003). Examining the linkages between team learning behaviors and team performance. *The Learning Organization, 10*, 228–236.

Chan, C. C. A., Pearson, C., & Entrekin, L. (2003). Examining the effects of internal and external team learning on team performance. *Team Performance Management, 9*, 174–181.

Chang, A., & Bordia, P. (2001). A multidimensional approach to the group cohesion – group performance relationship. *Small Group Research, 32*, 379–405.

Conley, S., Fauske, J., & Pounder, D. G. (2004). Teacher work group effectiveness. *Educational Administration Quarterly, 40*, 663–703.

Critchley, B., & Casey, D. (1996). Second thoughts on team building. *Management Education and Development, 15*, 163–175.

Dobbins, G. H., & Zaccaro, S. J. (1986). The effects of group cohesion and leader behavior on subordinate satisfaction. *Group & Organization Studies, 11*, 203–219.

Edmondson, A. (1999). Psychological safety and learning behavior in work teams. *Administrative Science Quarterly, 44*, 350–383.

Egberts, M. E., Verheul, A. D., Fisscher, O. A. M., & Vinke, R. H. W. (1993). *De manager als Coach* [The manager as coach]. Deventer: Kluwer Bedrijfswetenschappen.

Ellinger, A. D. (2003). Antecedents and consequences of coaching behavior. *Performance Improvement Quarterly, 16*, 5–28.

Ellinger, A. D., & Bostrom, R. P. (1999). Managerial coaching behaviors in learning organizations. *The Journal of Management Development, 18*, 752–771.

Ellinger, A. D., Ellinger, A. E., & Keller, S. B. (2003). Supervisory coaching behavior, employee satisfaction, and warehouse employee performance: A dyadic perspective in the distribution industry. *Human Resource Development Quarterly, 14*, 435–458.

Ellinger, A. E., Ellinger, A. D., & Keller, S. B. (2005). Supervisory coaching in a logistics context. *International Journal of Physical Distribution & Logistics Management, 35*, 620–636.

Ellis, A. P. J., Hollenbeck, J. R., Porter, C. O. L. H., Ilgen, D. R., West, B. J., & Moon, H. (2003). Team learning: collectively connecting the dots. *Journal of Applied Psychology, 88*, 821–835.

Engelen, A. J. A. (2002). *Coaching binnenstebuiten. Een onderzoek naar coaching van docenten door docenten [Coaching inside out. A study of peer coaching among teachers].* Nijmegen: University Press.

Forsyth, D. R. (1983). *Group dynamics.* Pacific Grove, CA: Brooks/Cole.

Garet, M. S., Porter, A. C., Desimone, L., Birman, B. F., & Yoon, K. S. (2001). What makes professional development effective? Results from a national sample of teachers. *American Educational Research Journal, 38,* 915–945.

Geijsel, F., & Meijers, F. (2005). Identity learning: the core process of educational change. *Educational Studies, 31,* 419–430.

Gittleman, M., Horrigan, M., & Joyce, M. (1998). 'Flexible' workplace practices: Evidence from a nationally represented survey. *Industrial and Labour Relations Review, 52,* 99–115.

Goleman, D. (2000). Leiderschap dat resultaten oplevert [Leading for results]. *HRMagazine, 46,* 35–49.

Hackman, J. R., & Wageman, R. (2005). A theory on team coaching. *Academy of Management Review, 30,* 269–287.

Houldsworth, C., & Mathews, B. P. (2000). Group composition, performance and educational attainment. *Education & Training, 42,* 40–53.

Huber, G. P. (1991). Organizational learning: The contributing processes and the literatures. *Organization Science, 2,* 88–115.

Isaacson, N., & Bamburg, J. (1992). Can schools become learning organizations? *Educational Leadership, 50,* 42–44.

Kasl, E., Marsick, V. J., & Dechant, K. (1997). Teams as learners: A research-based model of team learning. *The Journal of Applied Behavioral Science, 33,* 227–246.

Kidwell, R. E., Jr., Mossholder, K. W., & Bennet, N. (1997). Cohesiveness and organizational citizenship behavior. A multilevel analysis using work groups and individuals. *Journal of Management, 23,* 775–793.

Kluijtmans, F., Becker, B., Crijns, M., & Sewandono, I. (2005). *Anders leren, anders organiseren!? [Learn differently, organize differently].* Nederland: Open Universiteit.

Knight, P., Tait, J., & Yorke, M. (2006). The professional learning of teachers in higher education. *Studies in Higher Education, 31,* 319–339.

Lieberman, A. (2000). Networks as learning communities: Shaping the future of teacher development. *Journal of Teacher Education, 51,* 221–227.

Mackinnon, D. P., Fairchild, A. J., & Matthew, S. (2007). Mediation analysis. *Annual Review of Psychology, 58,* 593–614.

Michalisin, M. D., Karau, S., & Tangpong, C. (2004). The effects of performance and team cohesion on attribution: A longitudinal simulation. *Journal of Business Research, 57,* 1108–1115.

Montes, F. J. L., Moreno, A. R., & Morales, V. G. (2005). Influence of support leadership and teamwork cohesion on organizational learning, innovation and performance: An empirical examination. *Technovation, 25,* 1159–1172.

Moravec, M., Johannessen, O. J., & Hjelmas, T. A. (1997). Thumbs up for self-managed teams. *Management Review, 86,* 42–47.

Muncey, D. E., & Conley, S. (1999). Teacher compensation and teacher teaming: Sketching the terrain. *Journal of Personnel Evaluation in Education, 4,* 365–385.

Niemi, H. (2002). Active learning-a cultural change needed in teacher education and schools. *Teaching and Teacher Education, 18,* 763–780.

Osterman, P. (2000). Work reorganization in an era of restructuring: Trends in diffusion and effects on employee welfare. *Industrial and Labor Relations Review, 53,* 179–196.

Pettigrew, A., & Whipp, R. (1991). *Managing change for competitive success.* Oxford: Blackwell.

Pillai, R., & Williams, E. A. (2004). Transformational leadership, self-efficacy, group cohesiveness, commitment and performance. *Journal of Organizational Change Management, 17,* 144–159.

Popper, M., & Lipshitz, R. (1992). Coaching on leadership. *Leadership & Organization Development Journal, 13,* 15–18.

Pounder, D. G. (1999). Teacher teams: Exploring job characteristics and work-related outcomes of work group enhancement. *Educational Administration Quarterly, 35,* 317–348.

Prien, K. O. (2000). The effects of cooperative learning, cohesion, and commitment on team performance. *ProQuest Dissertations and Theses, 454*, 249.

Savelsbergh, C. (2010). *Team learning behaviors, role stress and performance in project teams.* PhD dissertation, Tilburg University, The Netherlands.

Seezink, A., & Van der Sanden, J. M. M. (2005). Lerend werken in de docentenwerkplaats: Praktijktheorieën van docenten over competentiegericht voorbereidend middelbaar beroepsonderwijs. [Learning and working within a 'teachers' workplace': Teachers' practical theories about competence-oriented prevocational secondary education]. *Pedagogische Studiën, 82*(4), 275–292.

Senge, P. (1990). *The fifth discipline.* New York: Doubleday.

Shaw, M. E. (1981). *Group dynamics: the psychology of small group behavior.* New York: McGraw-Hill.

Thornhill, A., & Saunders, M. N. K. (1998). What if line managers don't realize they're responsible for HR? *Personnel Review, 27*, 460.

Van der Linden, R., Teurlings, C., & Vermeulen, M. (2003). *De school als professionele Organisatie. Opbrengsten van vijf jaar kortlopend onderwijs onderzoek (1998–2002) [The school as professional organization. Results of five years of short term educational research (1998–2002)].* Tilburg: IVA beleidsonderzoek en advies.

Van der Vegt, G. S., Bunderson, J. S., & Oosterhof, A. (2006). Expertness diversity and interpersonal helping in teams: Why those who need the most help end up getting the least. *Academy of Management Journal, 49*, 877–893.

Van Eekelen, I. M., Boshuizen, H. P. A., & Vermunt, J. D. (2005). Self-regulation in higher education teacher learning. *Higher Education, 50*, 447–471.

Van Offenbeek, M. (2001). Processes and outcomes of team learning. *European Journal of Work and Organizational Psychology, 10*, 303–317.

Van Veen, K., Sleegers, P., Bergen, T., & Klaassen, C. (1999). Opvattingen van docenten in het voortgezet onderwijs over hun professionaliteit. *Pedagogisch Tijdschrift, 24*(4), 401–431.

Van Vianen, A. E. M., & De Dreu, C. K. W. (2001). Personality in teams: Its relationship to social cohesion, task cohesion, and team performance. *European Journal of Work and Organizational Psychology, 10*, 97–120.

Van Woerkom, M. (2010). The relation between broad professional identity, professionalization activities and a broad coaching style of teacher educators. In M. Van Woerkom & R. F. Poell (Eds.), *Workplace Learning. Concepts, measurement and application.* London: Routledge, pp. 200–215.

Van Woerkom, M., & Sanders, K. (2010). The romance of learning from disagreement. The effect of cohesiveness and disagreement on knowledge sharing behavior and individual performance within teams, *Journal of Business Psychology, 25*, 139–149.

Van Woerkom, M., & Van Engen, M. L. (2009). Learning from conflicts? The effect of task and relationship conflicts on team learning and team performance. *European Journal of Work and Organizational Psychology, 18*, 381–404.

Wageman, R. (1995). Interdependence and group effectiveness. *Administrative Science Quarterly, 40*, 145–180.

Wageman, R. (1997). Critical success factors for creating superb self-managing teams. *Organizational Dynamics, 26*, 49–61.

Wageman, R. (2001). How leaders foster self-managing team effectiveness: Design choices versus hands-on coaching. *Organization Science, 12*, 559–577.

Wageman, R., Hackman, J. R., & Lehman, E. (2005). Team diagnostic survey: Development of an instrument. *The Journal of Applied Behavioral Science, 41*, 373–398.

Williams, E. A., & Duray, R. (2006). Teamwork orientation, group cohesiveness, and student learning: A study of the use of teams in online distance education. *Journal of Management Education, 30*, 592–616.

Wilson, J. M., Goodman, P. S., & Cronin, M. A. (2007). Group learning. *Academy of Management Review, 32*, 1041–1059.

Yukl, G. (1994). *Leadership in Organizations*. New Jersey: Prentice-Hall.

Yukl, G. (1998). *Leadership in Organizations*. New Jersey: Prentice-Hall.

Zaccaro, S. J. (1991). Nonequivalent associations between forms of cohesiveness and group-related outcomes: Evidence for multidimensionality. *Journal of Social Psychology, 131*, 387.

Zellmer-Bruhn, M., & Gibson, C. (2006). Multinational organization context: Implications for team learning and performance. *Academy of Management Journal, 49*, 501–518.

Chapter 11
Learning with the Intention of Innovating: Eleven Design Principles for Knowledge Productivity

Suzanne Verdonschot and Paul Keursten

Our society is gradually becoming a knowledge society. Peter Drucker (1993) speaks of a revolution that is comparable to the industrial revolution that started in the 18th century. This means that the traditional factors of production, labour, land and capital make way for the factor of the production of 'knowledge'. By applying knowledge, people develop gradual improvement and radical innovations that lead to new products and services which provide for economic growth. This shift from an industrial society towards a knowledge society requires a change in the focus of learning in the context of work. In order to be successful in a knowledge economy learning with the intention of innovating becomes increasingly important.

Learning with the intention of innovating is a special form of learning. For a long time, learning in the context of work was organised serially (Nieuwenhuis & Van Woerkom, 2007): first learning, and then the application of this learning at the workplace. However, the effects of these training programmes in terms of the transfer of what had been learned to the workplace were disappointing (see, Baldwin & Ford, 1988; Burke & Baldwin, 1999). This was one of the reasons why the focus shifted from a training orientation to a learning orientation (Marsick & Watkins, 1990). Notions such as work-based learning, work-related learning and workplace learning emerged. Many of the learning processes that take place at work focus on helping employees to become better at their work. For instance, by observing a more experienced colleague at work, one can learn the intricacies of the profession. However, learning with the intention of innovating refers to another form of learning. It is not so much initiated from the perspective of learning (How can I become better at this task?), but rather from the perspective of work (How could we solve this problem?). This is the kind of learning that takes place when a difficult question or problematic situation arises for which no solution has been found yet. Then, learning and working coincide. To enable this process, the work environment should be a rich learning environment (Kessels & Van der Werff, 2002). In this case, learning is not seen as a means to support the work, but rather as something which itself adds value to the work by improving and innovating it.

S. Verdonschot (✉)
Kessels & Smit, The Learning Company, Utrecht, The Netherlands
e-mail: sverdonschot@kessels-smit.com

R.F. Poell, M. van Woerkom (eds.), *Supporting Workplace Learning*, Professional and Practice-based Learning 5, DOI 10.1007/978-90-481-9109-3_11,

The concept of knowledge productivity (Kessels, 2001) integrates the notions of learning and innovating. Knowledge productivity refers to the processes through which new knowledge is developed, contributing to the gradual improvements and radical innovations of products, services and operating procedures.

In environments in which the desired outcome is to achieve standardisation, repetitive routines and fixed procedures, the desired level of performance can be clearly described. In these environments a gap analysis helps to identify the required learning interventions. However, when the desired situation cannot be defined clearly, which is the case with questions whose answers are aimed at leading to innovative solutions, a clear path of interventions cannot be defined. Then, the desired situation cannot be defined clearly and a clear path of interventions cannot be defined in advance. It is not possible to systematically design a learning process that analyses the actual and the desired situation and to design a learning process to overcome the gap (Keursten, 1999). Learning with the intention of innovating is a process that happens in practice and that is about creating a context in which people participate and thereby acquire the abilities needed (Brown & Duguid, 1991).

This process of learning in practice for innovation cannot be managed systematically (Harkema, 2004; Van de Ven, Angle, & Poole, 1989). The term management implies control of processes that may be inherently uncontrollable (Von Krogh, Ichijo, & Nonaka, 2000). It is a learning process that takes place while working, driven by people who are motivated to find answers to the intriguing questions they encounter.

The aim of this research is to better understand the learning processes undertaken by employees with the intention of gradually improving or radically innovating their organisations' products, processes and services.

Problem Statement

The idea that people and learning processes are the only true source of competitive advantage in a world where products can so easily be replicated (Walton, 1999) and the fact that high levels of success can only be achieved in organisations that are able to develop creativity and innovation (Majaro, in: Walton, 1999) caused this study. The learning processes necessary for innovation cannot take place through training, nor can they occur through systematic management. Rather they are part of the daily work, during innovation and improvement processes. They are seldom deliberately planned as learning activities, but arise by organising the work environment as a learning environment in which new knowledge can be developed and used. This makes it important to learn more about the characteristics of a work environment in which learning with the intention of innovating is supported. The central question of our study, therefore, is

What are characteristics of a work environment in which learning for knowledge productivity is stimulated and supported?

Relevance

The present study aims to contribute to the existing knowledge about innovation and the related learning processes taking place in work environments. From the perspective of learning in the context of work, the present study builds on previous research that considered the work environment as a learning environment. These researches mainly focused on what and how people learn (e.g. Eraut, Alderton, Cole, & Senker, 1998), and on how to guide learning in the workplace (e.g. Billet, 2001). The present study aims to elaborate on these insights by exploring the specific learning processes that lead to gradual improvements and radical innovations in the workplace.

For a long time, research on innovation presented innovation as a linear process of design, development and implementation. Movement, interaction and feedback did not have a prominent place in the underpinning theories. If knowledge was acknowledged, the emphasis was on learning from external knowledge sources (Harkema, 2004). Currently, innovation is seen increasingly as a cyclical, interactive process in which learning plays an important role (Tidd, Bessant, & Pavitt, 2005). This requires a better understanding of the concept of innovation by conceiving it as a learning process, which the present study aims to contribute to.

For organisations, this research is relevant since the R&D departments are not the only – and maybe not even the main – places and sources for improvements and innovations. All departments, including marketing or finance, contribute to the process of innovation (Kanter, 2006), and besides product innovation, also process innovations are acknowledged as an important source for innovation (Volberda, Van den Bosch, & Jansen, 2006). Indeed, in a knowledge economy all members of an organisation contribute to the necessary and continuous process of improvement and innovation. This makes it increasingly important for organisations to know more about stimulating and facilitating these learning processes that lead to lasting success.

Theoretical Basis

A prominent concept in the theoretical basis that underlies the present research is that of knowledge productivity. This section explains this concept and describes the learning processes related to knowledge productivity. Furthermore, the concept of breakthrough that we used to focus our data gathering is introduced.

Knowledge Productivity

Kessels (1995) introduced the concept of knowledge productivity and described it as the process by which new knowledge is created in order to contribute to innovation in the workplace. Knowledge productivity refers to the process of tracing relevant information, using this information to develop new abilities and applying these abilities to the gradual improvement and radical innovation of products, services and work processes. The concept is inspired by the work of Drucker (1993). Drucker describes the important role of knowledge in the knowledge economy and the challenge for employees to become knowledge workers in their organisation (Drucker, 1999). These knowledge workers should contribute to the organisation's processes by developing gradual improvements and radical innovations. From this perspective the work environment is actually the learning environment in which employees develop the necessary abilities for the improvement and innovation of products, services and their working processes. Work processes then take on the characteristics of learning processes (Dixon, 1999; Kessels & Van der Werff, 2002).

Learning Processes Related to Knowledge Productivity

The process of knowledge productivity manifests itself in learning that can be characterised as developmental learning (Ellström, 2002) or double-loop learning (Argyris & Schön, 1978). Ellström describes developmental learning as opposed to adaptive learning. Adaptive learning refers to learning processes that cause changes within a given framework or a given organisational structure, whereas developmental learning causes changes 'that represent a break with the past and go beyond the given' (Ellström, 2002, p. 423). The difference between adaptive and developmental learning may be compared to the distinction made by Argyris and Schön (1978) between single-loop learning and double-loop learning. Argyris and Schön regard learning as the detection and correction of errors. Single-loop learning takes place when, in an attempt to correct an error, given goals, values and plans are operationalised rather than questioned. In double-loop learning, learners follow a different strategy. They question the governing variables, which may result in changing the goals, values and existing plans.

Knowledge productivity refers to learning processes in which learners break with the past and develop new approaches. Within this form of 'breakthrough' learning, another distinction can be made, namely, between the type of learning processes that precede the development of gradual improvements and the learning processes that precede the development of radical innovations. Following Ellström (2002), the first might be characterised as productive learning, and the second as creative learning. Productive learning is required when employees encounter novel situations for which no knowledge is available from previous experience. Learners then engage in a process of problem solving through experimentation in which they invent and test solutions (Ellström, 2002). Creative learning takes place when the learner comes across an unclear and puzzling situation. To develop a satisfactory way of dealing with this situation, it is necessary to question implicit taken-for-granted premises, and established definitions of problems, and then transform these.

Breakthroughs as Critical Learning Moments in Innovation Processes

In order to examine the learning processes undertaken by employees with the intention of innovating, it is necessary to take a closer look at those learning processes. Moments in which the learning process becomes visible are actually the breakthroughs in the innovation process. Breakthroughs are moments in an innovation process in which people break with their present way of working and start to think and act differently (Op de Weegh, 2004). Breakthroughs are conceptualised as a change in both 'thinking' and 'acting' leading to a step forward in the innovation process. The change in 'thinking' refers to the breaking of frames, which is necessary for innovation. Argyris and Schön (1978) describe how people have two choices, when the outcome of their work processes is not satisfactory. Either, they work with given or chosen goals, values or plans or they question these governing variables. The authors refer to the first option as single-loop learning, and to the second as double-loop learning. Double-loop learning may lead to an alteration in the governing variables and, therefore, to a shift in the way in which strategies and consequences are framed. As described in section 'Typical Questions That Form the Starting Point for Innovation', double-loop learning is the kind of learning associated with innovation (both the development of gradual improvements and of radical innovations). Senge (2000) refers to this process as the change of mental models, which is required for innovation. It is essential that innovation combines a change of governing variables (Argyris & Schön, 1978), mental models (Senge, 2000) or frames of reference (Hedberg & Wolff, 2001), with a change in behaviour. One must act based on these new ways of thinking (Hedberg & Wolff, 2001). This is the change in 'acting' that breakthroughs consist of.

Method

An inductive parallel study was carried out to learn more about the learning processes in ongoing innovation processes. Parallel research can be characterised as a prospective case study design (Bitektine, 2008). It is a form of case study research that studies ongoing processes. Along with the parallel study, an extensive literature review was conducted. The literature research was conducted in the fields of innovation, learning, and more specifically in the domain of learning to solve problems.

Context of the Parallel Study

The research took place at Habiforum (www.habiforum.nl), a network organisation that works on innovative solutions for land use in the Netherlands. An example of a pilot projects that the organisation initiated is the restructuring of an open and green area between two municipalities. Another example consists of local authorities of three big cities and three villages who want to develop and carry out a joint vision. In a pilot project stakeholders who are directly involved with the problem are invited to join (e.g. statesmen, inhabitants, shop owners). They meet regularly and are facilitated by someone from Habiforum's network.

Selection of Pilot Projects

In total, 10 pilot projects were part of the present study. The pilot projects were all characterised by a strong desire of the people involved to find an innovative solution for an intricate question or a solution for a long-standing issue. Since the study comprises an analysis of ongoing innovation processes, it was not known in advance whether these pilot projects would indeed come up with innovative solutions and ways of working.

Search for Breakthroughs

The most difficult aspect of a parallel study is determining what events to focus on in the data-gathering phase. How can one determine whether a situation occurring in the pilot project will turn out to be crucial for its success later on? In other words, how can these crucial situations be recognised at an early stage? In order to trace crucial moments in the innovation process, the data gathering in the parallel study was guided by the search for breakthroughs. Patriotta (2003) stressed that disruptions in the form of discontinuities are important indicators in innovation processes: 'in order to empirically observe how organizations create, use and disseminate knowledge, we have to look for disruptive events conceived as turning points in an ongoing flow of activities' (p. 69). The approach of tracing breakthroughs has similarities with the critical incidents technique as developed by Flanagan (1954) and Zemke and Kramlinger (1991). It was left up to the participants in the pilot projects to pass judgement on the extent to which a situation would qualify as a breakthrough.

Data Gathering

Table 11.1 presents an overview of the cases and the data-collection methods that were applied. With the collection of breakthroughs as the primary focus of data gathering, there is a risk of treating incidents as isolated episodes occurring at specific points in time (Patriotta, 2003). To prevent this from happening, 4 of the 10 cases were studied intensively and the events in these pilot projects were documented in a thick description (Geertz, 1973). Thick descriptions capture various aspects of the case and its context, aiming to give a rich description of the field that is examined, whereas thin descriptions only describe the aspects one is interested in.

Table 11.1 An overview of the cases that were part of the study

Case	Goal	Methods used for data gathering
Post-war district	To restructure a specific quarter in a city in the North of the Netherlands	Start-off face-to-face interviews with the facilitators of the pilot projects
Rhombus	To abolish the barrier in this area in order to give an impulse to the social development of this part of the city	Attending meetings of the pilot project
Industrial area	To restructure an industrial area in order to bring about economic dynamics and sustainable planning	Face-to-face interviews and telephone interviews with facilitators of pilot projects
Multi-layered area	To realise a multi-layered industrial area	Face-to-face interviews with other participants in the pilot project
Mounds	To develop 'mounds' to be safe for the rising water	
City harbour	To restructure the banks of the city harbour	Start-off face-to-face interview with the facilitators of the pilot projects
Hinge	To create a 'city-on-top-of-a-city'	
Health boulevard	To restructure the area between two municipalities	Regular short interviews via telephone with facilitators of the pilot projects to keep track of the process and to trace breakthroughs
Triangle	To make a joint vision – by six municipalities – and carry this out	
Polder	To find a sustainable solution to keep the polder dry	

Data Analysis

The breakthroughs that occurred in the pilot projects were input for the phase of analysis. In this phase an inductive analysis (Patton, 1990) was conducted. This is a process in which categories of analysis come from the data: they emerge out of the data rather than being imposed on them prior to data collection and analysis. Besides the breakthroughs, moments in which the process got stuck were used in the analysis of the data. These moments contributed to a better understanding of the themes that were related to the breakthroughs. The data emerged around 11 themes. These themes were compared with literature in order to better understand and interpret them. For an elaborate overview of the findings from literature, see Verdonschot (2009). The result of the analysis was a description of the themes in the form of design principles for knowledge productivity. The choice for design principles as a format to present the outcomes of a descriptive study is not self-evident. Indeed, design principles are usually seen as a yield of design research (Van den Akker, 1999). The reasons to choose for design principles as the format to present the results of the analysis of the present study are twofold.

First, the choice was made in anticipation of next research phases. The aim was to follow up the present study with a design study to find out the extent to which the factors identified in the present study could help participants in innovation processes to actively design their work environment to enhance innovation. The expectation was that by formulating the outcome of the present study in design principles, it would be easier to collect at an earlier stage reactions of possible future users with respect to the design principles. Second, design principles seemed especially suitable to do justice to the variation and complexity that was found in the themes.

These design principles aimed to express the effective aspects underlying the breakthrough moments in the pilot projects. Each breakthrough seemed to contain more than one of these effective aspects. This means that the success of each of the breakthroughs could be explained by more than one (often two or three) design principles.

Design Principles for Knowledge Productivity

This section presents the 11 design principles for knowledge productive work environments that emerged from the breakthroughs that were found in the pilot projects combined with the findings from literature.

Typical Questions That Form the Starting Point for Innovation

The breakthroughs in the cases showed that the formulation of the central question in the pilot project influences the outcome. Participants in the pilot projects formulated and reformulated the central problem. Breakthroughs occurred when they managed to formulate a question that somehow worked. Whether a question worked was related to the extent to which it was intriguing for the people involved. In the pilot projects, questions became intriguing when

- Participants formulated the question in terms of an appealing concept (e.g. a city-above-a-city or a multi-layered industrial area). Unusual concepts triggered their creativity;
- Participants formulated the question in the form of a complex problem they experienced and that triggered them and that left enough space for various perspectives and directions (e.g. How can this water be stored even though the country is so full already? How can we prevent this neighbourhood from becoming neglected?);
- Participants had questions that evoked their curiosity (e.g. an official who knew many people in a particular neighbourhood experienced that the beauty of the neighbourhood had died, and his personal involvement made him curious to find new perspectives on this problematic situation).

Besides the necessity of the question being intriguing for the people involved, the extent to which a question was experienced as urgent, seemed also relevant. In the Industrial area case the urgency of the question the pilot project worked on, remained unclear during the whole process. In the particular pilot project this led to long conversations, little activity in between meetings, participants who awaited developments and who asked many questions. Instances in which the urgency was clearly there, the process got an impulse and could go on.

Literature in the field of cognition affirms that the outcome of a problem-solving process is defined by the definition of the problem (Benjafield, 1997). Innovation can be seen as a special kind of problem solving that could also be referred to as problem finding (Getzels, 1979; Mackworth, 1965).

Design Principle 1: Formulate an Urgent and Intriguing Question

Developing an urgent and intriguing question is necessary for innovation. Such a question is not a given, it needs active development in interaction with key players and stakeholders. Urgency refers not only to a rational urge but also to the personal feeling that there is an urge. This means that the question must be formulated in such a way that the people who work on it have the feeling that the question cannot remain unanswered. An intriguing question refers to a question that entices people to develop new perspectives. A question can become intriguing when an unusual combination of concepts is made.

New Ways of Working That Deviate from the Traditional Approach

Many breakthroughs were characterised by a new way of working. Traditional meetings with agendas were traded off against open conversations with the individual involvement as the main topic of conversation. Information was not gathered by large-scale surveys with truth-finding as the main goal but rather by small-scale excursions by the people who joined the pilot project to understand the different perspectives from people involved in the area the pilot project was occupied with.

Theoretically, this can be explained by the idea that all learning integrates thinking and doing (Senge, Scharmer, Jaworski, & Flowers, 2005). Innovative solutions often require breaking with the actual way of thinking, and adopting a new frame of reference. The cases revealed that this new way of thinking can be stimulated by new ways of doing. Some 'old ways of working' provoke 'old behaviour'. They will not lead to solutions that break with the existing way of thinking. An official meeting with a chairperson, a secretary and an agenda that defines the procedure is not a setting that easily evokes new ways of thinking. In the pilot projects these ways of working were often traded off against forms in which individuals and their perspectives played an important role.

Example from the Polder Case

Participants in this pilot project experienced difficulties in explaining each other their interest in the pilot project. To overcome this, they hired a minivan and with a small group of people (each belonging to one of the stakeholder groups that had an interest in the polder environment) and they made a tour through the polder. There were inhabitants, farmers, environmentalists and people who represented the group of visitors who visited the polder for recreation. Each of these stakeholders got the key of the bus for 1 h. Within that hour they were free to show the others whatever they wanted. The idea was that everyone would guide the others through the polder, showing them what they found so attractive. The inhabitants, for instance, chose to have a coffee at a certain café in the polder where the view was exceptionally beautiful. In the afternoon they sat together and talked about the meaning of the polder to each of them. The outcome of this outing was that the various perspectives and interests became clear to everyone. This enabled them to facilitate their own process. The external facilitator was not needed as much as before.

Design Principle 2: Create a New Approach

To find new solutions ('thinking new'), a new way of working ('acting new') is necessary. Such a new approach can be realised by breaking with hindering structures (e.g. instead of talking about the problem in a formal meeting, making an excursion and showing each other what bothers you), and by designing an overall approach. The overall approach is characterised by a developmental approach: step-by-step designing of a process that deviates from existing routines.

Individual Motivation as the Basis for Creativity

The cases reveal that individual motivation is a powerful engine for innovation. Breakthroughs in the pilot projects were often preceded by a discussion of the participants' individual motivation. When the individual interests of the people involved were discussed, participants asked each other questions such as: 'What do you dream of?' 'What are you enthusiastic for?' 'What is your interest in this project?' and 'What do you want to realise?' See the example of the Industrial area case (below).

Example from the Industrial Area Case

An important milestone in this pilot project was the moment that the facilitator asked all of the attendants in the meeting to share what their personal stake in the project was. This conversation offered an attractive alternative for the behaviour that had not helped them until now. Instead of a formal meeting it became a personal conversation that stimulated the process. Not the formal positions of the people involved determined the agenda. Rather, the personal involvement determined the conversation. This led to a breakthrough in this pilot project.

Individuals are capable of special achievements when they work from individual motivation. This is confirmed by various authors. Authors refer to this kind of personal involvement with different concepts, such as intrinsic motivation

(Deci & Ryan, 1985), flow (Csikszentmihalyi, 1997), engagement (Nahapiet & Ghoshal, 1998) and passion (Amabile, 2000; Kessels, 2001).

Design Principle 3: Work from Individual Motivation

Individual motivation is a powerful engine for creativity and innovation. When people have the opportunity to work on things they find important, their creativity is stimulated. Therefore, it is important, in pilot projects, to explore and use the personal incentives of all participants and to allow them to formulate a personal goal. The personal incentives can be of an intrinsic nature (e.g. a passion for a specific theme) but they may also be of an extrinsic nature (e.g. recognition).

Novel Combinations as a Trigger for Innovation

According to Nahapiet and Ghoshal (1998), the creation of new knowledge, a process relevant for innovation, occurs by two processes: combination and exchange. These two processes can be recognised in the breakthroughs that were collected in the pilot projects that were part of the study.

Combination is a process that consists of combining elements previously unconnected or developing novel ways of combining elements previously associated (Nahapiet & Ghoshal, 1998). In the pilot projects this is recognised in the act of separating the main problem or sub-problem in different themes or perspectives that each offer a different perspective on the question at hand. For instance, in the postwar district case, in which the problems in a neighbourhood in the north of the Netherlands are central, the pilot project chose different perspectives to approach the question: economy and self-help among the inhabitants; cultural identity; social cohesion and initiatives of inhabitants. These perspectives all helped to take a different perspective on the situation. It showed that a new perspective on the situation leads to new ideas for the solution.

Exchange is a necessary process for knowledge creation when resources are held by different parties (Nahapiet & Ghoshal, 1998). The process of exchange occurs through social interaction and coactivity. This process is recognised in the pilot projects as well. In the pilot projects breakthroughs occurred when experts, invited by participants of the pilot project, gave their perspective on the problem at hand. Often, unusual combinations of subject matter expertise were made that contributed to the breakthrough: artists or architects were invited to give their perspective. See this example from the post-war district case (below).

Example from the Post-war District Case

This pilot project is concerned with restructuring a quarter in a city in the North of the Netherlands that is mainly inhabited by citizens originating from the Antilles. The participants in this pilot project invited an architect. This architect, who had lived in the Netherlands Antilles, developed new ways to design the quarter. He used the Antillean culture as a starting point and came up with 12 concepts for the redesign of the quarter. He had ideas such as transforming the neighbourhood into a street theatre, making a compound and a cruise quay. He used the Antillean culture and linked elements of that culture to ways of using the neighbourhood for living, recreating and working. Normally, the homogenous group of inhabitants was seen as the main problem, but the approach of the architect used a completely different starting point. The architect's proposals inspired the participants in the pilot project to take a new perspective on this 'problematic neighbourhood'. Participants could use this new perspective and add on their own expertise.

Design Principle 4: Make Unusual Combinations of Subject Matter Expertise

A surprising or not obvious admixture of different kinds of knowledge can help to establish new connections between elements that were not linked before. These new connections are necessary for innovation. A fruitful way to establish new connections is by choosing new or uncommon perspectives or metaphors to look at the question at hand, or by inviting experts who have new or uncommon perspectives.

Connecting Different Interests by Working from Mutual Attractiveness

Typical for innovation processes are the different, and often opposite, interests at stake. In order to develop an innovative solution, it seems necessary to combine these opposite interests. Imagine a municipality that wants to arrange more parking spaces whereas the inhabitants wish to preserve the green park. A solution, in which these different stakes are successfully combined, is the development of an underground parking lot. The search for a solution that meets varying stakes is an important aspect of innovation.

In the pilot projects that were part of the present study, breakthroughs occurred at moments in which participants succeeded in combining different interests. For instance, by collaborating with a party with which they previously did not want to collaborate because of their competing activities. They realised that collaboration was necessary, and instead of seeing them as competitors they worked as partners. Kessels (2001) previously referred to this principle as mutual attractiveness.

The principle of mutual attractiveness is considered to help participants in pilot projects to design a collaboration in which each of them can hold on to their own interests, and in which they use the varying interests to come up with new solutions for the problematic situation at hand. This is expressed in the fifth design principle.

Design Principle 5: Work from Mutual Attractiveness

Typical for innovation is that different and often opposite interests are at stake. To develop an innovative solution, it is necessary to combine these opposite interests. In a pilot project the personal interests must be central, and not a general goal or an abstract organisational goal. When everybody holds on to their own interests, and when people actively seek for ways to collaborate on a basis of reciprocity, breakthroughs are likely to occur.

A Positive Approach

Breakthroughs in the pilot projects were caused by what could be called a 'positive approach'. Not failures, shortcomings or gaps were central to the breakthroughs, but rather qualities, achieved successes and positive attention. In literature, this positive approach can be related to positive psychology (Seligman, 2005). The three ways in which this 'positive approach' was recognised in the breakthroughs include:

1. Using qualities as a starting point. Various pilot projects explicitly used the qualities of the area the pilot project was working on. See, for instance, the example below, taken from the city harbour case:
   Example from the City Harbour Case
   The participants made a presentation of 'lost and found objects' from the banks of the city harbour. The inhabitants collected beautiful pieces of nature but also some rusty objects. This made both the inhabitants and the market parties aware of how much the area actually had to offer. They realised that the area was not a blank field, but rather that there is much that is worth to protect. The perspective of the area as a 'problem' was changed into a perspective of the harbour as a promising area with various qualities. The facilitator of this pilot project described this as a breakthrough.
2. Reflection on previously achieved successes led to a lot of energy and at the same time it helped the group to learn more about their own abilities.
3. Working with the qualities of the context. In various cases the qualities of the context (e.g. the rare plants growing in the old city harbour) were taken as a starting point for new developments.

Design Principle 6: Build on Strengths

People's talents, successes achieved by the group, and the qualities of a context provide a valuable starting point for the pilot projects. Paying attention to the strengths of individuals, the group and the context offers an attractive starting point for reflection and for the design of follow-up steps. Furthermore, it is likely to contribute to the self-efficacy of participants, which may enhance their performance.

Beyond a Polite Conversation by Creating Something

In the pilot projects that were part of the study, there were groups that experienced difficulties in interacting with each other in such a way that it would help them to develop new perspectives. They kept having polite conversations, agitated discussions and reflections. The kind of conversation observed in the pilot projects is related to the type of communication that Scharmer (2007) refers to as 'download-ing'. Operating effectively in such conversation requires the participants to exchange polite phrases with one another, not telling one other what is really on their mind. These kinds of conversations reproduce existing rules and phrases and do not help to create something new.

In the pilot projects in which groups started to make things, for instance, concrete products or prototypes, they succeeded in going beyond these polite conversations. They were then able to move from ongoing analysis and reflection to a phase of design. Instead of explaining why things are as they are, they started to inquire each other's perspectives and connected them to each other. Examples of products that were made in the pilot projects are a model, a map for the area they were working in, and a flyer that announces a gathering they organised for inhabitants in the area. See the example of the Industrial area case (above).

Design Principle 7: Create Something Together

In pilot projects participants often spend quite a lot of time exchanging their points of view and discussing them. However, polite conversations or agitated discussions alone do not lead to innovation. For innovation it is necessary to examine each other's perspectives and to find out the points on which the various perspectives differ. Creating something together supports this process. Examples of products include a workshop, a photo-exhibition, a scale model or a poster.

Sensitivity for Weak Signals

Sensitivity (Walz & Bertels, 1995) and sagacity (James, in: Benjafield, 1997) refer to the ability to become aware of signals or information that people previously did not see but that could offer relevant clues for the problem to solve. Mindfulness (Langer, 2005) refers to the ability to play with context and interpretation in order to change the meaning of situations, people's actions and things. These two abilities, as became clear from literature that was reviewed, are relevant to innovation. In the pilot projects participants used these abilities as well. Participants used and devel-oped their sensitivity by doing interviews with people whom they would normally not have involved (e.g. interviewing a group of inhabitants). Using their genuine curiosity in an interview provided the opportunity to imagine other people's per-spective. This helped them to become aware of new information or new signals. Mindfulness is also recognised in the pilot projects. Participants searched for new words and metaphors in order to play with interpretation and to switch contexts. See, for instance, the example from the Rhombus case (below).

Example from the Rhombus Case

This pilot project deals with restructuring a region in order to improve its social development. The region had always been labelled as 'messy'. The highway that crossed this region was seen as something that stands in the way of innovating the area. As soon as people in this pilot project labelled the highway as a 'gateway' they started to see new perspectives. It helped them to get ideas to organise the area in a completely new way.

The eighth design principle refers to the development of sensitivity.

Design Principle 8: Entice to See New Signals and to Give Them New Meaning

People interpret the world around them all the time. For innovation it is necessary to reconsider existing interpretations and to develop new ones. In order to do so, people must become sensitive to new information and clues. Furthermore, playing with the interpretation of this information and these clues is necessary in order to assign new meaning to them. The use of new words and metaphors facilitates this process of playing.

The Pilot Project Versus the Unit of Adoption

In the pilot projects attention was paid not only to the development of new ideas and concepts, but also to the connection of them with the context for which they were developed. Several strategies of connecting the pilot project to the context outside led to breakthroughs:

1. Involving influential people by, for instance, letting them judge or test the developed ideas. See the example from the multi-layered area case (below).
   Example from the Multi-layered Area Case
   In this pilot project the participants connected their ideas with the world outside by composing an expert group consisting of experts from outside the pilot project. These experts were influential people within the context. They were asked to reflect on the vision the participants developed within the pilot project. The experts were especially interested in one of the ideas. Because of the involvement of experts in this phase, the participants in the pilot project had the opportunity to develop this idea further.
2. Another strategy was the involvement of important stakeholders that were left out before (e.g. the inhabitants or the shop owners in a certain area).
3. Also, positive attention from persons with a certain status, or attention from media, helped to establish a connection with the world 'outside'. In the pilot projects articles in newspapers, a visit from the royal family and radio interviews offered the participants the opportunity to connect the two worlds.

To be successful, it is necessary to establish a connection between the world inside the pilot project and the world outside. The ninth design principle refers to the connection that must be established between the pilot project and the organisations, groups or individuals for whom the innovation could mean a substantial benefit.

**Design Principle 9: Connect the World Inside the Pilot
Project to the World Outside**

Participants in pilot projects must establish a connection with the organisations, groups or individuals for whom the innovation they are working on could mean a substantial benefit. Indeed, this supports the implementation of the proposed innovation. Such a connection can be established by involving influential people (e.g. experts) or important stakeholders (e.g. inhabitants or users) in the pilot project.

The Innovation Process as a Social Process

The facilitators do show awareness for the social and communicative process in the pilot project. One of them said: 'When participants talk a lot about the minutes, for me that is a clear sign that things are not going well. And I want things to go well. A lot of fuss about minutes means that something else is going on. Let's talk about that then'. The facilitators also mention interventions that they initiated with respect to the social and communicative process:

1. Putting the process on hold and check: are we all talking about the same thing, do we understand each other?
2. Acknowledging the input of a group of participants who did not have the feeling being taken seriously.

Interventions concerning the social and communicative process seem to be conditional for breakthroughs, rather than directly causing breakthroughs. In literature, the importance of conversations for innovation processes is stressed as well (Scharmer, 2007; Steyaert, Bouwen, & Van Looy, 1996; Von Krogh et al., 2000).

Design Principle 10: Pay Attention to the Social and Communicative Process

Innovation is a social process. Social and communicative skills are the vehicle for this process. Therefore, it is important that participants in pilot projects pay attention to the quality of the interactions.

The Innovation Process as a Learning Process

The facilitators in the pilot projects that were part of the study had sometimes explicit attention for the development of competences that they needed in the innovation process. See, for instance, the example taken from the Hinge case (below).

Example from the Hinge Case

In a meeting with an important politician and the director of the development company the participants of the pilot project did not want to use a PowerPoint presentation. They were decisive to use the opportunity to start the conversation differently, unconventional. They did not want the politician and the director to lean backwards with an attitude of 'please convince me'. This motive created the urge to learn and practice a new technique. They practiced the 2×2 technique (a way of asking questions) in advance and then they used it in the meeting. Their motive for doing it like this was their desire to organise a new kind of conversation that would have a new outcome.

At the same time, participants in the pilot project found it difficult to facilitate their own learning and that of others. Some participants and facilitators found it easier to take over a specific activity than to help others to learn it themselves. Design principles 1–10 are pointed towards the innovation process itself. The eleventh design principle focuses on the crucial and lasting role of learning in this process.

Design Principle 11: Actively Support the Development of Competences

The learning processes undertaken with the intention of innovating are primarily focused on the improvements and innovations that the people involved aim to bring about. However, participants in pilot projects must pay explicit attention to the learning processes as well. They could do this by defining the competences that they need to develop and by developing approaches that stimulate learning in that direction. They should regularly reflect on these learning processes since that could enhance learning.

Conclusion and Discussion

This section circles back to the research question and discusses the practical implications of the study at hand. A reflection is offered on the generalisability of the findings. What are characteristics of a work environment in which learning for knowledge productivity is stimulated and supported?

The parallel study in 10 ongoing pilot projects tracked down breakthroughs. These breakthroughs were expected to represent the 'critical learning moments' of these pilot projects. The analysis of these breakthroughs led to 11 recurring themes. These themes were compared with literature in order to better understand and interpret them. Literature in the fields of innovation and learning, and more specifically the problem-solving field of learning was used for this purpose. This resulted in a description of the themes in the form of design principles for knowledge productivity. These design principles represent the factors that were found to underlie the learning processes leading to gradual improvements and radical innovations. The design principles tended to be present in various combinations in the breakthroughs that were observed or reported by the participants.

The definition of knowledge productivity distinguishes between gradual improvements and radical innovations as results of the process of knowledge productivity. All pilot projects that were part of the present study had the intention to come up with innovative solutions, but the actual outcome was not part of the study. The parallel study followed ongoing innovation processes for which the outcome was yet unknown. The choice not to concentrate on the outcome of the process but rather on the breakthroughs that happen along the way made it impossible to reflect on the different learning processes that precede the development of both gradual improvements and radical innovations. A provisional conclusion is that the intention to find a solution for a difficult question accounts for the characteristics of the learning process more than the intention to develop either a gradual improvement or a radical innovation. In all cases the intention was to come up with an innovative solution for an intricate question or a long-standing issue. Participants never deliberately aimed at developing gradual improvements or radical innovations.

Practical Implications

The study aimed to contribute to practice by providing guidelines which could help organisations in the design of learning environments that support employees in the process of learning with the intention of innovating. The results of the research are useful for practitioners. The design principles clarify the factors that matter in the creation of breakthroughs in innovation practices. These principles might be used in daily practice as a means to reflect upon or analyse innovation projects. Furthermore, the cases studied provide examples of interventions that were carried out by participants in the pilot projects, and that contributed to the creation of breakthroughs. Although these principles and the concrete examples do not tell people exactly what they need to do, they do contribute to practice by showing underlying principles that can serve as examples (Wardekker, 1999). This can be helpful for participants who are occupied with innovation projects in practice.

Generalisability of the Findings

The results of this study are not simply generalisable to all organisations since the cases that were studied were not part of a random selection. The 10 case studies that were included in the parallel study took place in pilot projects which were initiated by a Dutch organisation that promotes innovative urban planning processes in the Netherlands. Different people, related to both public and private organisations, took part in these pilot projects.

An observation that could be made is that the type of work environment that was central in this study had typical characteristics, such as the type of problems that were central in the pilot projects, the motivation of the people involved for solving this problem and the fact that these problems were never theoretical, but always real. If these characteristics are translated to the kind of work environment to which the results of this study could be applied, the findings could be applied in a context in which the following three elements are present: (1) an intricate question, problematic situation or long-standing issue that requires an innovative solution, (2) a group of people from one or more organisations, all of whom are committed to solving the problem and (3) a concrete manifestation of the problem that is dealt with.

Situations in which the findings of the present research are not applicable include situations in which individuals did not choose to participate, situations in which individuals have no interest in solving the problem at hand and situations in which the group that aims to find an innovative solution does not have the freedom to experiment with new approaches. If groups need to comply with the rigid structures and procedures that organisations often deploy, the findings from the present research will not be easy to apply.

References

Amabile, T. M. (2000). Stimulate creativity by fueling passion. In E. A. Locke (Ed.), The Blackwell handbook of principles of organizational behavior (pp. 331–341). Malden, MA: Blackwell.

Argyris, C., & Schön, D. (1978). Organizational learning: A theory of action perspective. Reading, MA: Addison Wesley.

Baldwin, T. T., & Ford, J. K. (1988).Transfer of training: A review and directions for future research. *Personnel Psychology, 41*(1), 63–105.

Benjafield, J. G. (1997). *Cognition* (2nd ed.). Upper Saddle River, NJ: Prentice-Hall.

Billet, S. (2001). *Learning in the workplace: Strategies for effective practice.* Crows Nest, NSW: Allen&Unwin.

Bitektine, A. (2008). Prospective case study design, qualitative method for deductive theory testing. *Organizational Research Methods, 11*(1), 160–180.

Brown, J. S., & Duguid, P. (1991). Organizational learning and communities-of-practice: Toward a unified view of working, learning and innovation. *Organization Science, 2*(1), 40–57.

Burke, L. A., & Baldwin, T. T. (1999). Workforce training transfer: A study of the effect of relapse prevention training and transfer climate. *Human Resource Management, 38*(3), 227–241.

Csikszentmihalyi, M. (1997). *Finding flow. The psychology of engagement with everyday life.* New York: Basic Books.

Deci, E. L., & Ryan, R. M. (1985). *Intrinsic motivation and self-determination in human behavior.* New York: Plenum.

Dixon, N. M. (1999). *The organizational learning cycle: How we can learn collectively* (2nd ed.). Hampshire: Gower.

Drucker, P. F. (1993). *The post-capitalist society.* Oxford: Butterworth Heinemann.

Eraut, M., Alderton, J., Cole, G., & Senker, P. (1998). *Development of knowledge and skills in employment.* Sussex: University of Sussex.

Flanagan, J. C. (1954). The critical incident technique. *Psychological Bulletin, 51,* 327–358.

Geertz, C. (1973). *The interpretation of cultures.* New York: Basic Books.

Getzels, J. W. (1979). Problem finding: A theoretical note. *Cognitive Science, 3*(2), 167–171.

Harkema, S. J. M. (2004). *Complexity and emergent learning in innovation projects, an application of complex adaptive systems theory.* Breukelen: Universiteit Nyenrode.

Hedberg, B., & Wolff, R. (2001). Organizing, learning, and strategizing: From construction to discovery. In M. Dierkes,A. Berthoin, Antal, J. Child, & I. Nonaka (Eds.), *Handbook of organizational learning and knowledge* (pp. 535–556). New York: Oxford University Press.

Kanter, R. M. (2006). Innovation, the classic traps. *Harvard Business Review, 84*(11), 72–83.

Kessels, J. W. M. (1995). Opleiden in arbeidsorganisaties. Het ambivalente perspectief van de kennisproductiviteit. *Comenius, 15*(2), 179–193.

Kessels, J. W. M. (2001). *Verleiden tot kennisproductiviteit* [Tempting towards knowledge productivity]., Enschede, Inaugural Lecture University of Twente.

Kessels, J. W. M., & Van der Werff, P. (2002). What is beyond knowledge productivity. In T. Van Aken & T. M. Van Engers (Eds.), *Beyond knowledge productivity, report of a quest* (pp. 19–28). Utrecht: Lemma.

Keursten, P. (1999). Het einde van strategisch opleiden? *Opleiding&Ontwikkeling, 10*, 27–33.

Langer, E. (2005). Well-being: Mindfulness versus positive evaluation. In C. R. Snyder & S. J. Lopez (Eds.), *Handbook of positive psychology* (pp. 214–230). New York: Oxford University Press.

Mackworth, N. H. (1965). Originality. *American Psychologist, 20*(1), 51–66.

Marsick, V. J., & Watkins, K. E. (1990). *Informal and incidental learning at the workplace.* London: Routledge.

Nahapiet, J., & Ghoshal, S. (1998). Social capital, intellectual capital and the organizational advantage. *Academy of Management Review, 23*(2), 242–266.

Nieuwenhuis, L., & Van Woerkom, M. (2007). Goal rationalities in work-related learning. *Human Resources Development Review, 6*(1), 64–83.

Op de Weegh, S. (2004). *How to break through, a research on knowledge productivity focussing on breakthroughs at Habiforum innovation projects.* Enschede: University of Twente.

Patriotta, G. (2003). *Organizational knowledge in the making: How firms create, use, and institutionalize knowledge.* New York: Oxford University Press.

Patton, M. Q. (1990). *Qualitative evaluation and research methods* (2nd ed.). Newbury Park, CA: Sage.

Scharmer, C. O. (2007). *Theory U, leading from the future as it emerges.* Cambridge, MA: SoL.

Seligman, M. E. P. (2005). Positive psychology: Positive prevention, and positive therapy. In C. R. Snyder & S. J. Lopez (Eds.), *Handbook of positive psychology* (pp. 3–9). New York: Oxford university press.

Senge, P. (2000). *The fifth discipline: The art and practice of the learning organization.* New York: Doubleday.

Senge, P., Scharmer, C. O., Jaworski, J., & Flowers, B. S. (2005). *Presence: Exploring profound change in people, organizations and society.* London: Nicholas Brealey.

Steyaert, C., Bouwen, R., & Van Looy, B. (1996). Conversational construction of new meaning configurations in organizational innovation: A generative approach. *European Journal of Work and Organizational Psychology, 5*(1), 67–89.

Tidd, J., Bessant, J., & Pavitt, K. (2005). *Managing innovation, integrating technological, market and organizational change* (3rd ed.). West Sussex: Wiley.

Van de Ven, A. H., Angle, H. L., & Poole, M. S. (1989). *Research on the management of innovation, the Minnesota studies.* New York: Harper & Row.

Van den Akker, J. (1999). Principles and methods of development research. In J. Van den Akker, R. M. Branch, K. L. Gustafson, N. Nieveen, & T. T. Plomp (Eds.), *Design approaches and tools in education and training* (pp. 1–14). Dordrecht: Kluwer.

Verdonschot, S. G. M. (2009). *Learning to innovate: A series of sudies to explore and enable learning in innovation practices.* Doctoral dissertation, University of Twente, Enschede.

Volberda, H. W., Van den Bosch, F. A. J., & Jansen, J. J. P. (2006). *Slim managen en innovatief organiseren.* Rotterdam: Erasmus Universiteit.

Von Krogh, G., Ichijo, K., & Nonaka, I. (2000). *Enabling knowledge creation, how to unlock the mystery of tacit knowledge and release the power of innovation.* New York: Oxford University Press.

Walton, J. (1999). *Strategic human resource development.* Harlow: Pearson Education.

Walz, H., & Bertels, T. (1995). *Das intelligente unternehmen: Schneller lernen als der wettbewerb.* Landsberg: Moderne Industrie Verlag.

Wardekker, W. (1999). Criteria voor de kwaliteit van onderzoek. In B. Levering & P. Smeyers (Eds.), *Opvoeding en onderwijs leren zien, een inleiding in interpretatief onderzoek* (pp. 50–67). Amsterdam: Boom.

Zemke, R., & Kramlinger, T. (1991). De critical incidents methode [The critical-incidents technique]. *Opleiders in Organisaties/Capita Selecta, 8*, 69–80.

Chapter 12
From Function-Based Development Practices to Collaborative Capability Building: An Intervention to Extend Practitioners' Ideas

Marika Schaupp

Distinctive and difficult-to-imitate capabilities have been recognized as the key source of firms' competitive advantage (Teece, Pisano, & Shuen, 1997; Newbert, 2007) and have gained much attention in recent years (Eisenhardt & Martin, 2000; Ambrosini & Bowman, 2009). This line of research is still, however, relatively young. Researchers have mainly tried to categorize and illustrate types of capabilities, and to show how capabilities change over time. Little attention has been paid to the systematic and intentional development of capabilities or to practitioners' active contribution to capability building.

This chapter introduces a developmental intervention conducted at a Finnish road-building company as an endeavor to purposefully create a new understanding of the nature of capabilities, and to develop new collaborative capability-building practices among functional specialists, such as HRD practitioners and systems developers. The goal was to critically evaluate the current system of capability building, to break away from the traditional function-based division of work among specialists in development activities, and to find a more systemic and concurrent form of capability building.

Contradiction Between the Systemic Nature of Organizational Capabilities and the Functional Organization of Development Activities

Until recently, the development of organizational activities has been dominated by the ideas of mass production; innovations in information and communication technology have been radically changing the situation since the 1990s (see, e.g., Freeman & Louçã, 2001; Perez, 2002). However, the functional division of work, separation of planning and production, and phased development models based on functional expertise still prevail in organizations as a legacy from the mass-production era (Hamel & Breen, 2007). However, as Hamel and Breen (2007, p. 12)

M. Schaupp (✉)
Finnish Institute of Occupational Health, Helsinki, Finland
e-mail: marika.schaupp@ttl.fi

R.F. Poell, M. van Woerkom (eds.), *Supporting Workplace Learning*, Professional and Practice-based Learning 5, DOI 10.1007/978-90-481-9109-3_12,
© Springer Science+Business Media B.V. 2011

point out, a strong paradigm is often the victim of its own tools and concepts. The general tendency to divide organizational learning challenges, on the basis of functional specialization, into partial problems, such as technological problems, HR issues, process problems or leadership issues, now prevents the development of a more systemic view of organizational capabilities.

Human resource development (HRD) practitioners have traditionally been responsible for defining training needs on the basis of the management's strategic choices and arranging course-based training for personnel in order to fill competence gaps. Later, as organizations have recognized the growing importance of change management and capability building, HRD practitioners have increasingly been involved in organizational change efforts. Even so, they have remained disconnected from other experts' work of analyzing the emerging learning challenges in business and developing new capabilities. Instead they have been preoccupied with the development of individual skills and know-how. As work practices are becoming more complex, it is increasingly difficult to clearly define jobs, and the skills that people should possess in order to manage their jobs, or to point out separate factors affecting the firm's competitive advantage. The traditional approaches to HRD seem to be becoming increasingly inadequate for keeping up with the pace of change of organizational activities, and for grasping the qualitative transformations of the capabilities needed.

The Concept of Organizational Capability

The concept of capability was introduced as an object of research by representatives of the evolutionary theory and the resource-based view of the firm (Nelson & Winter, 1982; Dosi, Nelson, & Winter, 2000). The concept is useful in that instead of individuals' skills, it takes the observable capability as a whole as the unit of analysis, and turns attention to the collective mastery of a particular kind of operation. Such a mastery is not an additive aggregate of the skills and competences of individuals, but also comprises organizations' systems, structures, and processes. It implies a certain level of generalization and conceptualization that lessens the need for building solutions from scratch. This makes the concept of capability different from many other approaches to organizational learning, which take learning as a universalistic phenomenon independent from what is being learned and why (Ahonen, 2008). Representatives of this approach see organizational routines as the essential building blocks of capabilities (Nelson & Winter, 1982, p. 14, Dosi et al., 2000). While the concept of routine nicely captures the organizational nature of learning, and the artifact-mediated dimension of capabilities, it does not, however, help us understand the dynamics of change in capabilities or the role of *practitioners' agency* in capability building and the related dynamics. It does not explain how organizational capabilities can be developed systematically (see, e.g., Miettinen & Virkkunen, 2005).

Since Teece et al. (1997, p. 516) introduced the concept of *dynamic capability* as "the firm's ability to integrate, build and reconfigure internal and external competences to address rapidly changing environments," a growing literature has emerged, which emphasizes an organization's need, from time to time, to renew its capability base to be able to meet the changing conditions of the business environment and to maintain the competitive advantage. Ambrosini and Bowman (2009, p. 30) note in their review that "while many fields address change related issues (e.g., organizational learning, cognition, innovation etc.) none, except the dynamic capability perspective, specifically focuses on how firms can change their valuable resources over time and do so persistently." The empirical work in this area is, however, still in its infancy (Newbert, 2007) and analytical descriptions of concrete, agentive processes of dynamic capabilities almost non-existent. Ambrosini and Bowman (2009, p. 37) note that all the examples concerning dynamic capabilities that they analyzed in their review are, with only one exception, "either conceptual ideas or derived from secondary data and are essentially results of quantitative studies" and that "[the studies] also by and large describe broad organizational processes; they do not delve into the detailed, micro mechanisms of how these capabilities are deployed or how they 'work'." The empirical work concerning people's agency in the processes is also strikingly lacking here. Most of the studies place the responsibility of developing dynamic capability solely on the managers.

Fujimoto (2000, p. 246) separates three levels of organizational capabilities: "(i) *static capability*, which affects the level of competitive performance, (ii) *improvement capability*, which affects the pace of performance improvements, and (iii) *evolutionary capability*, which is related to accumulation of the above capabilities themselves." Fujimoto notes that both the second and third level in the classification can be regarded as dynamic capabilities, but from the point of view of this study, the concept of evolutionary capability is especially interesting: Fujimoto defines it as a "non-routine meta-capability," in other words the capability of capability building.

Organizational Capabilities: An Alternative View

Although the need for a systemic and dynamic understanding of capabilities has been identified, the deep ontological presuppositions involved are not commonly recognized. Charles Tolman (1981) has described how ontological views have changed historically. He differentiates between "metaphysic" ontologies, which presuppose that objects exist independently of their relationships, and "dialectical" ontology, which is based on the idea that objects evolve in systems of relationships. Historically, in the beginnings of modern science, scientists sought control by defining the stable characteristics of existing things and explaining phenomena by referring to the qualities of objects. However, the explanatory power based on this *metaphysic of properties* reached its limits along with the development of science. An important advancement thereafter was the recognition that many qualities could not be understood as a property of an object but as something that emerges in the *relationship* between objects (like "color" between the viewing subject and the object).

Tolman (1981, p. 36), however, points out two limitations of the ontology of relationships: First, it assumes pre-existing unrelated things, and second it assumes that
the qualities that emerge in the relation are a function of the properties of the relating
things. This ontology is, thus, incapable of accounting for change or development,
because in it, change, movement or development can only stem from external relations, and the things that already exist before their mutual relations are regarded as
essentially static. They change, move, or develop only by coming into relation with
something else. Thus, it becomes impossible to explain how things have come about
in the first place and the question of development is reduced to only that of the first
mover.

In the dialectical ontology of developing systems, objects and qualities are seen
to co-evolve in systems of relationships. Phenomena are understood in their dynamic
motion, their emergence and evolution, rather than their mere existence at some
point of time. In this motion, the interconnections and relations are not considered as
external to the thing, but as inseparably constituting its existence and development:
". . .the relations in which the qualities of a thing emerge are not external to it, but
rather internal to it . . . . In short, the existing thing is something the essence of which
is constituted by its relations" (Tolman, 1981, p. 37).

Cultural Historical Activity Theory provides a way to conceptualize capabilities,
not as aggregates of externally linked elements, but as evolving activity systems.
The Activity Theory suggests that collective activity is motivated and defined by
the object and the outcome of the activity (Engeström, Miettinen, & Punamäki,
1999). The productive relationships between the acting subjects and the object of
the joint activity, as well as the various processes of distribution and exchange of
knowledge and intermediate products between the involved actors, are culturally
mediated. The mediators of the activity are the conceptual and practical tools used
in the activity, and the principles of the division of labor and rules, which are applied
in the work community (Engeström, 1987). In other words the system of collective,
object- and outcome-oriented activity as a whole defines the capability. People use
existing cultural artifacts and established tools and procedural models as resources
and mediators in their activity, but they also, from time to time, take distance from
existing practices and consciously change them in order to master the object of their
activity in changing conditions. Capability can thus be understood as *the mastery
of a specific object and outcome of an activity by a community of actors through a
specific system of joint activity, using specific conceptual and practical tools, forms
of division of labor, and rules of collaboration and exchange as mediators.* The
mastery of an activity can arise only as a unique system that integrates material
artifacts and human actors into a purposeful whole that cannot be reduced to its
elements or mastered as a mechanical aggregation of these elements.

An activity system is, as stated above, a dynamically evolving system. Its development can be conceptualized as cycles of expansive learning, in which inner
contradictions in the system emerge, causing aggravating situations which are then
resolved expansively by questioning the old activity and making qualitative changes
to the activity system (Engeström, 1987). According to Engeström (2001, p. 137)
"an expansive transformation is accomplished when the object and motive of the

activity are reconceptualized to embrace wider horizon of possibilities than in the previous activity." Thus, Fujimoto's (2000, p. 246) concept of evolutionary capability can be seen as the ability to master expansive transformations of the activity. Such ability requires boundary-crossing over functional boundaries and an analysis of the development of the activity system as a whole. In the following, I will describe a developmental intervention aimed at surpassing the functionally segregated form of development and creating a new, integrative form of capability building. In the next section, however, I will present the history of competence development and capability building in the case organization of this study to provide a background to the invitation I received to conduct an intervention concerning the development of the organization's capability-building practices.

History of HRD and Capability Building at Destia

In 2001, the Finnish National Road Administration was divided into two indepen-dent organizations: (1) an administrative office and (2) a state-owned production company—Destia, which operates in perfectly competitive road construction mar-kets in the same way as a private business. The following remarks on the history of the development practices in Destia and its predecessor are predominantly based on the firm's competence development team's reflection in 2002 on the history of their work, interviews, and analysis of historical documents.

In the beginning of the 1990s, the organization was a state agency governed by the principles of public-sector organizations. There were no official mechanisms to follow the development of the organization's competence needs, but development budgets were sufficient. The HRD department was free to plan the internal training programs, and the organization was famous for its efficient in-house training. The primary task of HRD practitioners who worked in the headquarters was to plan and develop courses and to coordinate their delivery. The practitioners characterized this period as the time of "head office's course factory."

The Finnish Parliament's decision to gradually divide the Finnish National Road Administration into an administrational and a business part started a long change process. As the process proceeded, it was found that the course-based system was too heavy and did not meet the new learning challenges. At the same time, com-petence building was increasingly being seen as a strategic task. The management gradually ran the training system down. It also abolished regional training officer posts and pre-planned course catalogues. A new team-based work structure was introduced to the whole organization. Team leaders were given primary responsi-bility for the development of their subordinates. In the mid-1990s, a company-wide project was launched to train "change coaches" to guide and help teams to manage organizational change by using collaborative group methods.

The change coach project failed, because the linkage between coaching methods and the ongoing operative transformation of the organization was weak, and most of the newly trained coaches felt that the training had not given them the compe-tence they needed. However, process-consultation remained part of the development work. The developers acted, for example, as facilitators in the company-wide managerial development programs which used collaborative methods. At the end of the 1990s, the organization's competence development team, which consisted of the old HRD department and some of the change coaches, started to search for new methods to be able help the organization encounter its new challenge: Soon work and income would depend solely on winning projects in the competition. One indicator of the new meanings attached to competence development was top management's decision to place the competence development team into the newly established "corporate planning" unit, in which the competence development specialists would work together with the research and development unit and IT-services unit.

The history of the development practices at Destia reflects a change from an expert-centered ("the head office's course factory") to a proceduralistic approach (e.g., the collaborative group methods). Moldaschl and Brödner (2002) criticize both approaches. They blame the expert-oriented paradigm for overlooking the true nature of open-ended organizational problems. On the other hand, they argue that the criteria-free proceduralistic processes leave the responsibility to the employees without, however, giving them proper tools to assess the consequences of their actions. Both approaches leave the underlying functional organization of development untouched.

In spring 2005, Destia's competence development team invited me to conduct a development intervention, with the help of which together we could investigate the new role that was offered to them through the removal to the corporate planning unit. The process was named "the developer workshop."

Theoretical Background of the Developer Workshop

The developer workshop intervention was based on the Change Laboratory method (Engeström, 2007), where the learning activity follows Lev Vygotsky's (1978) idea of double stimulation (see also Engeström, 2007). In Vygotsky's method, the first stimulus is the given learning task or problem, and the second stimulus is some auxiliary means for structuring the problem-solving process, which does not directly suggest the solution. In his experiments of children's learning, Vygotsky placed an essentially neutral object in the proximity of a child and followed how, when a problem-solving task exceeded the child's present capabilities, the child found a way to use the object as a tool for solving the problem. In the developer workshop, the first stimuli were created through carefully selected concrete material of present development practices (videotaped work situations, interviews, documents, etc.) that reflected the challenges of organizational capability building. The second stimuli, the mediating means, were formed by representations and models that depicted the organization and the object of capability building in various forms (see Figs. 12.1, 12.2, 12.3, and 12.4). The models, which are explained in the next section, were created on the basis of a hypothesis on what might create an expansive solution to the challenges. In this kind of structured intervention, the interventionist actively guides the participants' learning activity by, on the one hand, constructing the first stimulus by selecting material of the activity under scrutiny that shows the problems in it and, on the other hand, offering the possible means for structuring and solving the problematic situations. However, neither the specific content of the issues to be discussed and analyzed nor the solutions can be imposed on the participants by the interventionist.

The developer workshop created an arena for collective, cross-functional learning and development, in which together, the participants could explore capability-building processes and try to reconceptualize them. In order to do this, novel representations had to be collectively formed to grasp the capability as a new kind of shared object. The models used in the developer workshop aimed at presenting capabilities as a question of managing some productive activity as a dynamic whole. The idea was to help the participants expand their view of what capability building comprises and to surpass the narrow perspectives and categories of their traditional understanding of the object of their development activity. An expansion of the object of development would also mean that participants could see interdependencies between their respective objects of work, create new forms of collaboration between functionally specialized units, and see the development practices in a wider time frame.

Cross-functional development teams are not new in product development (e.g., in concurrent engineering), but they do not usually comprise HRD practitioners. In the developer workshop, the participant group consisted of HR developers (the competence development team) as well as other experts (also one manager) responsible for developing organizational concepts, systems, and knowledge. In total there were 13 participants. My role as the conductor of the intervention was to design and offer the participants first-hand data of the activities and analytical tools for reorganizing the problems in the present development practices in order to stimulate discussions that would open up perspectives for further development. All the learning tasks in the sessions involved three different elements, the selected "raw material" of the practices, the questions the interventionist posed in relation to the material, and the model as a novel representation of the practices, which helped the participants see the proposed problem in a potentially new light. The process comprised four 3-h sessions and an evaluation session, which I videotaped for further analysis. In the next section, I will present, in a general form, the developer workshop process focusing on the central models that we used in the sessions.

Warm-Up Session: Two Aspects of Capability Building

In the first session I introduced the participants to a system of co-ordinates (Fig. 12.1), in which the one axis was "human resource development" and the other "systems and organizational development." The idea was to get the participants to reflect on their own work and place themselves into the coordinate system based on how much time, in their own opinion, they spend on developing "people" and how much on developing "systems and operations models." At the same time, the

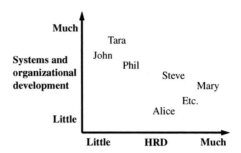

Fig. 12.1 "Me as a developer"

aim of the model was to imply that these are two aspects of the *same* activity—the development of *capabilities*.

Some participants started to reflect on their own careers and how their roles had been shifting between the two development tasks. Those who saw themselves more as systems experts located themselves in the model more straightforwardly, but the HRD practitioners, who a few years earlier had collectively investigated the historical development of their work in a similar kind of process, recognized a movement from "pure" HRD toward broader challenges of organizational learning in their work. They also realized that these two aspects were no longer so easily separable.

> M4: ...in my working history ... I've sort of moved in this direction, quite far, very far actually [*points at the HRD axis*] and then, over the last years the path has turned somewhat in this direction [*points upwards and to the direction of the systems axis*], but where exactly ...... I can't quite specify the direction of the path...
>   (Member of the Competence Development team, 9.3.2005)

The assignment did not require questioning of the customary expert roles and their boundaries but it did, however, place the two "carriers" of organizational capabilities, systems and people, as an object of development into the same picture and made the participants reflect on their past practices.

Second and Third Session: The Organizational Learning System

For the second session we gathered observational material, which mirrored the company's current development practices concerning project management and leadership, which are central capabilities in winning (or losing) new projects. Our material consisted of interviews, videotaped coaching sessions, and written documents, such as strategic policy papers. The material was collected together with the participants, and as the interventionist I selected the excerpts to be analyzed in the session. For the analysis I posed two questions: (1) In what way have different HRD actions, support systems, and company policies enhanced the ability of managers to lead projects? and (2) How coherent has the overall logic of these developmental actions been? The material concerning the development practices, together with the questions, formed the first part of the learning task—the "first stimulus" in Vygotskian terms. "The second stimulus," was the model I had created for the analysis, namely, the "organizational learning system" (Fig. 12.2).

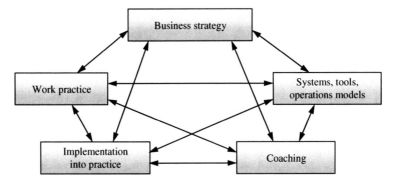

Fig. 12.2 Organizational learning system

The rationale of the model was to roughly depict the basic elements and types of actions involved in the development of organizational capabilities in Destia, and to offer the participants a horizon for investigating the development practices as a dynamic whole rather than only their specific function. The idea was to represent the connections between the elements in particular, and then analyze the possible contradictions and inconsistencies in the relationships between the elements. We had concrete data concerning all the elements in the learning system except for the work practice. The challenges of the actual project work were generated at the beginning of the session through brainstorming in pairs. However, as the data were collected from the elements separately, this proved to be a shortcoming compared to the session's learning task: The discussion stayed mainly within the separate boxes and did not as such tackle the question of the connections.

Two Cases: "Groundwork Construction" and "Managing of Data Flows"

For the third session the participants were divided into two groups, whose assignment was to build "an ideal learning system" around either some existing capability that should be supported more or some completely new capability that the organization would need in the near future. The first group chose groundwork construction capability, the development practices of which needed renewal. The second group chose the capability of managing data flows, a new capability, the building of which was part of a strategic knowledge management project. During the session, the groups presented their cases using the learning system model and were asked to comment on the solution the other group suggested. The cross evaluation of the cases interestingly brought up, for instance, the fact that even though the management of data flows was an established strategic project, it was very hard to define it in terms of whose capability was in question. A participant from the group, which had not been preparing the case, commented:

F1: I have a hard time understanding this, because the whole seems so abstract ... the questions, who really benefits from this [*the development of the capability of managing data flows*] and what is the target of this activity, the object of this activity, remain very vague. Because, if we want to build a [*learning*] system around this issue, we need to know what it's about and what the people are actually doing here ... whose learning this system supports and develops.

(Member of the Competence Development team, 19.4.2005)

Even though the model we used was the same as in the previous session, the difference was that the data was no longer about the separate elements. The focus was on how a learning system could be built to support the development of the two capabilities. This also opened up, in a new way, the question of how the different functions were connected. At the end of the session, I introduced the next model, which depicted the life cycle of a capability and the life cycle of the developmental practices related to it (see Fig. 12.3). As an assignment for the fourth session, I asked the participants to represent the two cases with the help of the life-cycle model.

Fourth Session: The Life Cycle of a Capability and the Development Forum

The organizational learning system was a static representation of organizations' developmental functions and their connections. In the fourth session we continued discussing the cases, but this time we focused on how the need to build some specific capability emerges and how the life cycle of a capability is managed, in other words, on the temporal aspect of capabilities (see Fig. 12.3). The model also presented the concept of capability more clearly as mastery of a specific object and outcome of an evolving productive activity. It carried the idea that development practices are always directed toward another activity and that this activity is a developing system, which has a dynamic of its own. Theoretically, the model of the life cycle of a form of an activity (and thus a capability) follows Engeström's (1987) theory of the cycle of expansive development.

The life-cycle model conceptualizes the evolutionary dynamics of a productive work activity as the object of the capability-building activity. In the model, the critical question is *how* and *by whom* the crisis of the old form of activity (as both a practical and a conceptual question) is detected and the required new capability is defined. The model suggests that capability-building methods also vary according to the phase of the life cycle of the work activity.[1] Defined this way, capability building requires new kinds of tools to analyze the developmental stage of the work activity in question, and its current developmental challenges. Even though this model is also "phased," as process models of development tend to be, the underlying idea is different: The analysis is directed to the developmental dynamics of the work activity, which offers more specific and contextual criteria for developmental actions. This also means that no functional expert group (or management!) can manage the

---

[1] Figure 3 shows the model in the form it was used in the intervention. However, later, the formulation of the life cycle of a development activity was changed to even more effectively highlight the dynamics of the capability in question.

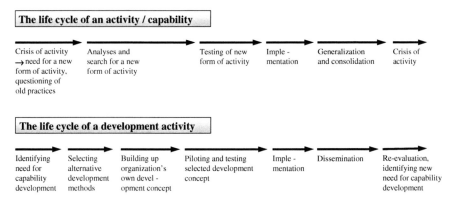

Fig. 12.3 Life-cycle model

capability-building process alone, nor can it be managed by coordinating different developers' actions without a shared analysis of the developmental stage of the activity in question.

As an assignment, the two groups constructed the capability-building cycles of the two case examples ("managing of the data flows" and "groundwork construction"). The model received an enthusiastic welcome, because it related the different developmental methods and goals to the work activity and business operations. Through this model, some of the questions discussed started to gain a more systemic form. The participants discussed, for example, why the development of the capability of managing of data flows should not be seen as a functional responsibility or a temporally delimited project:

> F4: ... a change in, like, learning and development, should really happen here. We can't think that we can start using information technology just by running through a project and then just stopping to check, like, "oops, where are we now", while the systems around us have changed and everything has to be started all over again. It's just too slow a process. Learning and developmental activity should be part of the whole process, a continuing practice...
>
> (R&D Manager, 28.4.2005)

The developer workshop contained the idea derived from the theory of expansive development, that the innovations generated in the workshop should also be experimented in practice, because reality is always more complex than any plan on paper. To create concrete pilot projects from the two cases, I offered the participants the idea of a development forum (Fig. 12.4) —a shared space for different developers for boundary-crossing analysis of work activities and capability building. It could be a permanent or temporary network, or another kind of collaborative structure of people with a shared idea of the object of development and tools to take distance from daily work and to engage in the collective learning and development activity. Here the expansive idea was that the development of a capability should be based on an analysis of the current learning challenges in the work activity, which should be done as a collective effort between different experts and the practitioners

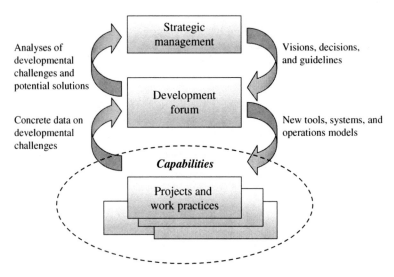

Fig. 12.4 Development forum as a collective structure for developing organizational capabilities

involved in the work activity itself. With proper tools and concepts for analyzing the local activities, a development forum would create a platform on which local innovations could be raised to the organizational level and also serve as an important link between strategic management and local dynamically evolving practices. On the basis of the development forum idea, the participants planned concrete experiments, which we gathered for evaluation in the fifth and last session of the process 3 months later.

In the next section I will analyze how the way of working presented above and the models in particular worked as stimuli for an expanded view of capability building. I do this by analyzing the discussions from the workshop sessions using Tolman's (1981) tripartite categories (ontologies of properties and relations and dialectics, see page 207). For the analysis I chose discussions in which we worked with the above-presented learning system and the life-cycle models. Because the data of the following analysis consists of videotaped and transcribed discussions, it is not possible to evaluate changes in practice. However, an analysis of the qualitative changes in the content of the discussions can reveal whether there were changes in not only the substantive conceptualization of learning challenges but also in the participants' ontological orientation toward conceptualizations with greater explanatory power, as suggested in Tolman's theory.

Structure of the Analysis

The first part of the discussion that I analyzed is from the second session and concerns the evaluation of the development practices of project leadership capability using the learning system model. The idea of looking specifically at project leadership came from me as the interventionist. The second part of discussion is from the third session and deals with the use of the same model in discussing the two cases chosen and generated independently by the participants. The third part is from the fourth session where the participants discussed the two abovementioned cases using the life-cycle model. As my interest was on the discourse relating to the models, I left a few short off-topic parts of these discussions out of the analysis.

Before moving to the analysis, it is important to note that the quality of the discourse was determined by the data that was discussed (i.e., the concrete material on the practices), the models that were used, and the learning assignments (i.e., the specific questions) that were given to the participants. Thus, the types of issues that were raised and the way in which they were brought up changed according to the assignments and the models, as we progressed from the learning system model to the hypothetically more expansive life-cycle model; a change that implied a change also in the unit of observation and analysis.

Because the learning task in the first analyzed discussion was to *question* the present organization of development activity concerning project leadership, the assignment steered the participants to bring up difficulties in present practices. Inevitably, this also meant that at the same time they suggested solutions and gave explanations both to problems and their possible solutions. Thus, I chose to analyze the discourse in this session by tracing all *problem statements* and *suggestions for solution* from the discussion. In general, the discussion could not be regarded as very dialogical: a great deal of the discourse was separate remarks that the participants made without directly continuing the previous speaker's ideas. Even shared themes did not provoke very long discussions. Only the theme of how the masses of data in internal databases could be better organized and managed in order to help people find what they need in their work engendered a lengthy discussion.

The same units of analysis also worked for the second discussion, even though it already had a slightly more dialogical nature and focused more clearly on six shared themes. However, in both of these discussions, only two of the themes that created dialog lasted over 350 words. The average amount of words per theme in the first discussion was 300, and in the second 400 (see Table 12.1). In the analysis concerning the first and the second discussions, I counted the statements/suggestions as follows: If a person mentioned some problem or idea twice during the same turn at talk, I counted it as one reference, but if the same person brought this problem or idea up again later, I counted it as a new reference. I defined *a turn* as Linell's (1998, p. 159) "a continuous period when one speaker holds the floor." The average

Table 12.1 Overview of analyzed data

Discussion	Participants	Shared themes	Statements & suggestions	Turns/theme (average)	Words/theme (average)	Participants/ theme (average)
1st	11	12	122	–	300	3.25
2nd	11	6	77	–	400	4.33
3rd	10	7	–	11	787	4.57

of statements/suggestions per person was 11 in the first discussion (within a range of 0–36) and 7 in the second (within a range of 1–23). Because pair and group work was used between the shared discussions, those who had the most statements or suggestions in their account had usually also spoken as representatives of a pair or working group.

The third discussion that dealt with the life-cycle model was quite different in nature. The average amount of words per theme in the discussion was 787, which was significantly more than in the previous discussions. The participants no longer expressed problems or suggestions as discrete remarks but the problems were connected to and developed as part of broader challenges. The discussion proceeded through seven larger themes, each of which had a very coherent, shared object of focus, with two or more participants taking part (the variation was between 2 and 8 speakers per theme). Thus, in this case I chose *the themes* as the unit of analysis. Each theme in the discussion was weighted by counting the amount of turns per theme, the average of which was 11 (within a range of 3–33).

In the following analysis, I use Tolman's categories to trace the qualitative change in how the learning challenges were conceptualized. First, I organized the statements/suggestions in the first and the second discussions, and the themes in the third discussion, into the three categories based on their ontological quality. Next I detected the proportional change in how the problems/suggestions and themes fell into these categories within the discussions. The principles I used for dividing the data into Tolman's categories were as follows: If a statement or discussion theme contained an assessment of a problem, challenge or potential new practice in capability building as a single quality or a stand-alone phenomenon of a thing, I put it in the ontological category of properties (e.g., "workers have the wrong attitude" or "IT-systems are poor"). If the statement brought up some problem or possibility for improved practice that concerned related things or the relationship itself, I put it in the ontological category of relations. According to Tolman, a dialectical way of perceiving things is to "grasp things in their self-movement, not merely in their external or mechanical movement" (1981, p. 38). Thus, if the statement or discussion contained a reference to a (historical) change of the internal relations or temporal development of the system as a whole, I put it into the category of dialectics (for a well-grounded introduction to the dialectical approach, see Glassman, 2000).

I tested the validity of the analysis by asking another researcher to test score the data. In the categorization concerning the first discussion, we had a difference of opinion in 30.43% of the cases, in the second discussion, 21.05% of the cases, and in the third discussion 14.29% of the cases. Most of the differences of opinion concerned situations were I had defined the case as belonging to the ontology of relations and the inter-scorer as belonging to the ontology of properties. This was because the inter-scorer based his evaluation on the data regarding the statements/suggestions and themes, which, in some cases, did not give enough context information for detecting the relationship reflected by the statement/suggestion in the discussion. After discussing the reasons behind the differences, a consensus was reached in most cases, only one problem statement and three suggestions for a solution remained non-scorable. In these few cases, the ontological quality was not clearly definable, because of the scarcity of information in the speech, which made it difficult to define what the speaker had really meant in her/his statement.

Analysis of Qualitative Changes in the Discussions

In the first discussion concerning the learning system of project leadership, most of the problem statements (72.73% of the 55 problem statements concerning 19 different issues) remained on the level of properties in Tolman's categories, whereas the rest reflected the ontology of relations (27.27%). A typical property-based interpretation of present problems was that poorly functioning practices in projects were due to employees' "wrong attitudes" (seven references). In other words, many problems were interpreted as a result of peoples' unwanted characteristics or lack of will. The participants argued, for example, that people easily claim that IT systems are a burden and do not provide enough support, just because they do not want to learn to use them. Other property-based arguments were that IT systems contain too much information or wrong logic of functioning (properties of the systems, eight references), the managers have not been able to make strategic choices or do not know how to lead (properties of the managers, five references), or that people lack competences or do not use existing ones to the full (properties of the workers, three references).

Among the suggestions for solutions, a majority presented the ontology of properties as well (49.25% of the 67 suggestions for solution concerning 27 different issues). The most common property-based suggestion was that "things should be done in a more systemic and orderly manner" (seven references). The relation-based suggestions (41.79% of the cases) usually dealt with the issue of how to better connect the systems or development practices to actual work practices, depicted in the learning system model as arrows leading to the "work practice" box. A typical suggestion in this category was that the operative business units should be better connected to the strategy processes (four references). In this discussion the suggestion to "improve interaction" (six references) remained non-scorable. Even if, in theory it emphasizes the relations between people, the sense in which it was used in the discourse gave it an intrinsic value of its own, thus it could not be defined properly. No statements representing the ontology of dialectics were found.

I argue that the first discussion remained mainly on the level of properties because the observational material was collected from the separate elements in the learning system model and thus focused the discourse on the existing functions and responsibilities rather than the relationships between them. Despite the two-headed arrows between the boxes, the participants read the model as just another static representation of the prevailing organizational structure. The lack of concrete cases also made the challenges more abstract, which was manifested in a large amount of passive talk ("the general competence level should be raised"), ascribing the responsibility of managing the challenges to some third party.

In the second discussion, in contrast, the participants presented two learning systems through concrete case activities which they themselves had selected. This also changed the dynamics of the conversation. The problem statements now mainly followed the ontology of relations (69.70% of the 33 problem statements concerning 21 different issues). The cases triggered discussions on, for instance, how ground work construction professionals could be more flexibly moved between the local projects and how the organizational control systems could better support participation in organizational competence networks. The question of how capabilities are managed was also more concretely present in the discussions than in the previous session. Character-based talk blaming either unmotivated or unskilled people or poor systems vanished almost completely. Nearly, all the suggested solutions belonged to the ontology of relations (90.91% of the 44 suggestions for solution concerning 17 different issues). The two most commonly suggested relation-based solutions concerned the question of whether the financial resources for competence development should be located in a centralized budget (13 references) or whether the local projects should carry the costs of training in their own budgets (six references).

In the third discussion, the participants elaborated on the two cases using the life-cycle model. The hypothesis was that the model would support dialectical thinking since dialectics highlights the evolution of activities in their mutual, inseparable relations. When reading the data it soon became clear that the discussion differed from the previous ones. Most of the initiatives for specific discussion themes came from the participants, not from the interventionist, and the discussion proceeded as a dialogue between the participants. Thus, in the analysis, it no longer made sense to count the separate suggestions and I concentrated on the themes and the amount of turns per theme in the dialogue. I defined the category of the theme by the ontologically most far-reaching idea that was expressed during the dialogue. Here many ideas of dialectical nature were also found. The participants noticed, for example, that development projects are special in that their objectives and goals usually change during the process when people learn more about the activity under development. Thus, the actors should be capable of reflecting and changing their actions and conceptions of what is being done, and why, during the process. In addition, the prerequisites for moving forward in the process should be critically evaluated in the transitions between the phases of capability building (a theme of eight turns). When continuing the theme from the previous session of flexible management of professional resources, the participants noted now that it would also require planning of the professionals' training in a longer time frame, and changes to the roles and forms of the developers' collaboration (a theme of 33 turns).

Figure 12.5 summarizes the above-presented findings. In the cases of the first and second discussion I put all the problem statements and suggestions for solutions reflecting the same ontology together, and counted their proportion in the discussions. In the case of the third discussion I put together the themes that represented the same ontological category and first counted the total number of turns per category, then their proportion of the total number of all the turns.

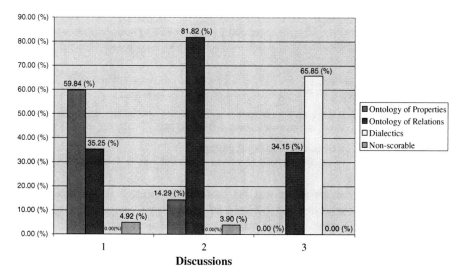

Fig. 12.5 Proportions of different ontological categories of thinking in the analyzed discussions

Development Forum and Planning of Concrete Pilot Projects

The new systemic ideas that emerged during the process were, however, easier to construct conceptually than to transfer into practice. The intention was to construct two developmental experiments, one concerning groundwork construction and one concerning the management of data flows, in which the participants could test the new ideas in practice. When we came to selecting the persons responsible for the experiments among the participants, the responsibility shifted back to the specialists present who, according to their official roles, were in charge of the activities the pilot experiments comprised. Their better substance knowledge of these activities gave them an advantage in negotiating for practical solutions, and other participants offered them the space to take the lead. In addition, as an organization already existed for the building of groundwork construction capability, the established division of work was hard to surpass in practice. Thus, the narrow conception of the competence developers' roles as "co-ordinative implementers" in development processes reappeared:

> M5: It's just a fact, that the competence development team, if we think of engineering and construction, or of this data flow case, that you don't really have the competence to define what the competence needs are here. The responsibility ends up being ours or theirs, [*the IT experts*], that's just the way it goes …
>
> (Leader of a business unit, 28.4.2005)

The management of the data flows, instead, turned out to be a challenge that could not be met within the framework of the prevailing division of work. By concentrating on a concrete data flow case, the practitioners saw the necessity of crossing the traditional professional boundaries.

M5: I think it would be good if we could focus [*the pilot*] on, like, the virtual construction plan and its link to the road building projects, I mean, the link between the planner and the builder, managing that link from the competence point of view ... To take it over by means of a concrete case.

M1: Should we change our [*first*] idea and take the virtual construction plan [*as a pilot experiment*], it would tell us more about what we are really lacking...

M5: And there is, in a way, one huge boundary, the planner—the builder, and mastering it through this virtual tool, and also the competence related to it...

M1: To virtually get rid of that boundary in practice.
                              (Leader of a business unit and Leader of a consulting team, 28.4.2005)

Unfortunately, from the pilots that the practitioners created in the last session, only the ideas concerning the building of groundwork construction capability were tried out in practice, as top management decided to postpone the strategic knowledge management project, making it no longer possible to continue the data flow pilot.

Conclusions and Practical Implications

This chapter discussed a developmental intervention, "the developer workshop," as a way of building new capabilities by introducing new concepts and boundary-crossing models to practitioners as a means to question and develop the structures, roles, and norms of present development activity. When evaluating the intervention process, the participants of the workshop affirmed that the models we used for analyzing the development practices had helped them create a more systemic view of the complex issue of capability building, offered them concrete tools to set a dialogue between different practitioners, and opened up new forms of collaboration. This development can also be seen in the qualitative changes of the discussions during the workshop. However, the intervention also showed how easily collectively created and accepted new ideas tend to dissolve into old practices, and how difficult it is to question the deep-seated functional structures of an organization and create a shared object of development. Understanding the object of activity as a dialectically evolving system calls for cross-functional agency. In this case, the contradiction between the organization that was based on the ontology of properties and relations (responsibilities divided according to function-based roles) and the new dialectical understanding of capability building was solved by retracting to old thinking.

From the dialectical point of view, a shortcoming of the developer workshop was that the historically developed contradiction of the present organization of capability building, which, according to the theory of expansive development, creates the need for change, and which manifests itself as aggravating situations in everyday practices, was not elaborated thoroughly during the sessions. We looked at how HRD specialists have traditionally participated in capability building and what perspectives of capabilities the traditional roles delimit from them, but we did not, however, discuss the history of the functional organization in a wider perspective, and its limitedness in managing the increasing pace of change in organizational activities and related capabilities. Without the understanding of the historically developed contradiction of the functional organization of capability building, the idea of, for instance, the development forum (see Fig. 12.4) as a platform of collective analysis did not come to life. However, although the developer workshop had these limitations, the conceptual idea of looking at capabilities through models that take the activity to be mastered as the object of inquiry has significant potential.

Concepts, models, and representations have a central role when people construct the object of their activity. The intervention proved that the kind of representations through which the object is analyzed is not insignificant, because the representations define (a) what can be seen as a manageable challenge, (b) how people interpret the causes of problems, and (c) how they construct the means to solve them. The more open and complex a challenge, the harder it is to manage it with tools and concepts that are based on the traditional, functional categorization of the nature of the problem. However, the model is not the only factor in the conceptualization, a link to the concrete practice is crucial: without a concrete real-life case, a model is an empty abstraction and subject to customary (or even mythical) explanations of the state of affairs. Thus, in order to achieve a new understanding of the intentional creation of organizational capabilities, the conceptualizations of capability must, on the one hand, surpass the models of the traditional paradigm of the functionally operating organization, and on the other, be reflected through a concrete real-life case in all its complexity. Concrete cases as shared objects turned the discussions in the developer workshop from disconnected and subjective observations to the deliberation of the complex relations of a concrete work activity. The way in which the practitioners conceptualized the object and ontologically oriented themselves to the challenges of capability building altered notably, as we progressed to more complex models and had more concrete cases that represented real-life challenges in their true, complex form.

The most expansive development of the discourse in the workshop was achieved by introducing the idea of the temporal evolution of capability, which stated that an activity, for the mastery of which it is required, is not static and cannot be managed by mere co-ordination and aggregation of function-based actions. The temporal mastery of historically formed activities and capabilities requires new forms of participation and agency from all involved in capability-building practices. For HRD practitioners, for example, this creates a particularly new challenge: their expertise, tools, concepts, and forms of collaboration should be directed toward a more theoretical mastery of the evolutionary dynamics of activities instead of the implementation of methods to predefined goals. What these new tools of HRD are in practice, and how the new forms of collaboration are achieved, is a central theme for future research. This would certainly also require that the representatives of related activities (e.g., other experts and management) also rethink and expand their views and conceptions of capability building, and create new tools better suited to the systemic and developmental view of capability than those currently available. Otherwise the predominant organization of activities will override any fragile new ideas.

Acknowledgments The author would like to thank Professor Jaakko Virkkunen for his valuable comments on different versions of this chapter.

References

Ahonen, H. (2008). *Reciprocal development of the object and subject of learning (in Finnish).* Helsinki: Yliopistopaino.

Ambrosini, V., & Bowman, C. (2009). What are dynamic capabilities and are they a useful construct in strategic management? *International Journal of Management Reviews, 11*(1), 29–49.

Dosi, G., Nelson, R. R., & Winter, S. G. (2000). Introduction: The nature and dynamics of organizational capabilities. In G. Dosi, R. R. Nelson, & S. Winter (Eds.), *The Nature and Dynamics of Organizational Capabilities* (pp. 1–22). New York: Oxford University Press.

Eisenhardt, K. M., & Martin, J. A. (2000). Dynamic capabilities: What are they? *Strategic Management Journal, 21*, 1105–1121.

Engeström, Y. (1987). *Learning by expanding.* Helsinki: Orienta Konsultit.

Engeström, Y. (2001) Expansive learning at work: Toward an activity theoretical reconceptualization. *Journal of Education and Work, 14*(1), 133–156.

Engeström, Y. (2007). Putting Vygotsky to work. The change laboratory as an application double stimulation In H. Daniels, M. Cole, & J. V. Wertsch (Eds.), *The Cambridge Companion to Vygotsky* (pp. 363–382). New York: Cambridge University Press.

Engeström, Y., Miettinen, R., & Punamäki, R. -L. (Eds.). (1999). *Perspectives on activity theory.* New York: Cambridge University Press.

Freeman, C., & Louçã, F. (2001). *As times go by. From the industrial revolutions to the information revolution.* New York: Oxford University Press.

Fujimoto, T. (2000). Evolution of manufacturing systems and ex post dynamic capabilities: A case of Toyota's assembly operations. In G. Dosi, R. R. Nelson, & S. Winter (Eds.), *The Nature and Dynamics of Organizational Capabilities* (pp. 1–22). New York: Oxford University Press.

Glassman, M. (2000). Negation through history: Dialectics and human development. *New Ideas in Psychology, 18*, 1–22.

Hamel, G., & Breen, B. (2007). *The future of management.* Boston, MA: Harvard Business School press.

Linell, P. (1998). Approaching dialogue. Talk, interaction and contexts in dialogical perspectives. Amsterdam/Philadelphia: John Benjamins.

Miettinen, R., & Virkkunen J. (2005). Epistemic objects, artefacts and organizational change. *Organization, 12*(3), 437–456

Moldaschl, M. F., & Brödner, P. (2002). A reflexive methodology in intervention. In P. Doherty, J. Forslin, & R. Shani (Eds.), *Creating Sustainable Work Systems: Emerging Perspectives and Practice* (pp. 179–189). London/New York: Routledge.

Nelson, R. R. & Winter, S. G. (1982). *An evolutionary theory of economic change.* Cambridge, MA: The Belknap Press of Harvard University Press.

Newbert, S. L. (2007). Empirical research on the resource-based view of the firm: An assessment and suggestions for future research. *Strategic Management Journal, 28*(2), 121–146.

Perez, C. (2002) *Technological revolutions and financial capital. The dynamics of bubbles and golden age.* Cheltenham: Edward Elgar.

Teece, D. J., Pisano, G., & Shuen, A. (1997). Dynamic capabilities and strategic management, *Strategic Management Journal, 18*(7), 509–533.

Tolman, C. (1981). The metaphysic of relations in *Klaus Riegel's "Dialectics"* of Human development. *Human Development, 24*, 33–51.

Vygotsky, L. S. (1978). *Mind in society. The development of higher psychological functions.* Cambridge, MA: Harvard University Press.

Chapter 13
Implications for Research and Practice

Rob F. Poell and Marianne van Woerkom

The 12 chapters preceding this final one have brought us a rich array of evidence-based insights from conceptual and empirical research around the following issues:

- Which interventions can organizations make to encourage workplace learning?
- How can social support contribute to workplace learning?
- What measures can be taken to stimulate collective learning in the workplace?

In this chapter we discuss what the various studies have taught us about these topics and what that means for further research into workplace learning and for organizational practice. We start, however, by discussing how our authors have defined workplace learning: what is learning in their view and what role does the workplace play in that respect?

What Is Workplace Learning?

A number of different views of what is workplace learning can be seen to emerge from the various chapters in this volume. Rob Poell and Marianne van Woerkom (Chapter 1) describe learning in the workplace as a natural and largely autonomous process derived from the characteristics of the work process and its inherent social interactions. In their view, learning in the workplace is often implicit and sometimes even hard to differentiate from doing the daily work. This perspective seems to be shared by Suzanne Verdonschot and Paul Keursten (Chapter 11), who describe learning for innovation as emanating from relevant work issues ("How could we solve this problem?"). In their view, learning and working coincide when a complex situation arises for which no solution has been found yet. Learning itself adds value to the work by improving and innovating it. In Chapter 8, Russ Korte starts from the related conception that a significant amount of learning in work settings occurs informally and relies on learning from others and from doing the work. He notes

R.F. Poell (✉)
Department of Human Resource Studies, Tilburg University, Tilburg, The Netherlands
e-mail: r.poell@uvt.nl

R.F. Poell, M. van Woerkom (eds.), *Supporting Workplace Learning*, Professional and Practice-based Learning 5, DOI 10.1007/978-90-481-9109-3_13,
© Springer Science+Business Media B.V. 2011

that recent developments in learning theories tend to emphasize the relational factors between the learner and the environment as an important influence on learning outcomes. Learning in the context of work can thus be conceptualized as a form of social exchange: a give-and-take relationship among "instructors" providing access to expertise and learners building their own expertise. Stephen Billett (Chapter 9), however, shows that while learning is ongoing through everyday work activities, often this occurs without access to more expert social partners. Employees even learn through everyday work activities typically and largely in the absence of direct guidance: by just doing their job, observing and listening to others, and the contributions of the physical workplace setting. In essence, then, the studies reported in the abovementioned chapters (all qualitative in nature, incidentally) propose workplace learning as expanding one's action repertoire by engaging in meaningful work experiences, a process largely driven by employees themselves in the context of everyday work and social interactions.

In a number of other studies in this volume, workplace learning is presented as a necessary companion to the learning that is supposed to occur in the context of training and development programs. Karen Oostvogel and colleagues (Chapter 2), for example, found that organizing such formal programs is still a major part of the job conducted by the HRD practitioners in their sample; workplace learning seemed to be an area that HRD practitioners deem important, but rather difficult to influence in their roles. Ronan Carbery and Tom Garavan (Chapter 3) focus on formal training and development activities and seem to assume that what participants learn in those situations will be transferred to the workplace. Chris Carroll and colleagues (Chapter 4) explicitly position workplace learning as an important mechanism in transferring skills and knowledge from the academic environment and embedding them within working practice. They see the potential offered by e-learning in bringing academic content and the workplace context together. In the abovementioned chapters, however, workplace learning does not transpire as a natural, ongoing process; rather, it is a way of making sure that what people have learned from organized programs is used on the job. Basically, Chapter 12 by Marika Schaupp also has a program-based view of learning; however, unlike Chapters 2 through 4 she focuses on producing collective learning and the development program aims to get participants to reflect on the way in which work is currently organized. Although the program offered employees concrete tools to have a dialogue and collaborate, old work practices and organizational structures were found to be rather difficult to change. Apparently it is quite hard for HRD consultants to "use" workplace learning as (part of) an intervention.

A third set of chapters in this volume focus on workplace learning as a process that may be brought about by coaching and mentoring activities of supervisors rather than by formal programs. Derk-Jan Nijman and John Gelissen (Chapter 6), however, combine the two in their quantitative study on the role of supervisory support in transferring learning results from training programs to employee's performance on the job. Supervisors are found to be able to influence the learning climate of the workplace. Andrea Ellinger and colleagues (Chapter 5) see the workplace as a place where adults learn and the learning itself as a daily ongoing process that is interwoven in and inseparably connected to the daily processes of work (cf. Chapters 1, 8, 9, and 11). Managerial coaching can facilitate workplace learning if managers recognize the catalysts that might stimulate coaching opportunities in their daily interactions with employees (cf. learning climate). Similarly, Andrew Rock and Tom Garavan (Chapter 7) present a relational perspective on mentoring and other developmental relationships in order to better understand their potential contributions to learning and career development. While their study focuses on everyday interactive processes, it is not as explicit about the learning itself. In Chapter 10, Marianne van Woerkom does quite clearly present a cognitivist perspective on team learning as a process of information acquisition, information distribution, information interpretation, and information storage and retrieval, by which teams may create knowledge for themselves or others. Her quantitative study shows that team coaching does not lead directly to team learning but is able to create conditions for team learning by helping the team members to build a collective commitment and to improve their interpersonal relationships. From the abovementioned chapters, it seems that the learning climate is a crucial context aspect of workplace learning that coaching and mentoring can influence.

Interventions for Workplace Learning

The interventions encountered in this volume range from corporate training and development programs to online courses in higher education, from team coaching to mentoring relationships, from HRD strategies to supervisory support, and from innovation projects to organization development workshops. The individual as well as the team and organization levels are dealt with across all chapters. Two chapters stand out: Stephen Billett (Chapter 9) shows how much of the learning in workplaces takes place in the absence of any kind of expert guidance and Russ Korte (Chapter 8) describes the socialization practices that occur among employees in engineering firms as newcomers learn the ropes. In both these cases, there is no "intervention" in the traditional sense, where an expert or authority figure attempts to influence an organizational process. Both authors are well aware, however, of the day-to-day interactions among colleagues in the workplace, which can actually be rather strong forces in getting employees to conduct themselves in certain ways.

In a way, of course, every action by any actor in the workplace can be thought of as an intervention, even though they may be more or less explicitly designed as such and even though their effect on other employees may differ strongly as well. This is implied by Poell and Van der Krogt (2010), who see individual employees as being capable of strategic action when it comes to their professional development. Based on their values and interests, and taking into account the social networks in which they operate, individual employees can more or less deliberately engage in activities to further their professional development.

Going back to the more "traditional" interventions that make up most of this volume, it is worthwhile to note that on the whole, the ones remaining closer to the primary work process (e.g., supervisory coaching and mentoring), involving employees and their managers, seem to be more effective than the ones that are program based, involving HRD consultants. HRD practitioners seem to be struggling with the question of how to connect their interventions with the learning that is already going on in the workplace. This was explicitly voiced in Chapter 2 by Karen Oostvogel and colleagues (which was a replication study of previous work in various countries showing similar findings). One possible way for HRD practitioners to get ahead in this struggle is attempting to make workplace learning more structured, more didactic, more formalized. Perhaps this is even what they have been trying to do over the last 15 years or so, without much success we should add. Another potential way forward is for HRD practitioners to accept that workplace learning is largely the realm of employees and managers and to create specific alliances with those actors for each work-based challenge, based on a thorough understanding of the dynamics of learning and the workplace and how it might be supported. The latter approach assumes that HRD practitioners team up with employees and managers to analyze work-related problems, (co-) develop (or recognize) relevant experiences for them to learn from, and find a suitable combination of on/off-the-job situations that will enable them to reduce their problems.

Measures for Collective Learning in the Workplace

Three chapters in this volume deal specifically with collective learning (all Part III). In Chapter 10, Marianne van Woerkom shows that team learning processes may be stimulated by creating team cohesion, which leads to more and better communication among team members. She also shows that team cohesion may be stimulated by team coaching, which leads to a collective commitment to the task. Teams with clear boundaries (identity) and high interdependency among members also experienced more team learning than other teams did. She concludes that stimulating the interpersonal relations in a team should be made an explicit goal for team leaders, who should also be selected and assessed on their coaching skills.

Suzanne Verdonschot and Paul Keursten studied innovation projects with a specific view of providing guidelines to help organizations in designing learning environments that support innovation projects. They present 11 design principles, which are described and illustrated at length in Chapter 11. Preconditions that innovation projects should have in place in order for these design principles to work fruitfully are (1) an intricate question, problematic situation, or long-standing issue that requires an innovative solution, (2) a group of people from one or more organizations, all of whom are committed to solving the problem, and (3) a concrete manifestation of the problem that is dealt with. Notions underlying the design principles seem to include double-loop learning, a strengths-based approach, learning by doing, encouraging creativity, and social capital (Harrison & Kessels, 2008). Interestingly, in view of the discussion raised in Section "What Is Workplace Learning?" of this chapter, these notions and the 11 principles seem to refer to strategies that HRD consultants could undertake rather well, albeit in constant interaction with employees and managers. They would, however, need to be HRD consultants with a thorough understanding of learning in the workplace as an ongoing process, with an eye for management as well as employee interests, with a high tolerance for ambiguity, and with a talent for bringing energy together and linking it to out-of-the-box creativity.

Chapter 12 by Marika Schaupp discussed a developmental intervention, "the developer workshop," as a way of building new capabilities by introducing new concepts and boundary-crossing models to practitioners as a means to question and develop the structures, roles, and norms of present development activity. When evaluating the intervention process, the participants of the workshop affirmed that the models we used for analyzing the development practices had helped them create a more systemic view of the complex issue of capability building, offered them concrete tools to set a dialogue between different practitioners, and opened up new forms of collaboration. This development can also be seen in the qualitative changes of the discussions during the workshop. However, the intervention also showed how easily collectively created and accepted new ideas tend to dissolve into old practices, and how difficult it is to question the deep-seated functional structures of an organization and create a shared object of development. Understanding the object of activity as a dialectically evolving system calls for cross-functional agency. In this case, the contradiction between the organization that was based on the ontology of properties and relations (responsibilities divided according to function-based roles), and the new dialectical understanding of capability building, was solved by retracting to old thinking.

From the dialectical point of view, a shortcoming of the developer workshop was that the historically developed contradiction of the present organization of capability building, which, according to the theory of expansive development, creates the need for change, and which manifests itself as aggravating situations in everyday practices, was not elaborated thoroughly during the sessions. We looked at how HRD specialists have traditionally participated in capability building and what perspectives of capabilities the traditional roles delimit from them, but we did not, however, discuss the history of the functional organization in a wider perspective, and its limitedness in managing the increasing pace of change in organizational activities and related capabilities. Without the understanding of the historically developed contradiction of the functional organization of capability building, the idea of, for instance, the development forum (see Fig. 12.4) as a platform of collective analysis did not come to life. However, although the developer workshop had these limitations, the conceptual idea of looking at capabilities through models that take the activity to be mastered as the object of inquiry has significant potential.

Concepts, models, and representations have a central role when people construct the object of their activity. The intervention proved that the kind of representations through which the object is analyzed is not insignificant, because the representations define (a) what can be seen as a manageable challenge, (b) how people interpret the causes of problems, and (c) how they construct the means to solve them. The more open and complex a challenge, the harder it is to manage it with tools and concepts that are based on the traditional, functional categorization of the nature of the problem. However, the model is not the only factor in the conceptualization, a link to the concrete practice is crucial: without a concrete real-life case, a model is an empty abstraction and subject to customary (or even mythical) explanations of the state of affairs. Thus, in order to achieve a new understanding of the intentional creation of organizational capabilities, the conceptualizations of capability must, on the one hand, surpass the models of the traditional paradigm of the functionally operating organization, and on the other hand, be reflected through a concrete real-life case in all its complexity. Concrete cases as shared objects turned the discussions in the developer workshop from disconnected and subjective observations to the deliberation of the complex relations of a concrete work activity. The way in which the practitioners conceptualized the object and ontologically oriented themselves to the challenges of capability building altered notably, as we progressed to more complex models and had more concrete cases that represented real-life challenges in their true, complex form.

The most expansive development of the discourse in the workshop was achieved by introducing the idea of the temporal evolution of capability, which stated that an activity, for the mastery of which it is required, is not static and cannot be managed by mere co-ordination and aggregation of function-based actions. The temporal mastery of historically formed activities and capabilities requires new forms of participation and agency from all involved in capability building practices. For HRD practitioners, for example, this creates a particularly new challenge: their expertise, tools, concepts, and forms of collaboration should be directed toward a more theoretical mastery of the evolutionary dynamics of activities instead of the implementation of methods to predefined goals. What these new tools of HRD are in practice, and how the new forms of collaboration are achieved, is a central theme for future research. This would certainly also require that the representatives of related activities (e.g., other experts and management) also rethink and expand their views and conceptions of capability building, and create new tools better suited to the systemic and developmental view of capability than those currently available. Otherwise the predominant organization of activities will override any fragile new ideas.

References

Harrison, R., & Kessels, J. W. M. (2008). *Human resource development in a knowledge economy: An organizational view* (2nd ed.), Hampshire/New York: Palgrave MacMillan.
Poell, R. F., & Van der Krogt, F. J. (2010). Individual learning paths of employees in the context of social networks. In S. Billett (Ed.), *Learning through practice: Models, traditions, orientations and approaches* (pp. 197–221). Dordrecht: Springer.

Index

A

Action domains, 3, 12, 16–24
Activity theory, 154, 208
Agency, 147, 149–150, 153–154, 157–158, 161, 206–207, 209, 222–223, 229–230
Attachment theory, 111–112, 114–115, 117–118, 122–123
Australia, 3, 11–24, 49, 155–156
Authenticity, 5, 111, 116, 119–120

B

Breakthrough, 185–195, 197–200

C

Capability, 3, 6, 72, 135, 142, 167, 205–224, 229–230
Capability building, 3, 6, 205–224, 229–230
Career decision-making, 107
Career development, 2, 12, 73–74, 107, 116, 122, 126, 142, 227
Career theory, 107
Case stories, 15
Case study research, 134, 146, 187
Change laboratory, 210
Changing roles, 11
Coaching, 71–82, 165–177, 213
Cohesiveness, 102, 168
Collective learning, 2–3, 5, 165–177, 183–201, 205–230
Compatibility, 5, 110, 116, 118–119
Constant comparative method, 15

D

Design principles, 6, 183–201, 228
Developmental relationships, 5, 74, 107–123, 227
Dialectics, double stimulation, 210, 216, 218–221

Dialogue, 5, 60, 76, 111, 113, 116, 120–121, 220, 222, 226, 229

E

E-Learning, 3–4, 47–64, 226
Evolutionary capability, 207, 209

F

Facilitating learning at work, 76
Feedback, 5, 15, 34–35, 54, 61–62, 73, 77–79, 90, 92, 100–112, 116–117, 120–121, 123, 166–167, 169, 185
Formal training and development, 3, 27–41, 226

G

Guided learning, 2

H

Higher Education, 5, 48–50, 54, 134, 165, 177, 227
HRD practitioners, 1–3, 6, 11–24, 109, 205–206, 209, 211–212, 223, 226, 228, 230
HRD roles, 14, 16, 18, 23
HRD strategies, 11–12, 15, 22–24, 227

I

Informal workplace learning, 4, 71
Innovation, 2, 6, 13–14, 155, 157, 165, 183–188, 190–194, 196–200, 205, 207, 215–216, 225, 227–228
Innovation practice, 200
Innovation process, 187–188, 190, 194, 198–200
Interdependence, 111, 116–119, 123, 132
Interpsychological processes, 149–150, 152, 154
Intervention, 1–3, 6, 11–24, 27–41, 47–64

R.F. Poell, M. van Woerkom (eds.), *Supporting Workplace Learning*, Professional
and Practice-based Learning 5, DOI 10.1007/978-90-481-9109-3,
© Springer Science+Business Media B.V. 2011

J
Job satisfaction, 81, 143

K
Knowledge economy, 1, 183, 185–186
Knowledge productivity, 3, 6, 183–201

L
Leader–member exchange, 95, 111–112,
    116–117, 123, 131
Leader–member exchange theory (LMX),
    111–112, 116–117, 123, 131
Learning culture, 2–3, 17–24, 34
Learning networks, 3, 11–14, 16, 20–21, 23–24
Learning-Network Theory, 3, 12–14, 16,
    20–21, 23–24
Learning programs, 12–13, 15–16, 18,
    23–24, 48
Learning through work, 5, 147, 150,
    154–155, 159
Learning at work, 1–6, 11–24, 27–41, 47–64,
    76, 226
Learning for working life, 148
Lifelong learning, 158

M
Managerial coaching, 4, 71–82, 166, 227
Mediation, 101, 160, 174–175
Mentoring, 2–5, 72–74, 107–123, 135–136,
    140, 226–227
Model, 3, 28, 30, 32, 36–37, 62, 72–74, 77–78,
    91–95, 97–101, 108–110, 131–132, 170,
    172, 174, 196, 211–220, 223, 229
Moderated learning, 56–57
Motivation, 4–6, 27, 31–32, 48, 57, 59–60, 81,
    89, 93–98, 100–104, 113, 115, 119, 157,
    192–193, 200

N
Networks, 13–14, 107, 109, 113–114, 140,
    157, 220, 227

O
Online learning, 47, 49, 56, 61, 63
Organizational socialization, 129–130, 142
Organizational types, 14

P
Participation attitudes, 4, 28–34, 37, 41
Participation in training and development,
    27–29, 31–37, 39–41
Path analysis, 184
Perceived behavioural control, 4, 27–31, 37–41
Personal agency, 154, 157–158

Personal epistemology, 149–150, 152,
    155–156, 158
Planned behaviour, 3, 27–41, 113, 184,
    209, 216

Q
Qualitative studies, 49

R
Reflection, 5, 56, 59, 109–111, 116,
    120–121, 123, 135, 138, 169, 195–196,
    199, 209
Relatedness theory, 111–112, 115, 117, 123
Relational, 5, 107–123, 130–132, 141–143,
    226–227
Relational interdependence, 111, 116–119, 123
Relationship building, 5, 111, 135,
    139–141, 143
Relative social isolation, 5, 147–161

S
Self-in-relation theory, 111–112, 115–119, 123
Situated learning, 59
Small business, 5, 147–161
Social agency, 147, 150
Social capital, 5, 110, 112–114, 117, 123, 228
Social cognition, 112
Social cognitive theory, 110, 112, 117–118,
    120, 123
Social exchange, 5, 130–132, 140–141, 226
Social experience, 143
Social norms, 5, 129–130, 133–136, 138, 140
Social support theory, 110, 112–113,
    117–118, 123
Student experience, 48, 50, 58, 61–62
Subjective norms, 4, 28–32, 34–37, 41
Supervisor support, 4, 89–104
Systematic review, 47–64

T
Teacher teams, 5, 165–167, 169–171, 173, 177
Team coaching, 5, 165–177, 227–228
Team leadership, 5, 94, 166–167, 169–171,
    176–177, 209, 228
Team learning, 5–6, 165–177, 227–228
Thematic analysis, 50, 139
Trainee, 4–5, 30, 33–35, 39, 89–91, 93–98,
    100–104
Training constraints, 28, 34, 37, 40
Training effectiveness, 89
Training intentions, 27–28, 32–34, 36–41
Training participation behavior, 3, 28, 37, 40
Training system expectancies, 28, 30–34
Transfer climate, 4, 35, 89, 93–98, 100–103

Transfer of training, 4, 89–104
Trust, 5, 79, 92, 109–111, 114–119, 123, 131, 136, 138–139, 141, 156, 167–168

U
United Kingdom, 3, 11, 14, 23, 48

V
Vygotsky, 149, 152–154, 210

W
Work, 20–22, 28, 31–33, 47–64, 112–116, 129–144, 186, 193–194, 213
Work experience, 15, 110, 226
Work group, 5, 102, 131–143
Working students, 51, 59
Workplace learning, *see* Learning at work
Workplace trainers, 12, 71